The Colonial American Origins of Modern Democratic Thought

This first examination in almost forty years of political ideas in the seventeenth-century American colonies reaches some surprising conclusions about the history of democratic theory more generally. The origins of a distinctively modern kind of thinking about democracy can be located, not in revolutionary America and France in the later eighteenth century, but in the tiny New England colonies in the middle seventeenth. The key feature of this democratic rebirth was honoring not only the principle of popular sovereignty through regular elections but also the principle of accountability through non-electoral procedures for the auditing and impeachment of elected officers. By staking its institutional identity entirely on elections, modern democratic thought has misplaced the sense of robust popular control which originally animated it.

J. S. Maloy is Assistant Professor of Political Science at Oklahoma State University, where he teaches courses in political theory and American constitutional law and writes on a wide range of topics in the history of political thought. He was born and raised in Austin, Texas, and educated at Brown University (philosophy), the University of Cambridge (history), and Harvard University (political science).

The Colonial American Origins of Modern Democratic Thought

J. S. MALOY
Oklahoma State University

CAMBRIDGE
UNIVERSITY PRESS

CAMBRIDGE UNIVERSITY PRESS
Cambridge, New York, Melbourne, Madrid, Cape Town, Singapore, São Paulo, Delhi

Cambridge University Press
32 Avenue of the Americas, New York, NY 10013-2473, USA

www.cambridge.org
Information on this title: www.cambridge.org/9780521514385

© J. S. Maloy 2008

This publication is in copyright. Subject to statutory exception
and to the provisions of relevant collective licensing agreements,
no reproduction of any part may take place without
the written permission of Cambridge University Press.

First published 2008

Printed in the United States of America

A catalog record for this publication is available from the British Library.

Library of Congress Cataloging in Publication Data

Maloy, J. S. (Jason Stuart), 1974–
The colonial American origins of modern democratic thought / J. S. Maloy.
   p. cm.
Includes bibliographical references and index.
ISBN 978-0-521-51438-5 (hardback)
1. Democracy – History.   2. Democracy – United States – History.   3. United States – Politics and government – to 1775.   I. Title.
JC421.M33   2008
321.8 – dc22   2008006770

ISBN   978-0-521-51438-5 hardback

Cambridge University Press has no responsibility for
the persistence or accuracy of URLs for external or
third-party Internet Web sites referred to in this publication
and does not guarantee that any content on such
Web sites is, or will remain, accurate or appropriate.

Contents

Preface		*page* vii
1	Introduction: Accountability and Democratic Theory	1
2	Radical Trust and Accountability in the Seventeenth Century	24
3	Fidelity and Accountability in Virginia and Bermuda	57
4	Politics and Ecclesiastics in Plymouth and Massachusetts	86
5	Constitutional Conflict and Political Argument at Boston	114
6	Democratic Constitutionalism in Connecticut and Rhode Island	140
7	Conclusion: Anglophone Radicalism and Popular Control	171
Bibliography		191
Index		205

Preface

This book originated in a curious fact about my move to England more than a decade ago: I quickly developed a previously unknown interest in studying the country from which I had come. Though I was not at that moment ideally situated for studying the history of American political ideas, I was well placed for learning about the places and intellectual traditions from which the reverse migration had first been made. Thus I started doing groundwork in English and to some extent European political thought from the sixteenth and seventeenth centuries. When I returned to the United States, I set out more directly on my path toward composing a first volume in the history of American political ideas.

That volume has yet to be produced. This book is the surprising result of my researches toward that project; it has not fulfilled the project itself. I wanted to acquire knowledge about American political ideas for its own sake, but along the way I discovered things about modern democratic thought which may be of interest even to people who find the other subject inherently uninteresting. Human affairs being as they are, to learn something important about the history of democratic thought is necessarily to learn something important about democracy itself. Thus I am deliberately offering a hybrid book, and I can only hope that seekers of knowledge about both the fields that it covers will find in it some reward for their pursuit.

Another curious feature of this book, and one that surprises those who know me well, is the amount of sustained attention I have given (not to say devoted) to matters of Christian theology – or, more precisely, ecclesiology. It is another subject considered by some to be inherently uninteresting, but I have found it to be both indispensable to understanding the seventeenth-century Englishmen who figure below and also powerfully explanatory in relation to the ideological origins of modern democracy. One of the hazards of doing intellectual history is that the most important lines of inquiry often diverge from the inquirer's personal favorites.

Notes on the Text

In the interest of simplicity, accessibility, and ease of reading, I have not reproduced sixteenth- and seventeenth-century English quotations in the exact form found in their original texts. Instead I have rendered them in modern American English spelling, but I have preserved original punctuation, capitalization, and italics except in a few cases where clarity seemed to necessitate a change.

Also in the interest of accessibility, I have preferred to cite modern editions and translations of sixteenth- and seventeenth-century texts if such exist, though I have attempted always to make clear the date and circumstances of original composition or publication in the text and Bibliography. For works by Plato and Aristotle, citations refer to Stephanus and Bekker pages, respectively. For parts of a book lacking numbered pages, citations refer to signature-page and folio; for example, A/2b stands for sig. A, fol. 2b.

Acknowledgments

While in England I had the pleasure of working with Jonathan Scott and John Dunn, who were not only helpful but even friendly – and not only during my two years there but also on the odd occasion since. I was also fortunate to know and to learn from Mark Goldie, Anthony Pagden, and Quentin Skinner.

My greatest debts are held in the United States, especially by Nancy Rosenblum and Thomas Skidmore, who provided early and formative support to my efforts to be a student and a scholar. Nancy has the dubious distinction of having been exposed to not only the latest but also the earliest instances of my writing on political theory. She has been among the chief supports for this book in particular, alongside John McCormick, Richard Tuck, Cary Nederman, Eldon Eisenach, and Russ Muirhead – all of whom provided vital assistance in both word and deed. Other colleagues who have helped with my work on this project in various ways over the years include Craig Borowiak, Bob Darcy, Noah Dauber, Yannis Evrigenis, Julian Franklin, Bryan Garsten, Jim Kloppenberg, Philip Pettit, and Thad Williamson. Special mention goes to two venues where I presented work-in-progress from this book: Oklahoma State University's Political Research

Seminar, including Vincent Burke, Jim Davis, Jason Kirksey, Jim Scott, and Mark Wolfgram; and Texas A&M University's Political Theory Colloquium, including Cary Nederman and his graduate students as well as Judy Baer, Lisa Ellis, Ed Portis, and Diego von Vacano. My only regret is that, had I availed myself of these valued colleagues more often, I might have avoided whatever errors are found in the text below.

Financial support for various phases of my research over more than ten years has come from the Marshall Aid Commemoration Commission in the United Kingdom, the National Science Foundation in the United States, the Department of Government at Harvard University, the Mark DeWolfe Howe Fund of Harvard Law School, and the College of Arts and Sciences at Oklahoma State University.

Finally, this book requires special tribute to be paid to an indispensable institution of human civilization: the public library. I am especially indebted to all those who have helped to maintain and to staff the Edmon Low Library of Oklahoma State University, the McFarlin Library of the University of Tulsa, and the Perry-Castañeda Library and the Tarlton Law Library of the University of Texas – each of which allows a person to enter, browse, and read. I am also grateful for the opportunity to use some less accessible but more magnificent instances of the genre: the University Library at Cambridge, the British Library in London, the Widener Library and the Houghton Library at Harvard University, the Boston Public Library, and the New York Public Library. Special thanks are also due to Lynn Wallace and the staff of the OSU-Tulsa library, on whom I relied heavily in the later stages of my research; and to Toby Wilson and Dan Crutcher at the Institute for Teaching and Learning Excellence at OSU-Stillwater, who helped with the book's illustrations.

I dedicate this book to my mother, Crista Kiefer McCormack, to whom I owe the love of knowledge for its own sake, among other debts too numerous to mention; and to my father, Jon W. Maloy, who has taught all his sons that the love of knowledge and the dignity of labor are compatible and complementary things.

Tulsa, Oklahoma, June 2008

1

Introduction

Accountability and Democratic Theory

Democracy appears to be the master concept of the world of politics today. Yet a treacherous terrain confronts those who would understand it – whether as students and theoreticians or as participants and practitioners, and equally in societies long known as "democracies" as in those newly embarking on "democratization." This book investigates a neglected phase of the history of ideas which can supply a useful compass for navigating the rough country of democracy and the scholarly literatures devoted to understanding it. It is based on research into various texts of the early and middle seventeenth century relating to colonization and constitutional design in the English-speaking Atlantic world. The magnetic north it proposes for democratic theory is the principle of accountability.

I will show how the principle of democratic accountability was adapted for and applied to modern political conditions, arguably for the first time anywhere, in England and America in the middle 1600s – perhaps surprisingly, in the colonies fully a decade prior to the metropolis. These conceptual developments accompanied and facilitated the founding of new states on the American continent by way of written constitutions. Some of these earliest colonial constitutions attempted to construct forms of government that may be regarded as genuinely democratic in modern terms: elective, representative, and constitutionally limited, but above all seeking popular control through non-electoral institutions of accountability. And the political debates of some of the colonists reveal, to an extent much underestimated before now, the theoretic underpinnings of these constitutional constructions.

These colonial American developments arguably represent the birth of modern democratic theory. At the very least, they gave rise to what has become the cardinal proposition of modern democratic thought – but also to an important alternative. Conventional thinking about democracy today rests on what might be called the electoral thesis of accountability: a democratic constitution is one that confers power on representatives who are held accountable to the people by regular elections. This proposition is most often associated, historically, with the revolutions and ensuing constitutional debates in America and France in the later eighteenth century. As I will show, however, it was originally the product of an ironic sequence of debates which began in New England in the 1630s. There the advocates of non-electoral forms of accountability were attacked by the self-conscious opponents of democracy with the notion that elections alone are sufficient to make officers accountable. Subsequently this anti-democratic argument was broached by radical elements in old England for their schemes of constitutional reform, over a century before it was eventually revived in the period of the great modern revolutions. In short, the cardinal proposition of modern democratic thought was originally designed to abort democracy's modern rebirth.

These seventeenth-century origins, specifically the colonial American democrats' alternative to the electoral thesis of accountability, should give today's student of democratic politics pause, for they supply resources for restoring the idea of popular control through non-electoral institutions of accountability from the margins of democratic theory to its center. These conceptual resources are encapsulated in three distinct models of accountability – the classical, the ecclesiastical, and the fiduciary – which I will briefly describe below and develop further throughout this book.

Resetting the compass of democratic theory by reference to the principle of accountability would reorient the field in several key respects. It would change the shape of debates around electoral arrangements generally, since they would be unburdened of a job of popular control to which they have in any case proved inadequate. It would lower the stakes for debates around representation more specifically, since the descriptive characteristics of a discretionary agent decline in (all but symbolic) importance when constituents acquire the means to hold that agent accountable. It would remove one of the leading arguments against rotation in office, or "term limits," since non-electoral means of popular control operate whether or not a representative is able to seek re-election. And it would bring to light, and might help to dissolve, lingering if often tacit worries about democratic participation, since it imagines forms of popular agency lying somewhere between the impotent act of voting and the improbable vocation of professional citizen.

In the bigger picture, the new historical light shed by this story of colonial American origins illuminates the considerable distance that democratic theory has traveled since its modern rebirth: away from popular control

Introduction 3

toward popular consent, away from accountable toward discretionary forms of authority. In this connection it not only reinforces a growing scholarly trend toward designing non-electoral democratic institutions but also shows the importance as well as the limitations of recent "deliberative" and "contestatory" elements of that trend. By depicting some of the grand rivalries of earlier eras – *logos* versus *kratos*, reason versus power, deliberation versus contestation – my analysis will help to clarify the moral and institutional stakes associated with their echoes in leading debates today. If the perspective of the first modern democrats arouses any sympathy at all, it appears that their insights must be incorporated in a quite different democratic theory from those versions that currently hold the field.

Historical Synopsis

Democratic norms and practices were in a deep sleep for almost two millennia between their ancient birth and modern rebirth. The primary normative requirement of popular control over public affairs was common to both moments of origin. Among the discrepancies between the two, however, the large territorial and demographic scale of modern states was not as significant as the language of legitimacy, consent, and representation in which their activities had come to be understood. If ancient democracy rested in part on the principle of accountability, modern democracy emerged from a new conceptual partnership of accountability with popular sovereignty.

The story of the colonial American origins of modern democratic thought begins, in Chapter 2, with the European context from which the first English settlers in America came. The ancient rivalry between discretionary and accountable conceptions of political authority, typically conducted in the language of "trust," was regularly rehearsed in sixteenth-century European debates on sovereignty and resistance and again in seventeenth-century England. During the English Civil War the accountable conception of trust was used, by the so-called Levellers, to develop the first political theories that were both distinctively modern and genuinely democratic. The Levellers' key theoretic moves were to orient the accountable trust toward genuinely popular bodies and to transfer it from the domain of war and resistance to regular constitutional processes, including elections. Whereas the English nation as a whole was to hold its parliament accountable through regular elections, local constituencies were to conduct recalls, audits, and impeachments of individual representatives by citizen juries.

But by the 1640s the institutional state of nature created by civil war in England had already been met by Englishmen in America. The process by which Anglo-American colonists came to anticipate key elements of the democratic revival begins, in Chapter 3, in the unlikely commercial colonies of Virginia and Bermuda. Settlers there and observers in England used the language of trust to understand both moral and institutional features of colonial life, and debate revolved, accordingly, around rival accounts of the virtue of fidelity and the principle of accountability. One plan for reorganizing Virginia's government, by John Bargraves in 1623, applied the principle of accountability to the colonies' internal government for the first time by proposing that officers in Virginia be subject to trials for state crimes by a kind of representative jury.

The classical-humanist dream of founding new commonwealths had played a significant role in the thinking of those associated with the Virginia Company, as of their Elizabethan predecessors, but conceiving American colonies in terms of the principle of popular sovereignty required the interaction of other intellectual traditions. The "Pilgrims" of New Plymouth, as Chapter 4 will show, combined the commonwealth values of classical humanism with conceptual tools taken from Bodinian jurisprudence and Calvinist ecclesiology. The result was a theory of church government which rendered officers accountable to the whole congregation, as typified by the writings of John Robinson, the "Pilgrim Pastor." Robinson explicitly compared these arrangements to ancient Athens and described them in the Bodinian language of a "popular state," and the Plymouth colony adopted similar institutional forms for civil government.

In Massachusetts Bay, meanwhile, lively debates over the colony's constitution gave rise to a persistent reform movement that pressed for nonelectoral institutions of accountability, as Chapter 5 will explain. Opposition deputies at Boston championed, on the one hand, classic Athenian practices like the auditing of magistrates and rotation in office; and, on the other, institutional features adapted from the most radical theories of congregational churches, notably a unicameral voting assembly as the ultimate power in the community. John Winthrop and the Boston elite denounced these demands as "democratic" even while skillfully moderating and co-opting them. By the end of Winthrop's reign the government of Massachusetts had evolved into an elective and bicameral constitution of the familiar modern sort: two separate voting assemblies, each possessing a veto over the other, and no accountability between elections. No one in New England mistook this regime for a genuine democracy.

Connecticut and Rhode Island, by contrast, were the first fully developed modern democratic states, and they are the subjects of Chapter 6. Their governments were set up by the voluntary and involuntary exiles from the Bay colony and were deeply marked by the Massachusetts opposition's reform program. Connecticut's leading figure, Thomas Hooker, directly challenged Winthrop's discretionary conception of political trust, and the colony's founding document instituted key reform proposals that had first been broached at Boston. Rhode Island's chief statesman, Roger Williams, presided over the establishment of a self-proclaimed "democratic" constitution which made representatives strictly accountable to the citizens of federated towns. Thus the New England democratic movement anticipated the Levellers' pioneering application of democratic accountability to representative, constitutional government.

The leading lessons of these stories of the first adaptation of ancient democratic ideas for modern settings have to do with the principle of accountability and its non-electoral institutional forms, especially audits and impeachments. Popular sovereignty was a necessary but not a sufficient condition of modern democratic thought; the principle of accountability was also needed. Accordingly, the parallel processes of consent and authorization, whether by regular elections or extraordinary ratifications, are necessary but not sufficient for a genuinely democratic theory; regular mechanisms of scrutiny and sanction are also needed. Even if perfect procedures of deliberation and consent could be obtained, or even if perfectly representative bodies could be assembled, no democracy could exist in the absence of regular accountability. This historical lesson has rather stark implications for the current priorities of academic political theory, as I will explain further below.

The centrality of accountability and of seventeenth-century Anglo-Americans to the origins of modern democratic theory also has implications for how key figures in the history of political thought are understood. Some famous names must be re-evaluated and other more obscure ones better illuminated. Bodin and the Levellers assume greater stature than is usually accorded them, while Hobbes and Locke appear just as significant for what was derivative and responsive as for what was innovative in their thought. Certain figures who loom large in colonial American history but not in the history of political thought – especially Capt. John Smith, John Winthrop, Thomas Hooker, and Roger Williams – must have both the nature and the importance of their political ideas re-evaluated. And other more obscure figures – especially John Bargraves, John Robinson, and Israel Stoughton – appear to deserve more scholarly attention than they typically receive.

The telling of this story, as of any episode of intellectual history, is circumscribed by certain parameters and shaped to some degree by previous tellings of similar stories. Before elaborating the current issues in political and legal theory on which I believe this story has special bearing, I must explain the conceptual parameters and the historiographies that frame the story itself.

Form and Substance

The crucial contribution of the seventeenth-century Anglo-American democrats has to do with a particular aspect of democratic thought which might be called formal rather than substantive: with "democracy" as a system of rule, not a way of life. This qualification is important because the heavily substantive character of thinking about democracy today has tended to obscure the seventeenth-century contribution.

There are two kinds of substantive criteria which have misled scholars in their assessment of modern democracy's theoretic origins: democracy as necessarily predicated on a liberal or inclusive conception of membership, in other words of the community's matter or substance; and democracy as necessarily embodying substantive ethical principles of liberty, equality, and rights. These two criteria refer to fundamental questions of democracy as a way of life: Who are we? How ought we to live together? Focusing on these questions allows us too easily to dismiss modern democracy's seventeenth-century origins because, for example, universal suffrage and religious toleration were ideas widely abhorred, or at best applied unevenly, prior to the later eighteenth and early nineteenth centuries.

Democracy as a system of rule may be considered an altogether less grand notion: not quite a way of living, merely a way of institutionally structuring relations of authority. The importance of institutionalized authority to social life is what makes democracy not merely an ethical but also a political concept. Famously, the ancient Greek inventors of the term differed among themselves and over time about how broadly or narrowly political membership should be drawn. They usually defined it more narrowly than the modern legatees of Judeo-Christian culture have done, but it would be absurd to allege on this basis that the Greeks misunderstood their own concept. What is distinctive about democracy on this view, and what could in principle unite it across ancient and modern differences on substantive questions of membership, are the formal principles of institutional structure by which power (*kratos*) may be said truly to belong to any given people (*demos*).

My analysis of the theoretic origins of modern democracy revolves around just such a formal principle. The adaptation for and application to modern political life of the ancient idea of democratic accountability – this is the key theoretic move in the story I tell. And this is the step for which the seventeenth-century Anglo-American democrats deserve credit.

Introduction

One assumption about the origins of democratic theory which is entailed by the formalistic parameters of my study may seem counter-intuitive: the restrictive suffrage qualifications and illiberal social legislation of the seventeenth century are not particularly relevant considerations. They are relevant to other concerns and inquiries, of course, and I would not in general deny the interest of universal suffrage and cultural pluralism for political theory. But I hope my study will illustrate how we lose rather than gain understanding of modern democracy by ruling the seventeenth century out of court on substantive grounds.

The Concept of Accountability

The concept of political accountability has received no general scholarly treatment to compare with the attention lavished on representation (e.g. Pitkin 1967), for instance, even though it appears to be in equally wide use today in various discursive contexts. For the purposes of this story, "accountability" can be defined in both historically and theoretically useful terms by reference to the ancient Greek practices (see Roberts 1982) that have come to be known by that modern Latinate term. Those practices, as we will see in more detail in Chapter 2, involved *scrutiny* and *sanction*: a cognitive or discursive act followed by a punitive act. Officers of government at Athens were subject to the combination of these two, apparently, in order to confer on the *demos* some measure of control over their conduct. To the extent that popular control was the etymological and remains the conceptual core of democracy (see Pettit 2008, 46), the concept of accountability must be regarded as essential to democratic thought.

Thus *accountability*, especially in its sanctioning mode, works directly to confer control, but it must be distinguished from *selection*, whose relation to control is more tenuous. Selection is an *ex ante* procedure involving a kind of scrutiny or judgment followed by a moment of choice; accountability is an *ex post* procedure in which scrutiny is followed rather by sanction. Whereas selection confers authority and grants license toward future conduct, accountability rewards and punishes past conduct. Despite some similarities, then, selecting is analytically a different thing from holding accountable (Fearon 1999, 58).

Yet *control* itself is only one facet of power; as we moderns are acutely aware, *consent* is another. The former uses rewards and punishments to give governors incentives to act in certain ways; the latter authorizes or legitimates their acting at all. The difficulty in distinguishing selection from accountability arises from the former's occupation of a region of conceptual overlap between consent and control (see Figure 1.1): authorizing one actor

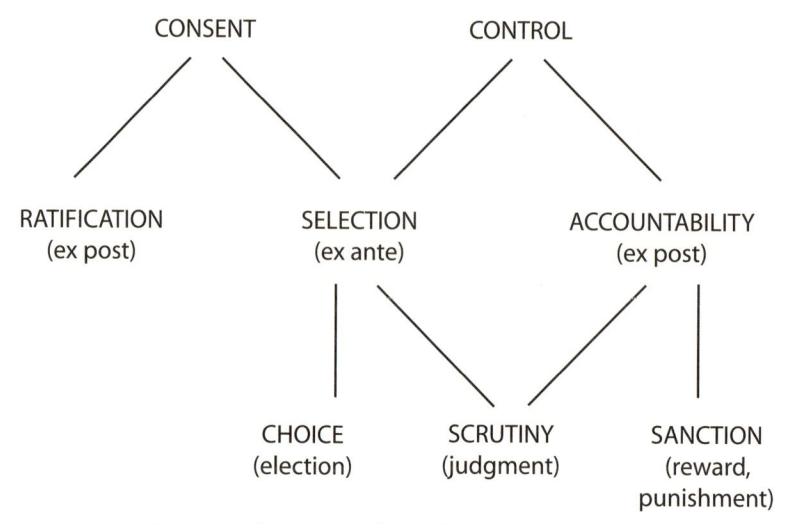

```
                CONSENT              CONTROL
               /       \            /       \
              /         \          /         \
             /           \        /           \
       RATIFICATION    SELECTION        ACCOUNTABILITY
        (ex post)      (ex ante)           (ex post)
            |             |   \           /     |
            |             |    \         /      |
            |             |     \       /       |
            |           CHOICE   SCRUTINY    SANCTION
                       (election) (judgment)  (reward,
                                              punishment)
```

FIGURE 1.1. Conceptual elements of popular power.

rather than another may be one way of exerting control over the actions that will ultimately ensue, but this is a fairly weak form of control compared to the alternatives. The early-modern democrats may provide an antidote to the late-modern dependence on this conceptual confusion. They were not satisfied with popular consent via ratification and selection, and they were not convinced that selection secures popular control. The distinctive lesson of their story is that even if plebiscites or referenda secured *ratification*, and even if elections secured *selection*, democracy would still require other procedures to secure *accountability*.

In light of the dubious potency of selection procedures generally, and periodic elections specifically, as mechanisms of control (Fearon 1999, 56, 68–9; Manin et al. 1999a, 50), moving accountability back to the center of democratic theory has not only historical but also contemporary warrant. The political ideas of the first modern democrats offer resources toward understanding and institutionalizing accountability on three conceptual registers: the *mechanics* of scrutiny and sanction as means of control, the composition of the *agency* charged with performing scrutiny and sanction, and the *rationale* or purposive force behind scrutiny and sanction.

Three mechanisms of accountability will emerge from the texts under consideration below: (a) *special inquests* into officers' conduct, such as periodic audits or episodic impeachments; (b) *general liability*, as when persons of authority are subject to the normal legal processes that apply to ordinary subjects; and (c) *deselection*, in other words revocation and replacement. Of course (c) carries elements of both consent and control, at least under conditions in which the bare revocation of power is construed as a harm with deterrent potential. These conditions involve peculiarly modern institutional and psychological assumptions: the conferral of authority on particular persons must be considered appropriately done by deliberate choice (election as opposed to lottery), re-eligibility must be favored, and selection and deselection must be perceived as significant forms of reward and punishment, respectively. These three assumptions cannot all be taken for granted for the early-modern period, and the last is particularly hard to gauge. But we will see that some thinkers began to bring these assumptions together and to apply the distinctively modern logic of elections as a mechanism of accountability. Equally significantly, however, other non-electoral mechanisms played a more important role in the first modern democratic theories.

Second, the composition of an agency performing scrutiny and sanction may vary from (a) a *universal* body (including every member of a political community) to (b) a *class*-specific one (either popular or elite, for instance) to (c) a *representative* one (a microcosm of the universal); class and representative bodies, in turn, may be selected by random sample (lottery) or election, or some combination of the two. Though the calling to account of governors by representatives or elites on behalf of the people has at times been called "democratic," my historical analysis will meet a more exacting standard by showing thinkers who proposed making representatives or elites themselves accountable to popular bodies. This issue of composition brings substantive questions of membership and the franchise into contact with the formal principle of accountability. One of the lessons of my analysis is that defining a regime according to how widely consent is solicited, or by who may vote, is no more important than doing so according to who has the right to exert more direct control over persons of authority, or by who may serve in agencies of accountability. On this view excluding any class of persons from service in agencies charged with the scrutiny and sanction of political officers would be just as anti-democratic as denying that same class the right to vote in elections.

Third, the *rationale* behind accountability might be popular control for its own sake, arising from a moral or ideological commitment to democracy itself, or it might rather revolve around higher ideals of truth, justice, righteousness, and so on. It is possible, of course, to make the first instrumental to the second: a government may for various reasons be considered more likely to pursue just or righteous policies if it is effectively subjected to popular control. But, as the stories below will illustrate, shifting the rationale

	MECHANISM	AGENCY	RATIONALE
CLASSICAL	special inquest	representative (election) or popular (lot)	public liberty
ECCLESIASTICAL	special inquest, deselection	universal	metaphysical truth
FIDUCIARY	special inquest, deselection, general liability	popular or universal	democratic legitimacy (et al.)

FIGURE 1.2. Three models of democratic accountability.

behind democratic accountability away from popular control itself toward higher substantive ideals tends to lead accountability away from its sanctioning component and more exclusively into its scrutinizing component – and ultimately away from control altogether and more exclusively into consent. This movement is arguably, as we will see below, what has happened recently as "accountability" has been reduced to a conceptual adjunct of "deliberation."

Three Models of Accountability

The assumptions, conceptions, and logics by which these various aspects of accountability relate to one another can be encapsulated in three recurring bundles of theoretic tendencies, or models of democratic accountability: the classical-republican, the ecclesiastical, and the fiduciary-legal. These may be taken as yesterday's offerings to today's conceptual toolboxes, and I will suggest further below some ways in which they might bear on current debates around elections, deliberation, and constitutional design. For now I will merely outline the three models (see Figure 1.2), but they will feature in greater detail throughout this book.

The *classical*-republican model of accountability drew its inspiration from historical examples of republics, usually ancient Greek or Roman, in which different political agencies check one another, by means including relations of scrutiny and sanction. The primary mechanism of control in this model is the special inquest, usually a kind of impeachment for crimes against the state. The agencies that adjudicated such cases were either representative or popular in composition, and they were typically guided by the purpose of defending public liberty or safety.

The *ecclesiastical* model of accountability was based on the Calvinist notion that every member of a particular church, including authoritative figures like ministers and elders, is subject to the scrutiny and "censure" of every other member. This model revolved around special inquests but also introduced the modern emphasis on merely revoking authority and replacing its holders (deselection). The primary agency of accountability is universal in composition, comprising the whole community. Ecclesiastical rationales tend to cluster around some kind of grand metaphysical truth, typically related to ideals of religious purity and communal harmony.

The *fiduciary*-legal model arose from the analogy of relations of public authority to private-law relations of agency such as guardianship and trusteeship, in which one party's power is created by and may be called to account by another. This model's potential mechanisms of control run the gamut of special inquests, general liability, and deselection, but the first two were particularly favored. Fiduciary accountability bears a strong bias against empowering elite bodies and even a suspicion of representative bodies, preferring instead either universal or class-based popular agencies of accountability. Its proponents often rationalized popular control as an essential criterion of legal justice, or of what might now be called "democratic legitimacy," but various other purposes ranging from natural rights to provincial liberties to providential design could also be accommodated within the model.

An important channel of access to these models of accountability ran through Jean Bodin's definition of sovereignty as ultimate and indivisible authority, including rights of both selection and accountability. Bodin himself was far from sympathetic to the democratic imperative of popular control. Yet, rather like ancient critics of Greek democracy (see Ober 2003, 18), he depicted the regime's institutional forms in such vivid terms that some of his readers found them more congenial than he did. As we will see, Bodin's analysis of democratic accountability surfaced in discourses related to all three models, but it was particularly pivotal for the fiduciary model's legalistic conceptual framework and its institutional versatility.

After the main story of this book has been told, I will more fully explore the theoretic ramifications of the three models of accountability for democratic theory today in the concluding Chapter 7. My conclusion will be twofold. First, elements of the classical and ecclesiastical models of accountability can be found in recent writings on democratic theory, but the aristocratic tendencies as well as other features of these two have been under-appreciated. Second, the fiduciary model offers an attractive third way around the difficulties of the other two, suggesting a new kind of democratic theory which not only preserves the value of popular control in some semblance of integrity but also orients it pragmatically toward problems of institutional design.

Terminological History

What makes the sorts of accountability contemplated by the three models "democratic" as opposed to, say, "aristocratic"? Contrary to a widely held belief about political terminology, "democracy" was not a universally pejorative term in the seventeenth century. The colonial American democrats supply examples of this under-appreciated fact in the history of political thought. Though some scholars have noticed this fact (e.g. Ball and Dagger 1999, 32), none has explored its theoretic significance. Every chapter of this book involves seventeenth-century debates over the meaning and valence of the term "democracy," and my analysis will show why it was not unheard of to favor it.

The key consideration for this question has to do with the widely disseminated terminological protocols of Bodin's *Six Books of the Republic* (1576). Bodin used the classic tripartite division of regimes into "monarchy," "aristocracy," and "democracy," but he distinguished two parts of a regime, *l'état* and *le gouvernment*. Roughly speaking, "state" corresponded to ultimate sovereignty and "government" to regular administration. Both the state and the government could be described by any of the three traditional labels, and it was possible for a single regime to be composed of a state of one type and a government of a different type. Thus, for example, a democratic state could have a monarchic or an aristocratic government while remaining "democratic" for purposes of classification (Bodin 1986, bk. 2, chs. 1–2, 7; Bodin 1962, 184, 199, 249).[1]

Bodin's *Six Books* was one of the most widely read works on politics in the seventeenth century, and it was a set text at the University of Cambridge

---

[1] Bodin 1986 is a modern reprint, in the original French, of the tenth edition of the *Six Books*, issued in 1593; Bodin 1962 is a facsimile edition of the only English translation of the entire work, made in 1606; Bodin 1992 is a recent English translation of selected excerpts. I always cite Bodin 1962 because it is the version of the text that was used by my seventeenth-century subjects.

(Greenleaf 1964, 125), where many of the most prominent New England colonists were educated. As I will explain in Chapter 4 and further illustrate in Chapters 5 and 6, many of them championed robust accountability in a democratic "state" in the Bodinian sense despite a reluctance to countenance a democratic "government." By ignoring Bodin's influence in this respect, scholars of colonial American political ideas have failed to notice a crucial distinction between two ways of endorsing a "mixed" political regime: whereas the traditional Aristotelian mixture (also Polybian and Machiavellian; see Pocock 1975, 273) allowed distinct segments of society to share power on more or less equal terms, the new Bodinian mixture allowed a "government" of one type of social composition to be wholly subordinate to a "state" of another type. The earliest colonial democrats sometimes referred to a "mixed" regime in the latter not the former sense, but that locution made their commitment to popular control no less radical.

Historiography

The Bodinian influence in New England is one example of the value of a broader contextual perspective in research on American political ideas. The materials under study represent not only a neglected chapter in the history of American political thought but also an important chapter in the history of democratic theory. There are two distinct historiographies, then, whose shape would be altered by the inclusion of my seventeenth-century subjects.

The political ideas associated with the first few generations of English colonization in America have received only scant and superficial attention in recent decades. I have concentrated my research on Virginia, Bermuda, and southern New England – at the expense of other English settlements in Barbados, St. Kitts, the Bahamas, Maryland, New Hampshire, Maine, Newfoundland, Nova Scotia, and elsewhere – because of the particular richness of their extant records. Even they have been neglected recently because "imperialist" scholarship and other forms of revisionism in the twentieth century, which attacked previous "patriotic" and "progressive" histories, inculcated the assumption that the political ideas of the earliest Anglo-American colonies were inert, unoriginal, and uninteresting. Dominant assumptions in the field of American puritan studies in particular, at least since the canonical work of Perry Miller and his students (Miller 1939, 1956; Morgan 1958), have obscured the true nature and interest of early New Englanders' political thought: understating their interest in worldly politics while overstating their maintenance of consensus. Miller's findings have been challenged by subsequent generations of scholarship on several counts (Hall 1987) but not on these two assumptions about political ideas. The effect has been virtually to remove the seventeenth century from the study of American political ideas (e.g. Block 2002, Butler 2004; but cf. Miller 1991), so that even a book about "the Protestant origins of American political thought" may focus on the revolutionary period while barely mentioning the puritans of the previous century (Shain 1994). Timothy Breen's *Character of the Good Ruler* (1970) has been called "the only serious study of political theory in seventeenth-century America" (Murrin 1984, 421), and no comparable work has been published since. Thus mine is the first sustained examination of its subject in almost four decades.

The remedy for this neglect of the earliest colonies is older than the malady itself. Herbert Osgood long ago advised that "to works on religious polemics we must go to find the beginnings of American political literature. These together with the important public documents of the time are the storehouses of the ideas which guided the puritans in their work" (Osgood 1891, 2). My attempt to take this advice, particularly in Chapters 4 and 6, is something of a historiographic novelty. Another aspect of needed revision is, even more simply, to remember and to probe the real conflicts that existed in and among civil governments around New England; this I have done primarily in Chapters 5 and 6.

The results of my researches echo one of the favorite whipping boys of Miller and his vast progeny. The first volume of Vernon Parrington's *Main Currents in American Thought*, titled *The Colonial Mind* (1927), remains unique to this day in its endeavor to take seriously and engage critically the political ideas of figures like Winthrop, Hooker, Williams, and others in the first few generations of New England settlement (Parrington 1987, chs. 1–5). Though Miller's sneer that "Parrington simply did not know what he was talking about" (Miller 1956, 17) has carried considerable weight with colonial historians, I will show that Parrington was correct to recognize fundamental ideological disagreements and to describe them in the language of "democracy" and "aristocracy," since many of his subjects understood themselves in those terms (Parrington 1987, xviii, 16–18, 47, 52–3, 57). But I have tried to make my analysis contextually more sensitive and textually more extensive than Parrington's; as a result, my broadly similar conclusions rest on somewhat different grounds.

Parrington's analysis was merely a more trenchant and more celebrated (Pulitzer-winning) variation on a theme of predecessors like Osgood, Charles Borgeaud, and J. T. Adams (Osgood 1891, Borgeaud 1894, Adams 1921): the thesis that seventeenth-century New England puritanism gave birth to modern democracy in Connecticut and Rhode Island after overcoming the aristocratic tendencies of Massachusetts. My analysis will show that this thesis is formally correct but substantively faulty, since it stakes the conflict between democracy and aristocracy on grounds that are either incomplete or anachronistic. Whereas Parrington and his precursors understood democracy in terms of social class, civil liberties, and procedures of consent, I will show that the New England democrats' key differences with their ideological rivals implicated another consideration altogether: the formal principle of accountability as a vehicle of popular control.

My analysis, then, overturns the historiographic conventional wisdom that "truly democratic ideas ... are difficult to find" before the Revolution (Main 1966, 391; see also Lokken 1959), and it accentuates the irony lurking beneath the finding that the seventeenth-century partisans of aristocracy championed what has passed for "democracy" since the middle twentieth century, if not before (see Brown 1954). It would be wrong, of course, to mistake the details of seventeenth-century ideological conflict for those of later, more familiar periods in American history. Instead we may simply confirm Eldon Eisenach's suggestion that recurring patterns of "political-cultural conflict" in American life do indeed have important roots in the seventeenth century, without reducing the later conflicts to the earlier (Eisenach 1978, 90–3).

Rewriting and expanding the opening chapter in the history of American political ideas in the way I propose would also have an impact on how the history of democratic theory more generally is conceived. In short, conventional accounts of modern democracy's ideological genesis must be revised backward from the post-revolutionary milieux of France and America in the later eighteenth and early nineteenth centuries.

In the last decade several books on the historical origins of ideas of representative democracy have made valuable contributions to an important subject. Bernard Manin has argued that government by elected representatives was originally intended to replace rather than enhance democratic power, or at least to lend it an aristocratic admixture, while using the idea of consent to satisfy the requirements of popular sovereignty (Manin 1997). John Dunn has suggested that the word "democracy" was enlisted in this cause by a gradual process of related intellectual and economic developments by which it began to be construed according to the "order of egoism" rather than the "order of equality" (Dunn 2005). Nadia Urbinati has argued, somewhat in contrast, that representation was conceived in the later eighteenth century to enhance democratic deliberation and is still needed today to rescue democracy from faulty interpretations of popular sovereignty and direct participation (Urbinati 2006). All three, notwithstanding their differences, converge on the post-revolutionary constitutional debates in both America and France as the decisive historical moment when the theory of modern democracy came into its own.

Without denying the importance of those debates generally, I wish to suggest an earlier theoretic birth for modern democracy. The current consensus appears to rest on interpretive criteria that under-value the principle of accountability, focusing instead on substantive criteria of broadly distributed rights of membership and formal criteria confined to popular consent and the election of representatives. Of course opinions vary on the minimal criteria of modern "democracy," and some would hold that popular consent is both necessary and sufficient while popular control is too dangerous to be allowed. This was the view of Joseph Schumpeter, for instance, who held that modern democracy both begins and ends with the selection of governments through periodic elections (Schumpeter 1942, chs. 21–2). What is interesting is that both the minimalist (consent only) and the populist (consent plus control) interpretations of democracy have their origins in the seventeenth century, where the former was first invented as a counter to the latter. If Madison and Sieyes were the sires of Schumpeter, they were the heirs of Winthrop.

As Chapter 2 will show, for the conjunction of popular sovereignty and accountability historical precedence appears to belong to the Levellers in England in the middle seventeenth century. The Levellers are often noticed for their substantive views on suffrage, participation, and natural rights (Hanson 1989, 73–4; Kateb 1992, 9; Rabb 2003, 41, 50, 54; Urbinati 2006, 19–20), but rarely for the formal principle of accountability. Once popular control is considered as essential as popular consent to this story, the Levellers must be seen in a new, more searching light. But the conceptual contours of the Levellers' proposed constitutional reconstruction of war-torn England in the late 1640s had already been developed for some proposed and some actual constitutional constructions in the American colonies, particularly in New England in the 1630s. And over the course of the 1640s, in the Rhode Island settlements, these constitutional features were for the first time gathered under the rubric of "democracy." If the New England democrats make a claim for an expanded first chapter in the history of American political ideas, they also make a claim for a chapter of their own in the history of democratic theory.

Accountability and Elections

The lessons of these new or rediscovered chapters in the history of democratic theory revolve around not only the principles of popular sovereignty and accountability but also their institutional expression. Voting and elections are the institutional practices most directly associated with consent, but today they are usually burdened with the double expectation of simultaneously effecting popular control. This expectation has been a staple of modern democratic thought in general but especially of its American strand. Madison defended the U.S. Constitution of 1787 by arguing that it combined "the elective mode of obtaining rulers" with "such a limitation of the term of appointments as will maintain a proper responsibility to the people" (*The Federalist*, no. 57: Hamilton et al. 2005, 309). Even the more populist elements of the American tradition have often accepted the electoral thesis of accountability, as in Thomas Paine's suggestion that representatives' "fidelity to the public" could be secured by the deterrent incentives of periodic elections (Paine 1987, 68). When Thomas Jefferson, in retirement, referred to "popular election and control" as the cardinal criteria of republican government, it was not obvious that he saw any distinction between the two (Jefferson 1979, 87). Today the case is little different, since the assumption that elections deliver democratic accountability prevails not only in political science generally (Manin et al. 1999b, 4) but also in democratic theory in particular (see Cohen 1996, 99; Carter and Stokes 2002, 1).

The inadequacy of elections for this task, however, now appears to be both an empirically and a theoretically compelling proposition (Manin et al. 1999a, 44, 50; Manin et al. 1999b, 22, 24). The historical association of elections with aristocracy prior to the nineteenth century, combined with the apparent domination of elite interest groups over politics today, has recently prompted the rediscovery of the notion that modern electoral systems were never designed to effect popular control in the first place (see Manin 1997, McCormick 2006). No little impetus has been added to the anti-electoral trend of thought, presumably, by the evident practical difficulties of ensuring fair procedures and accurate counts in modern mass elections – as witnessed by recent voting scandals and (non-frivolously) contested elections in several states around the world, including at least one of the older and more prestigious "democracies."

The perspective of the first modern democrats suits this anti-electoral trend because they refused to conflate procedures of selection and of accountability. The refusal required a conscious choice because the conflation was being proposed to them by defenders of the discretionary against the accountable conception of political trust in order to undermine institutional reforms toward popular control in New England. John Winthrop invented the proposition that regular elections are sufficient to control the elected precisely in order to take non-electoral forms of accountability off the table. Not all his hearers took the bait at the time, but subsequently many "democrats" have done so. To the extent that the bait is losing its appeal, the old distinction between selection and accountability that was present at the birth of modern democratic thought promises now to figure in efforts to prolong its vitality.

But my findings are more congenial to some aspects of the broadly antielectoral trend in political theory today than others. This trend belongs to a tradition of critiques of "aggregative" conceptions of democracy which confine democratic politics to majoritarian voting and interest-group bargaining. Arguably the anti-aggregative tradition is well over thirty years old (e.g. Pateman 1970), but it has flourished recently on the backs of comprehensive philosophies of liberal justice, republican freedom, and "communicative ethics" – in the form of "deliberative," "contestatory," and "discursive" theories of democracy, respectively. Despite their differences, what these recent theories all have in common is a passion for taming power with reason (Habermas 1996, 28–9; Sunstein 2001, 7; Warren 2002, 189; Pettit 2003, 138); many of them exhibit a corresponding hostility to "direct" popular participation (Sunstein 2001, 7; Pettit 2003, 154; Gutmann and Thompson 2004, 30–1).

The new generation of anti-aggregative theories also tends to seek refuge in non-electoral institutions (Gutmann and Thompson 1996, 143, 145–51; Habermas 1996, 28; Pettit 2000, 127–33; but cf. Thompson 2002). The colonial American origins of modern democratic thought generally affirm that anti- or at least non-electoral posture, but they also suggest a significant realignment of it. As I will explain further in the concluding Chapter 7, the first modern democratic theories were tilted more toward power than reason: what they sought for the *demos* was more *kratos* than *logos*, authoritative control above and beyond the right to ask questions. They have more in common with non-"deliberative" skeptics of electoral procedures who have begun to explore innovative non-electoral institutions – not for shaping and refining democratic judgment but for giving it practical effect (e.g. McCormick 2006).

Accountability and Deliberationism

Those recent variants of the anti-aggregative critique which have gathered under the banner of "deliberation" often invoke a preference for "a genuine republic" or "a republic of reasons" over "direct" democracy (Sunstein 2001, 7, 239). But the theoretic puzzle remains how exactly a "republic of reasons" is to be wedded to structures of popular power (Habermas 1996, 28–9) – if indeed such structures are meant to be included at all. The question stems from the subordinate place of democracy in the normative scheme of deliberationism, as in the goal of the keystone work of the genre that "democracy might be made safe for deliberation" (Gutmann and Thompson 1996, 347).

The concept of accountability is a register of deliberationism's ambiguous relation to democracy. Compared with the seventeenth-century democrats' conception, deliberationist accountability has a smaller stature and a different character. The frequency of deliberationist invocations of the term "accountability" has not been matched by the clarity of its use, as I will explain in Chapter 7, but it appears that they embody the discursive, rationalist facets of accountability at the expense of its coercive, sanctioning core. To be sure, some political theorists have recognized the need for deliberationism to deal more directly with the concept of authority (e.g. Warren 1996), and others have contemplated "contestatory" challenges with adversarial procedures and binding results (e.g. Pettit 1999). But these gestures toward *kratos* have appeared only in fits and starts. For the most part deliberationism has concentrated on the most narrowly etymological sense of "accountability": *compter* or *conter*, "to count" or "to tell." The first modern democrats, by contrast, understood democratic accountability to require authoritative action over and above talking.

Among the more trenchant criticisms of deliberationism is that it fails to account for the realities of power (see Shapiro 1999; Fontana et al. 2004, 15–18); the same could not be said of the principals of this book. To be fair, deliberationism arose in the 1980s and 1990s in response to the evident difficulties of moral disagreement in pluralistic societies. Though the cultural and intellectual life of seventeenth-century New England was in fact less homogeneous than it is often assumed to have been (as my analyses of ideological rivalries in Chapters 4, 5, and 6 will suggest), it may be true that problems of pluralism often require taming power with reason. But events in the first decade of the twenty-first century have arguably gone some way toward deflating the currency of "reasoning together" and reorienting the perceived theoretic needs associated with accountability: what it means today surely must have more regard to teeth than tongues. Recent political experience suggests that averting disaster often requires that the people be able actually to control their rulers, not just to talk to them and be listened to. This is the sort of world in which the first modern democrats still make for profitable study.

Democracy and Constitutionalism

The central place of power and authoritative decision-making in the idea of democracy raises questions about the structuring of power and the procedures of decision – in other words, about institutional design. The designs of the first modern democratic states were borne by written constitutions setting out both fundamental rights and procedural requirements: the first modern democratic theories were also theories of constitutionalism. But the relation between democracy and constitutionalism today often appears reluctant, troubled, even hostile – and there is good historical and conceptual warrant for the tension. My analysis of the colonial American origins of modern democratic thought suggests a unique angle of vision on the relationship. This perspective reveals the basis of a limited alliance between democracy and constitutionalism, which I will introduce here and discuss in more detail in Chapter 7.

Four aspects of modern constitutionalism appear to supply its main points of contact with democratic theory: (a) constituent power, or the idea that the people is legally superior to the government that it creates or constitutes; (b) legal limitation, or the constraining of governmental actions by written rules; (c) judicial review, by which governmental actions may be confirmed or invalidated by judges; and (d) multicameralism, or "checks and balances" among differentiated agencies of government. My analysis below will suggest an understanding of the relation between democracy and constitutionalism which restricts the meaning of constituent power in a democratic context, reveals distinctive arguments for reconciling democracy with legal limitation, and undermines the democratic credentials of judicial review and multicameralism.

At first blush the idea of *constituent power* appears the least problematic with respect to democracy: it reflects the legal supremacy of the people over the government by enshrining the popular will in constitutional laws that are harder to change than ordinary statutes, which reflect the governmental will. But the prime mechanism at work here, "entrenching" constitutional law by prohibiting alterations or else by allowing them only through extraordinary procedures (such as super-majority voting), has recently been shown to be both historically and conceptually a profoundly anti-democratic practice (see Schwartzberg 2007) – even when constitutional laws genuinely embody the people's will rather than some other agency's. The first modern democrats did not resort to legal entrenchment or the logic of "precommitment," by which entrenchment is construed as formally democratic when it represents the people's binding itself for the future (e.g. Holmes 1995, ch. 5). Instead they showed a simpler way to uphold the idea of constituent power: subjecting governmental agencies to regular accountability before popular ones.

Legal entrenchment is often associated with but remains conceptually distinct from *legal limitation*, by which the actions of governmental agents are constrained by law. Among modern strategies for reconciling legal limitation with democracy, one is to identify substantive rights, like free speech, that deserve constitutional protection from governmental violation because they are essential to a distinctive "democratic" morality (Kateb 1992, 26; Sunstein 2001, 7). Another, more procedural approach focuses on protecting those rights that appear to be empirical preconditions of democratic process (Holmes 1995, 169–72; Pettit 2000, 127–30). The first modern democrats' embrace of legal limitation had nothing to do with uniquely "democratic" rights but, as I will explain further in Chapter 7, obeyed a distinctive logic of its own which foreshadowed the notion of uniquely democratic procedures.

Judicial review is merely one particular (and relatively recently devised) mechanism of enforcement for the idea of legal limitation. It was unknown to the first modern democrats but is usually considered an essential feature of any democratic constitution today. My analysis not only shows how popular control was institutionalized in a world without judicial review but also suggests an intriguing context for understanding the significance of the landmark rationalization of judicial review as a mechanism of democratic accountability. Famously, *The Federalist*, no. 78, attempted to associate legal limitation with the democratic logic of constituent power by making the federal judiciary out to be an intermediary that vindicates the rights of the people as principal against Congress as agent. But this claim was an ironic polemic gesture, not a genuine argument for democratic accountability, as I will explain in Chapter 7. The story of the colonial American origins of modern democratic thought supplies a context of recurring Anglo-American debates on "democracy" in which to understand the irony. What no. 78 did for judicial review against the Anti-Federalists, Winthrop had already done for regular elections against his rivals: to gain acceptance of an aristocratic institutional practice (which one favors) by arguing that it serves democratic political ends (which one's opponent favors). Not one but two of modern democracy's cardinal propositions about institutional design, then, originated in the American tradition of anti-democratic irony.

Finally, another institutional staple of modern democracy warrants skeptical attention from the first modern democrats' point of view: *multicameralism*, which typically involves inter-agency "checks and balances." The division of the legislative assembly into two distinct voting bodies was the *bête noire* of seventeenth-century democrats on both sides of the Atlantic. Though the Levellers famously proposed reducing the English parliament to the House of Commons in the later 1640s, reformers in New England took chronological precedence. There the "negative voice" of the magistrates over the deputies was repeatedly attacked beginning in the 1630s. In fact the Massachusetts opposition's debate with Winthrop on this question forecast the leading themes of the later, post-revolutionary debate on unicameralism versus multicameralism between Paine and John Adams (Maloy 2007).

In summary, the New England democrats' constitutionalism offers critical resources for re-evaluating the relation of democracy and constitutionalism. The central consideration suggested by my historical analysis is one closely related to some of the foremost concerns of institutional design and constitutional reform in political science and legal theory today (e.g. Cook et al. 2005, Levinson 2006): a written constitution can be an instrument of democracy to the extent that it can give structure and stability to practices of regular accountability enabling popular control. Once this proposition is explicated and ramified, the seventeenth-century perspective appears to offer a kind of third way between the paradigmatic liberal quest to tame democratic power and the extreme anti-constitutional view of "fugitive democracy" (Wolin 1989, 11–13; Wolin 1996).

In the context of the broader Anglo-American tradition of constitutionalism, Paine and the Anti-Federalists, notwithstanding their differences, inherited from the original American democracy its intense suspicion of aristocratic power (Hoffert 1992). Because they lost resoundingly in the constitutional debates of the later eighteenth century, the conventional assumption that modern democracy originated in those debates has lent an aura of supremacy to the victorious institutional designs of that era. Once modern democracy's clock is turned back to an era of more even conflict and more mixed results, however, a more balanced sense of the vital (though far from total) role of democratic accountability in Anglo-American constitutionalism becomes possible.

In one of the most useful books in democratic theory in the past decade, Manin, Przeworski, and Stokes have noticed that "there has been a broad and stable consensus over representative institutions" for the past two hundred years (Manin et al. 1999b, 3). Given the accountability deficits that are rampant in modern politics, and are the theme of their collection (Przeworski et al. 1999), they go on to suggest that there is now a need for renewed creativity in institutional design (Manin et al. 1999a, 50–1). That renewal might begin by escaping the two-hundred-year frame in which democratic theory has been stuck and sampling the institutional-design resources of earlier eras.

2

Radical Trust and Accountability in the Seventeenth Century

> Let not your *King* and *Parliament* in *One*,
> Much less apart, mistake themselves for that
> Which is most worthy to be thought upon;
> Or think they are essentially the STATE;
> ...
> But let them know, 'twas for another thing,
> Which they but *represent*; and which, ere long,
> Them to a strict account will doubtless bring,
> If any way they do it willful wrong:
>   For that, indeed, is really the *Face*,
>   Whereof they are the *shadow* in the glass.
>   George Wither, 1645 (Wildman 1645, 8)

The political ideas of seventeenth-century Christendom were shaped by the historical, philosophical, and theological literatures of European societies going back over two millennia. The cumulative lessons of these literatures were usually understood to endorse variations on the theme of one-man rule, and the contemporary prevalence of large and legally centralized monarchic jurisdictions was treated, in print, with broad approval. There were numerous ways of qualifying and limiting monarchic sovereignty, of course, and it was also true that the republics of ancient Sparta and Rome, or of contemporary Venice and Geneva, were lauded by some commentators. But the archetypal democracy of ancient Athens was scarcely considered either a viable or a desirable constitutional option. Macedonian and then Roman hegemony had marked the end not only of Greek democratic practice but also, it seemed, of serious democratic thinking in the West.

This was the intellectual world from which the first English colonists in America came. But the generally anti-democratic consensus of early-modern political thinking was by no means monolithic or invulnerable. Indeed a massive lacuna in the history of democratic theory was about to be closed, as the basic conceptual toolbox for constructing modern democratic states was being assembled and applied for the first time in the middle seventeenth century. The political thought and practice of small and generally insignificant Anglo-American colonies played a surprising and pioneering role in the modern democratic revival, and that story will unfold in succeeding chapters. Appreciating the significance of the American colonists' rehabilitation of democratic thought requires first noticing and investigating the political and intellectual world they left behind.

There are both historical and conceptual reasons for regarding the adaptation of the principle of accountability as the crucial turn in the modernization of democratic thought. Historically, as I will soon show, the scrutiny and sanction of persons of influence or authority by popular bodies were among the essential practices of ancient Greek democracy. Making this essence compatible with modern conditions had to do with accommodating changes less in territorial scale than in intellectual framework – less to do, that is, with the physical than the conceptual setting of modern representative government. As Madison long ago pointed out, the ancient Greeks knew what it meant to delegate power from primary to secondary agencies; what made them different from the moderns was simply that their citizen assemblies delegated authority for administrative not legislative functions (*The Federalist*, no. 63: Hamilton et al. 2005, 340). In a modern state covering a large territory, where legislative power is exercised by a representative assembly that is smaller and more orderly than the entire political community, the rules of accountability could in principle apply much as they did between citizens and magistrates in Athens. It is rather the conceptual furniture that accompanies the modern state, not its sheer physical necessity, that requires significant adaptations of ancient democratic ideas. The peculiar notions of legitimacy, sovereignty, and consent must be accommodated. These conceptual constraints arguably helped to undermine some essential aspects of ancient democracy, notably selection by lottery (Manin 1997, 89–91); by contrast, the ancient principle of accountability could be construed as supplementary to the modern principle of consent. This was the achievement of certain anglophone writers in the middle seventeenth century.

The two facets of Greek accountability were scrutiny and sanction: the first, a discursive act involving inquiry followed by judgment; the second, a punitive act involving harm. The modern notion of consent, by contrast, involves a discursive act resembling judgment, in some respects at least, but without a punitive companion. The theoretic defense of the stronger conception of popular control represented by accountability was mounted for the first time in the context of a modern state by radical publicists during the English Civil War. In addition to building on the revival of ancient ideas of accountability in the sixteenth century, the Levellers made two distinctive moves with respect to other treatments of popular sovereignty and representative assemblies. Previously the principle of accountability had usually been applied to monarchs on behalf of elite bodies; the Levellers applied it to both monarchs and representative councils on behalf of the whole people, using a radicalized language of "trust." And previously, even on those rare occasions when accountability was conceived in democratic rather than aristocratic terms, it had been applied to extraordinary situations of war and resistance; the Levellers applied it to regular constitutional processes. Thus the theoretic origins of modern democracy, in terms of formal principles of institutionalized control, are to be found in the middle seventeenth century; not, as dictated by substantive questions of how widely consent is solicited, in the later eighteenth and early nineteenth centuries.

This new account of modern democracy's ideological genesis runs counter to widespread assumptions about not only the history of democratic ideas in general but also the concept of representation in particular. The rival conceptions of political trust doing battle in the story below, the discretionary and the accountable, resemble Pitkin's two formalistic theories of representation, one of "authorization" and the other of "accountability" (Pitkin 1967, ch. 2). The former, which Pitkin has dated from Hobbes, in fact had important prior expressions in European political debate; and, as we will see, the supposition that champions of accountability have always been merely reacting against Hobbes and Hobbism (57) is arguably the exact converse of the truth. Equally suspect is the supposition that the language of trust and the notion of trusteeship have always implied discretion rather than accountability in a political agent, and that therefore trust in a formal sense is inimical to democracy (128–30). This mistake perhaps follows from regarding the idiosyncratic Burke as a model theorist of political trust – an implausible place for him at least within the anglophone political tradition (see Gough 1950, ch. 7; Paine 1987, 288–9). Contrary to expectations derived from the view that trusteeship and guardianship have little to do with political representation (see Pitkin 1967, 131), the principle of accountability which had been infusing ideas of political trust in the later sixteenth and early seventeenth centuries was during the English Civil War joined precisely to the renascent language of representation (see epigraph above). This combination, as I hope to show, was behind the first attempts to modernize the ancient democratic norm of popular control by making representatives accountable to the represented.

This chapter, then, offers the English side of a new story about the modernization of democratic thought and sets the table for subsequent chapters, which will examine the colonial American side. Two aspects in particular of this chapter's analysis of English and broader European traditions are indispensable to understanding the thought of the first English colonists in America: general ideas of political trust and specific components of the classical, ecclesiastical, and fiduciary models of accountability (see Chapter 1 above).

Ancient Greece

The principle of accountability was of prime importance in the operation of the aboriginal democracies of ancient Greece. This fact was more clearly perceived and more amply remarked by the Greeks themselves than it has been by modern democratic theorists.

Perhaps the first recorded definition of democracy appears in Herodotus's classic account of a speech in favor of the power of the *plethos* (the multitude) (Herodotus 1938, bk. 3, ch. 80); later in his text Herodotus referred back to this as a declaration for democracy (*demokratia*) (bk. 6, ch. 43). The speaker was Otanes, a Persian, who argued that in his favored regime type "all offices are assigned by lot, the holders are accountable for what they do therein, and the general assembly arbitrates on all counsels" (bk. 3, ch. 80). Not long after this speech was supposed to have been made (521 B.C.), the regime bearing the name of *demokratia* began at Athens (508 B.C.), including the three institutional characteristics named by Otanes. The prime organ of public decision was the *ekklesia*, the assembly which all citizens were entitled to attend and speak to. Most officers were selected by lottery, the notable exceptions being the military commanders (*strategoi*), who were elected by vote of the assembly. But all officers, both lotteried and elective, were made accountable to the people by various institutional mechanisms.

The rules and procedures governing relations between the Athenian people and their officers constitute the earliest evidence of democratic accountability (see Roberts 1982, ch. 2; Hansen 1999, 193, 210–11, 218–22, 307–10). Magistrates were subject to scrutiny and sanction by popular jury courts after their terms of service by the process of *euthynai*, an audit backed by monetary and other penalties. They could also be removed in the middle of their term, by either a vote of no confidence (*apocheirotonia*) or a trial of impeachment (*eisangelia*) before the whole assembly of citizens. The latter extended to elective as well as lotteried officers, and even orators with no formal position could be prosecuted via the *graphe paranomon*. The juries that adjudicated these audits and impeachments were popular in composition, being selected by lottery from among the pool of citizens over the age of thirty.

Otanes' reference to "answerability" suggests that these various procedures of accountability were considered essential to ancient democracy. This view was far from eccentric: Aeschylus also shared it (Roberts 1982, 5–6), Plato's *Statesman* specifically named *euthynai* among democracy's alleged faults (Plato 1995, 299a), and Aristotle repeated Otanes' three characteristics of democracy in his own discussions of that regime type. The famous account in the *Politics* names ten distinct institutional features as characteristic of democratic regimes, including a supreme citizen assembly, the selection of magistrates by lottery, and the auditing of officers by popular bodies (Aristotle 1998, 1317b).

Famously, Aristotle himself had mixed feelings about democracy, but accountability is a constant theme of his analysis of that regime type in all its variations. In the worst kind of democracy, for instance, Aristotle claimed that "all offices are destroyed" because the people are allowed to judge impeachments (1292a). In another place, however, he included among the best kind of democracy's features the fact that magistrates "will rule justly because the others have authority over the inspection of officials" (1318b). Though he clearly believed it could be carried to excess (a point on which most modern writers have agreed), the ability of the *demos* (people) to scrutinize and sanction their magistrates was for Aristotle essential to their *kratos* (power). Yet the complexity of his thinking about democracy tended not to impress his medieval and early-modern readers. Aristotle and his students often treated democracy favorably as a counterbalance to the oligarchic schemes of some of their contemporaries (Ober 1998, chs. 6–7). But his use of the term *demokratia* to denote one of the bad or "mistaken" forms of government (Aristotle 1998, 1279b) was seized on by Aquinas and other readers in the thirteenth century (the first ones in Europe to read the *Politics* since ancient times) and transmitted to posterity as reducing democracy to the oppression of the rich by the tyrannical poor (Skinner 1992, 59–60).

Tuck's important finding must be noted that the *Politics* was occasionally used in a manner favorable to democracy, by dint of revaluing certain elements of the "extreme" form of democracy which Aristotle himself had condemned and using it to describe the Roman republic (Tuck 2006,

176–83). But the overwhelming verdict of classical wisdom, in the eyes of the early-moderns, seemed to hold that just and benevolent rule required bearers of authority to be unaccountable to popular agencies. Luminaries on the order of Plato, Cicero, Seneca, and Augustine all left written evidence of their understanding of political power as a kind of guardianship which allowed wide discretion to pursue the common good. This dominant discretionary legacy of ancient philosophy may explain why, for a period of almost two millennia, writing about democratic accountability was as rare as practicing it. But formal principles of accountability similar to those associated with Greek democracy were more abundantly preserved in and more favorably received from another department of ancient literature.

Roman Law

The rules and procedures governing guardians and other fiduciary agents in Roman law preserved a model of accountable authority that would prove more accessible to future generations than the fragmentary records of Greek political life. When medieval jurists and early-modern publicists turned to the private law of ancient Rome for analogies to illuminate the public law of the kingdoms and empires of their own day, or even of the "natural" laws of politics in general, the principle of accountability was one of the main conceptual tools to hand.

Three areas of Roman law were particularly relevant in this respect: agency, property, and liability. The Roman guardian (*tutor*) was held accountable for the protection of his ward (*pupillus*) by judicial processes in which a finding of deceit, negligence, or incompetence could result in his removal; a bare accusation suspended the guardian's authority (Buckland 1950, 160). Guardians were also subject to double damages for the embezzlement of their wards' estates and to the loss of some civil and legal rights in cases ranging from gross negligence to simple inaction (Buckland 1931, 79). A *curator* took charge of a person of legal majority who suffered some mental defect unrelated to age, such as insanity, and was also subject to damages for mismanagement, as well as being required to offer security before assuming his post (82–5). Between persons of full legal competence, the bearer of a mandate (*mandatus*) answered to his principal via the *actio mandati*, and his powers were revocable at pleasure (*ad bene placitum*); the *procuratio*, a position of estate management, was an early version of the mandate (278–80).

Roman models of accountable agency arose out of not only the law of persons but also that of property. The *fiducia* was an obligation appended to a conveyance of property which functioned like a covenant in modern times, as "a direction or trust as to what was to be done with [the property conveyed]" (Buckland 1950, 431). Roman rules of liability supplemented contract law with a range of standards for determining when an agreement had been breached. The basic rule of *bona fides* (good faith) originally required *dolus* (deceit) in order to trigger liability; over time the rule slackened to include *culpa* (negligence or carelessness). The shift from *dolus* to *culpa* liability required agents of all kinds to exercise an active, prudent management of their principals' property, as if the principals were managing it themselves (Buckland 1931, 302–5). These principles of Roman law involved various mechanisms of scrutiny and sanction, including the taking of security *ex ante* and the inflicting of deterrent punishment *ex post*, as well as various criteria of abuse related to the rationale of fiduciary authority: the welfare of the ward or principal. Thus they were a prime source of the versatility of what I have called the fiduciary model of accountability.

The Roman-law language of fiduciary agency was seized on for larger political purposes by medieval and early-modern writers who were interested in analogizing the public authority of kings and popes to that of trustees in private law. By the fourteenth century legal scholars were describing political authority as "a guardianship over wards" (*tutela pupillorum*) and "the estate-management of the public realm" (*procuratio reipublicae*); by the sixteenth century it was not uncommon for jurists to characterize "public office" (*officium publicum*) generically as a guardianship (*tutela*) (Gierke 1900, 141–2, 148). But this fiduciary idiom could serve either a *discretionary* or an *accountable* conception of political trust. Those interested in defending the former insisted on the moral imperative of keeping faith (*fides*) by ruling for the common good but held that breaches thereof (*laesio fidei*) were answerable only to God in the hereafter (36, 144–5). Indeed what was usually taken as the aboriginal precedent of popular sovereignty, the *lex regia* by which the Roman people had granted power to their emperors, was often construed as the irrevocable alienation of popular rights of agency (Lloyd 1991, 255). Other prominent writers like Bartolus and Marsilius considered, on the contrary, that popular sovereignty was generally delegated (*concessum*) rather than alienated (Skinner 1978, 1:62–5). Bartolus, who would be best known to posterity for his defense of tyrannicide, traced a pathway of accountability from prince to people running in the opposite direction of, and logically correlative to, the original grant of power. In the early sixteenth century the "Sorbonnists" Mair and Almain, following the formula of John of Paris (ca. 1250) in characterizing authority as *dispensatio* or *ministerium* (stewardship) rather than *dominium* (ownership), were the most prominent heirs to the thesis of delegation not alienation (2:119–22), and Salamonio used it to reinterpret the *lex regia* itself as a conditional and revocable grant of power (2:130–4).

Resistance Theory

Debates between the discretionary and the accountable conceptions of trust assumed new importance later in the sixteenth century, when the civil wars associated with religious reformations and counter-reformations lent new urgency to questions of sovereignty and resistance. In these debates fluid circumstances mattered as much as fixed principles, and by the turn of the century Catholic strategies for justifying resistance had assumed the same contours as Protestant ones (Figgis 1998, 138–9, 144). Though the notion of alienated sovereignty was formally associated with absolute and irresistible rule, it could be made to accommodate substantive exceptions legitimating revolt. Thus Suarez, a harsh critic of Bartolus's "false doctrine" that sovereignty is delegated and therefore revocable (*De Legibus*, 3.4.6; in Suarez 1944), was nonetheless a notorious "monarchomach" (king killer) by dint of his call for English Catholics to overthrow the Protestant King James. The narrowness of the grounds of Suarez's resistance theory is indicated by the title of his most famous polemic, *Defensio Fidei Catholicae* (1613): "a defense of the Catholic faith."

Nederman has noticed, in differentiating medieval from modern conceptions of constitutionalism, a distinction between moral and theological, or substantive, limitations on power and formal limitations (Nederman 1996, 187). In this respect both Catholics and Protestants in France in the later sixteenth century took a modern turn away from Suarez by seeking out the wider latitude for resistance afforded by the formal properties of delegated sovereignty. The Calvinist "Huguenots" analyzed the French monarchy not only by reference to customary law, as in Hotman's *Franco-Gallia* (1573), but also by the avid use of Roman-law models of accountable trusteeship to defend resistance. Theodore Beza's *Right of Magistrates* (1574), for example, likened God's designation of rulers over nations to the judicial assignment of guardians over wards (Franklin 1969, 103). "Stephanus Junius Brutus," the pseudonymous author of the *Vindiciae contra Tyrannos* (1579), argued that kings should be regarded *de jura tuentibus* (according to the law of tutorship), "as guardians rather than as usurpers" (Garnett 1994, 19). The claim that political power generally resembles Roman-law guardianship was frequently reiterated in the *Vindiciae* (123, 127, 159). In this connection Brutus alluded to the practice of *rationem reddere* (literally, "to render account"), which a Roman guardian had to perform before a magistrate at the end of his term of service, using it to argue that kings lay under the same kind of obligation to account for their government before God (lxxxi, 17).

Like the Huguenot publicists, the Scottish humanist George Buchanan used arguments from Roman law to defend violent resistance as a form of political accountability, but Buchanan's theory was more radical in several respects. In *De Jure Regni apud Scotos* (1579) he defended the view of sovereignty as delegated and revocable by specifically denying, in Bartolist fashion, the traditional account of the *lex regia* as an alienation of the Roman people's sovereignty (Buchanan 2004, 93). He went on to argue that, even if a king had secured a contract from his people authorizing him to rule arbitrarily and abusively, deceit and fraud would be grounds for invalidating the agreement: "the laws also grant full restitution to those outwitted by fraud, and this principle they think should apply particularly to minors" (99). Buchanan was here referring to *actio furti*, a legal procedure applicable to a wide variety of agents in Roman law, including depositees and custodians, when they defrauded their principals for their own profit; *restitutio in integrum* ("full restitution") was one of the remedies associated with this judicial process (Buckland 1931, 327–30; Buckland 1950, 560–1). The fiduciary language of Roman law also figured in Buchanan's definition of tyrants as those who "wield power not for their country but for themselves... and who see their kingship not as a commission [*procuratio*] entrusted to them by God but as plunder for the taking" (Buchanan 2004, 87).

This fiduciary-legal idiom was used to make a general point about the obligations attached to political power, and the thesis of delegation not alienation, entailing that authority transmitted by the people must remain accountable to them, promised a more radical and permissive resistance theory. But the question of who exactly can call rulers to account depended on further specifications. Both Buchanan and the Huguenots identified God as the fountain of political power as often as they did the people, and the Huguenots in particular exploited the idea of guardianship to make resistance the exclusive preserve of an elite of "ephors" reminiscent of ancient Sparta (Garnett 1994, 49, 80). After all, guardians exist because children are incapable of representing themselves in a legal capacity, and this fact fit nicely the Huguenots' wary stance toward popular agency.

Where Buchanan and later the Jesuit Juan de Mariana departed from the Huguenots was, first, in their broader, more populist notions of who may call a tyrant to account (Skinner 1978, 2:343–8), but also in their emphasis on regular constitutional mechanisms of accountability rooted in local traditions. Buchanan claimed that in Scottish history "many [kings] who used their office cruelly and scandalously were called to account by their subjects, that some were condemned to imprisonment for life, others punished in some cases with exile, in others with death" (Buchanan 2004, 95). These local customs had the sanction of natural reason by dint of a transitive logic, "since the law is more powerful than the king... and the people more powerful than the law" (135). Mariana's remarks on regular accountability had an Athenian flavor, as in his recommendation of the regular auditing of magistrates: "it would be very salutary to demand an accounting of the public trust" because rulers "would necessarily become accustomed to live with the others equitably under the law" (Mariana 1948, 268). But the model for this "guardianship of the Commonwealth" (333) came from medieval Spain rather than classical Greece, for Mariana contemplated a larger project of resurrecting defunct Spanish institutions like the *cortes* as bulwarks against the encroaching centralism of the previous century of military empire – typified by the Inquisition, which Mariana knew from bitter personal experience (Lewy 1960, 11–13, 22, 112).

By the end of the sixteenth century, then, the Roman law had served as a vehicle for bringing not only the principle of popular sovereignty but also the principle of accountability to the fore of political debate in Europe. Yet seldom was the composition of agencies of accountability allowed to be popular rather than elite. The willingness of many theorists of resistance to claim the people as the original fountain of power while treating them as a legal minor incapable of independent action amounted to a brief flirtation with democratic accountability followed by a nervous retreat. In short, popular sovereignty and accountability were simultaneously present but rarely integrated. Buchanan and Mariana offered momentary glimpses of how genuinely popular bodies might be incorporated into the fiduciary model of accountability; others contributed toward widening this view into a more steady gaze.

Bodin and Althusius

The resistance theories of the sixteenth century, particularly the French, had a significant influence around Europe for decades to come, particularly in England (Salmon 1959, chs. 1–2, 5). By the middle seventeenth century some Englishmen, more in the manner of Buchanan and Mariana than of the Huguenots, would join popular sovereignty and accountability in firm partnership. The *Vindiciae* had claimed that the people as a body "transferred to them [its representatives] all its legal capacity" (Garnett 1994, 49), but the

1648 English translation of the *Vindiciae* simply omitted this phrase (Laski 1924, 99). Clearly the Huguenot resistance theories had a lasting influence, but equally clearly the rebels of a later era were no longer committed to a complete defect of popular agency.

In significant measure the terms of debate within which this English innovation took place were shaped by Bodin and Althusius, two of the most renowned analysts of sovereignty and most cited authorities during the English Civil War (Salmon 1959, 85, 88). Bodin's attack on theories of resistance, responding precisely to the *Vindiciae* and its ilk (Franklin 1973), was included in his massive and wide-ranging *Six Books of the Republic* (1576). There he conceived political power in such a way as apparently to exclude the accountable conception of trust. He famously defined sovereignty as "the most high, absolute, and perpetual power," thereby ruling out conditional or even temporary tenure (Bodin 1962, 84). All "men put in trust," he claimed, hold power for a fixed term and "hold nothing of themselves, but are to give account of their doings unto the prince or the people of whom they had the power so to command; whereas the prince or people themselves, in whom the Sovereignty resteth, are to give account unto none but to the immortal God alone" (84, 86). Bodin was especially concerned with the perpetuity of office, for he appears to have assumed that any temporary post was necessarily burdened by accountability, presumably because returning to the station of an ordinary subject exposed a former ruler to legal liability. Thus even the ten-year magistrate (*archon*) of pre-democratic Athens could not be regarded as sovereign because he was "yet [ac]countable of his actions unto the people, his time being expired" (86). Bodin went on the defend the view that a people could alienate its entire authority (88) and to deny that a genuine sovereign could be held accountable in the extreme form of violent resistance (221–5), unless he were acting from a condition of captivity or insanity (95).

Bodin's remarks on the classification of regime types also revealed important aspects of his views on sovereignty and accountability. On his view a democracy or "popular state" exists where "such power given unto the magistrates belong[s] unto the people, and... is not given but as in trust unto the magistrates" (Bodin 1962, 185). On this view a democratic state would repose both the election and the correction of governors in the people, as confirmed by Bodin's further remarks about identifying sovereignty in historical examples. Ancient Rome was a democracy, on Bodin's view, because the tribunes were more powerful than the senate and consuls (188–90); specifically, the tribunes had the right to call consuls to account for state crimes through special inquests resembling impeachment (477). In another example, Geneva as it existed under its 1528 constitution (before Calvin), Bodin again found the sovereignty to be democratic, despite the elite character of the magistrates there, because of a kind of annual audit: "the censuring of every one of them every year is still reserved unto the Citizens, which is most straightly looked unto" (233).

The protocols for Bodin's classification of regimes are more fully explained in book 2, chapter 7. Having distinguished "state" or sovereignty from "government" or administration (Bodin 1962, 199), Bodin explained that the classification of a regime should depend on the former not the latter, since the sovereign might vary the form of administration but not vice versa. Rome, on this view, was a democratic state with an aristocratic government (249), as was Geneva. The reputedly novel state/government distinction appears to have been intended as a way to undermine the Aristotelian "mixed" regime by replacing it with a new sort of mixture: not a dividing and sharing of sovereignty itself but a discrepancy in the compositions of sovereign and administrative bodies (Franklin 1963, 75).

Althusius's *Politica Methodice Digesta* (1603) was an equally ambitious work, whose implications for the debate over resistance were made explicit in its preface. Althusius announced that his analysis of sovereignty was "the exact opposite" of Bodin's, since he would conclude that the "supreme magistrate" was merely the "steward, administrator, and overseer" of sovereignty, while the whole community had "ownership" of it – this was the old distinction between *ministerium* (or *dispensatio*) and *dominium* taken from John of Paris and the Sorbonnists. Althusius further concluded that only a people not a prince could hold sovereignty in perpetual succession, and he denied that a people could alienate it (Althusius 1995, 7). Chapter 9 of the *Politica* made good on these promises and spelled out their implication that "the supreme monarch is required to give an account of his administration ... and can even be deposed" (73). Althusius went on to defend the usual Calvinist position that resistance may normally only be performed by an ephoral elite, with the reservation that ordinary subjects may resist unjust acts of violence by lesser magistrates (196).

On the question of regime types, in a further departure from Bodin, Althusius insisted that the best government was of the conventional mixed sort (Althusius 1995, 204–5). He observed no Bodinian distinction between sovereignty and administration but classified regimes according to the "prevailing part" of a constitution; thus Althusius's scheme of classification savored more of the conventional approach associated with Aristotle, Polybius, or Machiavelli. At the same time Althusius's defense of resistance, perhaps not altogether ironically, involved much weaker references to regular, peaceful means of accountability than Bodin's anti-resistance analysis had done. For Althusius "the state or magistrate is democratic when certain persons elected alternately and successively from the people for definite periods of time rule all the others" (206). This definition put the whole burden of "democracy" on popular consent via elections and none on popular control via non-electoral procedures of accountability; Bodin, albeit for analytic not normative purposes, was much more explicit about the essential role of regular accountability.

The *magna opera* of Bodin and Althusius appeared to represent (among other things) the two principal contending views on questions of sovereignty and resistance. But Salmon and Franklin have perceptively argued that this was less true of the first question than of the second. Despite his own advertisement of "exact" opposition, Althusius in a sense accepted Bodin's indivisible sovereignty, differing only in holding that it necessarily lies in the whole community (Salmon 1959, 47–50; Franklin 1991, 312–13; Salmon 1996, 507); in short, he implicitly assumed that the locus of sovereignty must always be "popular" or "democratic." The Bodinian conception of sovereignty, after all, was not inimical to accountability per se: the sovereign was simply (and by definition) the *only* unaccountable agency in society, to which *all other* powers were to be held accountable. This is the connection in which the legacy of Bodin and Althusius would reach beyond the context of resistance theory and into the later development of ideas of democratic accountability. Whereas their legalistic analyses of primary and derivative powers would inform the fiduciary model of accountability, the examples of historical republics discussed in Bodin in particular would inform the classical model.

It was Bodin more than Althusius who would influence seventeenth-century developments in England, where his *Six Books* was used as a textbook of legal and political theory and an encyclopedia of political history. Both authors considered democracy to be far from ideal, violently so in the case of certain passages from the *Six Books* (see Bodin 1962, bk. 6, ch. 4), but both also treated it as a potentially viable if relatively rare form of government. Ironically, Bodin would figure more prominently in the modernization of democratic theory: the uncompromising picture he painted of unmixed "popular states" would be viewed much more favorably by some of his readers than by Bodin himself. If his defense of unaccountable sovereign monarchs would find favor with one side of the coming English debates on sovereignty, the mechanisms of regular accountability which he associated with popular states like Rome and Geneva would find favor with another.

Trust and English Law

Though discourses of Roman law and resistance theory helped to supply the century of the Levellers, Hobbes, and Locke with idioms of trust and ideas of accountability, there was an important vernacular tradition around "trust" which would play an equally vital role. This tradition featured the insular developments of English law which seeped into political theory in the Tudor and early Stuart periods. Gough's impressive survey of the uses of "trust" in English political thought from the sixteenth century to the Victorian theory of empire played down the significance of the technical legal trust (Gough 1950, ch. 7). Yet this was one of the principal engines of English legal development in the sixteenth and seventeenth centuries (Holdsworth 1927, 4:408–17), and it was only natural that it would have broad effects on England's legalistic political culture.

The roots of English trust law lie in the "use," which functioned much like the *fiducia* of Roman law, as an agreement attached to a conveyance of land. When a landholder "enfeoffed" his property to another, he could require that part or all of it be held "to the use of" a third party. In theory the "feoffor" could thereby retain control over both the property and the "feoffee"; in practice, however, the feoffor and the third-party beneficiary of a use were both at the mercy of the feoffee's discretion, and legal remedies to uphold their rights at common law were few and cumbersome. For this reason the use, by around 1500, had become a central part of the equitable jurisdiction of the court of Chancery, where parties who felt they had been wronged by the rigors of common-law procedure appealed for relief (Holdsworth 1927, 1:454, 4:408–17).

Over the course of the sixteenth century the beneficiary (also called the *cestui que use*) became "Chancery's darling" (Maitland 1936, 174), despite the effort of the Statute of Uses (1535) to make the proprietary interests of beneficiaries enforceable at common law in order to divert some of Chancery's booming business to other courts (Holdsworth 1927, 1:455, 4:409). As a result, feoffees were increasingly held liable for their beneficiaries' well-being. This same kind of development was evident, from an earlier period, in the law of guardianship. Like the Roman *tutela*, English guardianship began as a position more of privilege than responsibility, and it was widely viewed as a legitimate source of profit. But the legal guardian in England was over the course of the fourteenth and fifteenth centuries made more and more accountable, until he was, on one observer's view, "no better off than a servant" (Pollock and Maitland 1899, 1:481, 2:435–44):

in this sense "guardianship... developed into a trusteeship" (Holdsworth 1927, 3:66). And ideas that came out of the law of uses naturally gathered under the rubric of "trust": as Bacon said in his "Reading on the Statute of Uses" (1600), "*Usus est dominium fiduciarium*: Use is an ownership in trust" (Bacon 1864, 14:291). More broadly the term "trust" and its derivatives could refer to fiduciary relations of power among not only guardians but also bailiffs, commercial agents, executors of wills, and feoffees of land (Holdsworth 1923, 370).

In general the procedures of accountability applicable to fiduciary agents in English law resembled those of Roman law. As the great common-lawyer Coke recognized, an English guardian "shall be accountable whensoever it shall please the heir to call him to account after the age of fourteen" (Coke 1650, 27), and in any case he had to give security, keep an inventory, and render up his accounts "when the wardship is out" (Cowel 1651, 34, 49). In charitable trusts, in which a general public interest supplied the absence of an identifiable beneficiary, the chancellor had since Elizabethan times had authority to appoint commissions to audit trustees and to assess compensatory damages for "abuses," "breaches of trust," "negligences," fraud, and mismanagement (Herne 1663, 10–16).

These developments were very gradual, and the records of their key moments are fragmentary, but it is clear that the positions of guardian and trustee were being assimilated as accountable not discretionary figures by about 1500. In the sixteenth century, then, the political valence of "trust" in England derived not only from its referents in classical or Christian ethics but also from the important role it had assumed in English law. The fiduciary idea was first radicalized – that is, not only construed in accountable terms but also referred to popular agencies – in the context of counter-reformation and Protestant resistance in which Englishmen were implicated as well as their continental coreligionists.

Tudor and Stuart England

An important predecessor of the resistance theories of the Huguenots and Buchanan was John Ponet's *Shorte Treatise of Politike Power* (1556), the first piece of political writing in English to employ "trust" in a call to resistance and perhaps the earliest articulation of the ecclesiastical model of political accountability. Ponet was among the "Marian exiles" who fled England after the accession of the Catholic Queen Mary in order to practice their uncompromising brand of Protestantism in continental havens like Emden, Frankfurt, and Geneva in the 1550s. He wrote to agitate the deposition of Mary from the English throne. His keynote is sounded in his epigraph, taken from Psalm 118: "It is better to trust in the Lord than to trust in Princes" (Ponet 1972, title page). Though the substantive moral relation of *fides* appears thereby to be given pride of place, in fact the *Shorte Treatise* exploited the dual meaning of "trust" by connecting personal confidence with formal, legalistic relations of accountability.

The premise of Ponet's analysis (prefiguring Buchanan) is that personal confidence is always perilous where human governors are concerned. It was all too common that "he that maketh suit to be a deputy for the multitude seemeth to sue for his own vainglory and profit" and "meaneth not the benefit of them that he would serve" (Ponet 1972, J/8b-K/1a); "such an evil governor properly men call a Tyrant" (G/3a). Ponet's notion of what makes a ruler trustworthy depended on a formalistic conception of authority. Thus the language of "office and charge" (B/1b) is even more frequently used in conjunction with "trust" than that of moral or other psychic relations: governors are described as being "put in trust and authority to make statutes and laws" (B/1a), "being put in trust in Courts and parliaments to make laws and statutes" (B/1b), and holding "an office upon trust" (G/6a).

The hallmark of this notion of political trusteeship, above and beyond moral confidence, was the principle of accountability, which supplies procedures for the principal's satisfaction in case the agent's fidelity fails. Thus "all laws do agree that men may revoke their proxies and letters of Attorney when it pleaseth them; much more when they see their proctors and attorneys abuse it" (Ponet 1972, G/6a). The justified avenues of correction and punishment of wicked rulers might even reach to tyrannicide; hence "it is lawful to kill a tyrant" as part of the "account and reckoning" which "the body of the whole congregation or commonwealth" are entitled to exact (G/5b). This equivalence of church and state power signaled the advent of the ecclesiastical model of accountability, in which power-holders are under the control of all the members acting as one body. For, unlike the Huguenots, Ponet did not dabble in Roman-law guardianship's denial of rights of action to one side of the fiduciary relation; he preferred the common law of agency in which principals may revoke their agents' power at pleasure.

It was in the reign of James I, the third cousin of Ponet's target Mary, that political trusteeship first became overtly the subject of domestic debate in England. In contrast to medieval characterizations of English monarchs as guardian-like and discretionary figures (see Lockwood 1997, xx–xxii), there was by 1600 little question about whether political trustees were generally accountable for their fiduciary duties, for developments in the law had made that a rock-bottom assumption in English political culture. The Chancery had established, and common-lawyers like Coke had accepted, that guardians can be held liable for injuring their charges' welfare. To the extent that holders of political authority were likened to guardians, then, the great problem was *how* and *to whom* they were accountable.

James himself was a party to these polemics. He had repudiated Buchanan, his former tutor, and engaged in a polemic battle against Suarez's call for him to be overthrown as a heretical prince, and therefore was intimately familiar with the uses of the fiduciary idea in debates on resistance. James followed Bodin's normative view of monarchic sovereignty in maintaining, in a speech before Parliament in 1610, that the king is "accountable to none but God only" (Sommerville 1994, 181–2). In *The Trew Law of Free Monarchies* (1616) he further described his position in terms congenial to the fiduciary idea, while in the same breath denying any temporal accountability to human agencies: "a loving father and careful watchman, caring for them more than for himself, knowing himself to be ordained for them, and they not for him; and therefore accountable to that great God, who placed him as lieutenant over them, upon the peril of his soul to procure the weal of both souls and bodies" (65). James meant to defend these principles against "Levellers" and others with a "Puritanical itching after Popularity" (222, 227), and his way of polemically defending discretion by apparently honoring accountability established the bedrock logic of Stuart absolutism in England.

James's arguments were not uncontroversial, as evidenced by the fact that the debate continued under his ill-fated son and successor. As Charles I's attorney general Robert Heath queried in the Five Knights' Case (1627), "who shall call in question the actions or the justice of the king, who is not to give any account of them?" (Gardiner 1906, 60). Charles himself supplied what he considered the only possible answer when he dissolved Parliament in 1629, asserting that "princes are not bound to give account of their actions but to God alone" (83). In the parliamentary debates of the previous year, which had resulted in the Petition of Right but also had precipitated the fateful dissolution, Heath had elaborated the royal case in the fashionable terms of "reason of state": the secrets of the kingdom (*arcana regni*) could not be inquired after by Parliament (White 1979, 248–50). In reply Edward Coke insisted that "trust," if construed in a "parliamentary way," must dispel such secrecy, since submitting a petition for grievances was the time-honored method for Parliament to uphold Magna Carta and the English liberties associated with it (261–3). Coke was defending a regular process of making the king answer to the people's representatives, but even this purely discursive form of accountability was met with royal rejection. Within a little over a decade events turned Englishmen's minds to forms of accountability that were coercive rather than discursive and extraordinary rather than regular.

Civil War

The English Civil War carried the debate around trust into a climate of emergent politics, but the regular constitutional trust of democratic accountability would emerge from the rubble. "Trust" was radicalized again in the manner of Ponet, not only made accountable but also oriented toward popular bodies, but this time the most innovative move involved the further step of proposing the accountable trust to reconstruct what it had previously been used to destroy: a regime of legal order.

"Trust" was flourishing mightily in English political discourse in the years leading up to and during the Civil War: it was applied to the king, his ministers, both houses of parliament, military commanders, and judicial and administrative officers. Parliamentarians, on the one hand, justified their demands for policy change and constitutional reform "in discharge of the trust which we owe to the State, and to those whom we represent"; on the other, they accused various royal counselors of abusing the trust they held from the king (Gardiner 1906, 201–5). After the start of armed conflict Henry Parker, the prolific pamphleteer for the parliamentarian cause, justified resistance to Charles in part by alleging that the king's abuse of power constituted a breach of trust (Mendle 1995, 83). Because parliament was the true representative of the people, Parker insisted, it could resume original sovereignty in such an emergency (Sharp 1983, 143). Though this conjunction of ideas of trust and representation enabled parliament to hold the king accountable, it simultaneously denied any accountability as between parliament and the people. In Parker's hands the right of resistance was confined to the people's appointed guardians, much as in the Huguenot theory.

The near defeat of parliamentary forces in 1642, however, led others to speculate about the legitimacy of popular resistance against parliament itself in case the latter failed to fulfill its own trust (Wootton 1990, 659–63). The Levellers revived and ramified this line of thought in 1645–6, when the menace of parliamentary betrayal had more to do with religious persecution and other perceived injustices than with military failure. They sought to make not just the king but also parliament subject to the accountable trust. Thus Richard Overton told parliamentarians that "the edge of your own arguments against the King in this kind may be turned upon yourselves"

(Sharp 1998, 56), referring to the conjunction of the accountable trust with the ubiquitous formula *salus populi suprema lex* ("the people's safety is the supreme law"). If the common good was the prime object of legitimate authority, the accountable trust might justify resistance against parliamentary as well as royal violators. In a similar vein William Walwyn attacked "that common and thread-bare doctrine that Kings were accountable only to God.... No, they are but corrupt and dangerous flatterers that maintain any such fond opinions concerning either Kings or Parliaments" (McMichael and Taft 1989, 150). In their first major collective effort in print, *A Remonstrance of Many Thousand Citizens* (1646) on behalf of their imprisoned comrade John Lilburne, the Levellers advised members of parliament that "we possessed you with the same power that was in ourselves.... But ye are to remember, this was only of us but a power of trust – which is ever revocable, and cannot be otherwise"; in short, "we are your principals, and you our agents" (Sharp 1998, 33–4).

In shifting the locus of accountable relations of trust in this way, the Levellers were in effect appropriating the Bodinian conception of sovereignty from Parker and other supporters of the so-called Long Parliament, which had raised its standard against Charles. The parliamentarians had themselves taken the Bodinian idea of "arbitrary, absolute" sovereignty from the Stuart kings and simply relocated it to a representative assembly (Mendle 1995, 87–8), somewhat as Althusius had done from Bodin himself. Though their pamphlets sometimes echoed Parker by describing parliament's power in Bodinian terms (e.g. Sharp 1998, 131, 133), the Levellers went on to deny that the people's representatives wield a purely discretionary authority with which the people may not interfere. They insisted, as Ponet had done, that principals may sanction their agents and even revoke their commissions: this was what the *Remonstrance* meant in declaring on its title page the petitioners' intent of "calling these their commissioners in parliament to an account" (33).

The Civil War language of trust was inspired in part by the republication and citation of the Huguenot resistance tracts (Salmon 1959, ch. 5) as well as of Ponet's *Shorte Treatise* (Hudson 1942, 210), and one observer claimed that "whereas in the beginning Buchanan was looked on as an oracle, he was now slighted as not anti-monarchical enough" (Gooch 1927, 98). But often ideas of accountability were couched in terms of property and agency under English law. It was claimed, for example, that "there is a difference between disposing of things by way of donation or sale, and disposing of things by way of trust"; this was the difference between a straight conveyance, or alienation, and a fiduciary conveyance, "as in the case that a Steward be trusted with a man's house" (Bridge 1643, 41). The parliamentarian news sheet *Mercurius Britannicus* referred to the king's "fiduciary interest of trust and depositoriness" as inferior to the proprietary interest of the people (Worden 1995, 314), and William Ball made the same point against parliament by an extended analogy of its authority as a "Lease of Trust" (Malcolm 1999, 296). John Goodwin brought this kind of legal analogy to the point of violent resistance when he argued that the people retain a liberty of "removing of such persons, whom they have chosen for Guardians to their Estates and Liberties, from these places of trust, when they evidently discern a direct tendency in their proceedings to betray them" (Goodwin 1649, 13).

Goodwin's and others' militancy had been shared, intermittently, by the Levellers. What made this militancy possible in practical terms was the rise of the New Model Army. By 1647 the army appeared to be the most viable vehicle for democratic accountability against the Long Parliament, which for the Levellers' taste was becoming too friendly with defeated royalists while remaining too intolerant of religious sectarians. Thus Overton claimed that the army was "the *natural Head* of the *Body natural* of the people at this present" (Overton 1647, 27). Tragically for the Levellers and their supporters, army leaders – specifically, Oliver Cromwell and his son-in-law and lieutenant Henry Ireton – also appeared guilty of betrayal by dint of stifling radicals' hopes for wide-ranging political and legal reform. The Levellers became desperate for peace, doubtless reflecting the yearnings of thousands of soldiers and civilians alike; but, more specifically, for peaceful means of achieving justice through regular rather than extraordinary accountability.

The Agreement of the People

The Levellers' strategic alliances varied according to the political, military, and diplomatic ebbs and flows of the later 1640s, but what united Lilburne, Overton, and Walwyn throughout this turbulent period was the goal of achieving a peaceful settlement through new constitutional forms of accountability. From the summer of 1647, shortly before the famous army debates at Putney, until late in 1649, under the post-regicide Cromwellian regime, the Levellers' commitment to a program of constitutional reconstruction was as central to their activities as the substantive ethical commitments (especially freedom of conscience) which had first brought them together.

Elections were at the core of the Levellers' formal, institutional program. They hardly missed an opportunity to complain of the Long Parliament's continuance in light of the fact that, as Lilburne saw it, "many of the members betrayed their trust" (Lilburne 1645b, 33). Therefore they demanded in the first instance a new parliament to be selected by new elections, but for the longer term they also insisted that the provision of regular elections at intervals fixed by law was "so essential to their freedom that without it they are no better than slaves" (Fairfax 1647, 14). This program found its ultimate expression in what became their trademark document: the so-called Agreement of the People. In its three versions the Agreement was conceived as a trust-deed detailing the general purposes and specific conditions against which the people could judge the performance of their trustees. "The people are to declare what their power and trust is – which is the intent of this Agreement" (Sharp 1998, 97): the first version sought thereby to remove the "obscurity and doubtfulness" of the nature and extent of the people's commission to their governors (96). It was later described as "an Agreement between those that trust and those who are trusted" (141) and was the first of several attempts in seventeenth-century England to substitute for war and resistance a "pacified" politics (see Baumgold 1993).

The first Agreement briefly laid out what would remain the stable nucleus of the Levellers' constitutional program: a representative, frequently elected, unicameral parliament was to be the supreme legislative power of the nation, "without the consent or concurrence of any other person or persons" (Sharp 1998, 94). Against the prevailing common-law norms of changing law by incremental and judicial rather than purposive and legislative means, the Levellers were the first Englishmen to say that such an assembly should have comprehensive powers to revise or repeal old laws and to create new ones (Schwartzberg 2007, 75–91). The first Agreement's other clauses included a vague provision for proportionality and "equal representation" in electoral districts, a more specific one for biennial elections, and a list of "reserved powers" which representatives were not to meddle with, including freedom of conscience and freedom from conscription. These essential features of Leveller constitutionalism remained unchanged, though modifications to electoral districts and terms of office were made in the second and third iterations of the Agreement.

Thus the Levellers' Agreement of the People put forward what is perhaps the most basic feature of a recognizably modern sort of democratic constitutionalism, the idea of constituent power: a constitution embodies the will of the people, which is superior to that of their governors. The specific characteristics of the supreme legislature – that its seats be apportioned according to population, that its members serve for short terms, that it operate as a single chamber – were all justified as corollaries to popular control, both over parliament itself and over potential sources of corruption within and without it. It is clear that regular elections not only were the prime institution of selection but also had a role to play in the regular accountability of the representatives to the people; yet in this latter capacity they were only one of several institutional forms put to work. Thus, though the Levellers offer an early approach to the electoral thesis of accountability (see Chapter 1 above), we must carefully consider not only how close they came to the familiar modern logic but also how far they stopped short of it.

Leveller Accountability

The Levellers' understanding of the relation between elections and accountability had a distinctly discursive or deliberative dimension, yet their sense of the need for coercive, punitive, and deterrent power summoned the supplementary presence of non-electoral institutions of accountability. Since the prime purpose of a written constitution was pacification, its ability to make governors accountable naturally hinged in the first instance on discourse and judgment. As the first Agreement explained, "when our common rights and liberties shall be cleared, their endeavors will be disappointed that seek to make themselves our masters" (Sharp 1998, 93): that is, declaring the terms of government's fiduciary power offered a basis for appeal – petitioning was the marrow of Leveller politics – and a definitive guide to political judgment, "that there may be no grounds for future quarrels or contentions" (96). This is what might be called the judgmental element of a constitution's capacity to induce accountability, and it was not so much embodied as occasioned by elections. For these moments of selection required the joint presence of both the representative, back from Westminster, and his constituents, away from their shops and fields; hence Lilburne's remark that the people should have annual elections "to renew and inquire once a year after the behavior and carriage of those they have chosen" (Lilburne 1645b, 33). In the absence of such a shared moment in time and space as the early-modern hustings provided for political principals and their agents, it is difficult to imagine what the Levellers would have made of modern elections: viewing advertisements before casting a ballot in a private booth.

But the Levellers were concerned with not only reason but also power, not only consent but also control. Accordingly their search for orderly procedures of accountability included a coercive or deterrent phase, as in the claim that the Agreement's provisions would "lay an impossibility upon all whom they [the people] shall hereafter trust of ever wronging the commonwealth in any considerable measure without certainty of ruining themselves" (Sharp 1998, 145). This reliance on deterrence might explain why Lilburne believed electing new representatives amounted to "call[ing] their predecessors to a strict account" (Lilburne 1648, proem), and it would in this sense constitute the first ever formulation of the "electoral connection" that has figured so centrally in academic political science (see Mayhew 2004). There is something to be said for the Levellers as theorists of a democratic accountability that deters by playing on governors' self-interest. In a remarkable passage from one of the group's last public pronouncements, issued from the Tower of London in 1649, they defended the Agreement in terms foreshadowing 1787:

And whereas 'tis urged that if we were in power we would bear ourselves as tyrannically as others have done: we confess indeed that the experimental [experienced] defections of so many men as have succeeded in authority, and the exceeding difference we have hitherto found in the same men in a low and in an exalted condition, makes us even mistrust our own hearts and hardly believe our own resolutions of the contrary. And therefore we have proposed such an establishment as, supposing men to be too flexible and yielding to worldly temptations, they should not yet have a means or opportunity either to injure particulars or prejudice the public without extreme hazard and apparent danger to themselves. (Sharp 1998, 164–5)

In these explanations of their constitutional reforms, of which regular elections were the nucleus, the Levellers offered the first articulation of the general idea of electoral accountability through deterrence. But they did not in fact consider regular elections to be a sufficient or even a primary mechanism of democratic deterrence; that job required other, non-electoral procedures. Thus, when Lilburne wrote of the people's need "annually at least to choose new Parliamentmen, to call their predecessors to a strict account," he explained that "the people that are willing in the several Shires, Cities, and Boroughs may call home their Parliament men, and send new ones in their places, to call them to account, and to make Laws to punish such betrayers of their trust" (Lilburne 1648, proem). His suggestion, in other words, contemplated not only regular elections but also inter-electoral recall (in the middle of a term) and general legal liability. In a similar vein Overton proposed that special commissions be set up in the counties to hear constituents' petitions against their representatives, so that corrupt ones could be subject to "impeachment" trials "for falsifying and betraying...their Country's [constituency's] trust" (Overton 1647, 33). These commissions would have functioned like grand juries, examining evidence and issuing indictments before the trial stage.

Thus the "extreme hazard and apparent danger" of which the Levellers spoke as a deterrent to tyrannical rule was not to be supplied by elections alone. In fact Overton's and Lilburne's judicial proposals from 1647–8

Radical Trust and Accountability 47

arguably came to eclipse elections in their quest for accountability as their frustration with Cromwell and his Council of State grew over the course of 1649. Lilburne's attack on the young republican regime in *England's New Chains* (1649) called for all officers of government to be made "frequently and exactly accountable" by "strict prohibition and severe penalty" for breaches of trust (Sharp 1998, 154), and later the third Agreement called for representatives found to have violated its terms to be prosecuted for high treason (177).

Crucially, situating accountability at the local level reflected a key difference between the Levellers' fiduciary model of accountability and the parliamentarians' classical model revolving around centralized, national agencies, and the notion of elections as a sole and sufficient mechanism of control could only have been accommodated in the latter. By contrast, of the three mechanisms of accountability, special inquests and general liability were meant by the Levellers to be as threatening to an unfaithful trustee as the prospect of failing to secure re-election. For this reason the third and final version of the Agreement, drawn up after the regicide and while the Leveller principals were imprisoned on Cromwell's orders, introduced one significant change: the membership of parliament was to be completely rotated every year, since annual elections would now exclude incumbents (Sharp 1998, 171). The Levellers became more and more preoccupied by the need for strict legal accountability in 1649 just as they moved against re-eligibility for consecutive terms in this way. Such a "term limit," of course, is now usually taken to vitiate electoral deterrence (e.g. Manin et al. 1999a, 34n), which relies on the vanity and ambition that would be dashed by losing a vote but which typically excludes legal liability for official conduct. Yet the Levellers continued to believe that representatives could be held accountable even after they imposed term limits because for them elections could confer popular control only in tandem with general liability and special inquests. It was not their deficient theoretic sophistication, then, but rather their different theoretic framework that prevented them from regarding the mere possibility of electoral defeat as a deterrent robust enough to effect popular control.

The Levellers' distinctive approach to these issues is perhaps best encapsulated in a phrase reminiscent of Aristotle's definition of properly "political" citizenship, as "ruling and being ruled in turn" (Aristotle 1998, 1259b). The first Agreement intended that elected representatives "shall be in a capacity to taste of *subjection as well as rule*, and so shall be equally concerned with yourselves in all they do... when the laws shall bind all alike, without privilege or exemption.... The parliament must then make your relief and common good their only study" (Sharp 1998, 96–7; emphasis added). In 1649 Lilburne put it more succinctly: "by frequent Elections men come to taste of subjection as well as Rule (and are thereby obliged for their own sakes to be tender of the good of the People)" (Lilburne 1649, 162). "To the end all public officers shall be certainly accountable and no factions made to maintain corrupt interests," the third Agreement justified its requirement that elected representatives give up their positions in the army, in the treasury, or at the bar by insisting "that all persons may be capable of subjection as well as rule" (Sharp 1998, 171). This ancient formula was meant not to encourage subjects from all classes to take the reins of power – very few were willing to follow the Dutch author of the *Fraternal Warning* (1581) (Gelderen 1992, 195–6) in this regard, apart from the millenarian radical Lawrence Clarkson (Sharp 1983, 187–8) – but rather to establish a basic equality of liability to legal hazard. This explains why the Levellers failed to see that any significant difference was made for the mechanics of accountability by the rule against re-eligibility: a representative had to anticipate scrutiny and sanction for his conduct each time he returned from parliament, regardless of whether or not he had the opportunity to return there.

The formula of "subjection as well as rule" had a busy career in Leveller writings but also beyond them. The radical zeal for constitutional reform survived through the Commonwealth period, and making representatives accountable to the people remained the priority of some reformers. Thus Edward Billings advocated that "every man may taste of subjection as well as Rule," but not by the Leveller rule against consecutive terms; rather, Billings would have allowed a representative to stand for re-election only after the Athenian expedient of "giving a complete account of his last year's trust" – going before commissions of examination to be judged as to his fidelity to his constituents (Billings 1659, 10). Billings's frequent elections and judicial audits used ideas from Lilburne and Overton without the militant tone of the Levellers' final proposals of 1649.

It is noteworthy that, though the Levellers contemplated what has become the conventional wisdom about modern electoral "democracy" – that regular elections allow the people to "call to account" their representatives – they went even further in quest of popular control by insisting on non-electoral procedures of accountability which have by now largely subsided in democratic theory and practice. Regular audits, ad hoc impeachments, and general legal liability were all part of the Levellers' fiduciary model of accountability. As we will see in Chapter 5, earlier debates in the American colonies had already thrown up the electoral thesis of accountability, but in a context that made it an alternative rather than a complement to these non-electoral mechanisms.

"Democracy"

The Levellers pioneered the deployment of certain formal principles of ancient democracy in a modern setting, but they never called themselves "democrats" and rarely even uttered the term "democracy" in their writings. The question of terminology, though secondary in interest to the theoretic substance of their politics, requires the results of historiographic mishandling to be cleared up. Considering the Levellers in relation to two contemporary discursive contexts will help to explain how far they may genuinely be considered democrats: Calvinist ecclesiastics and classical republicanism. The question of the breadth of the franchise, which has until recently dominated modern interpretations of the Levellers' politics, is an utterly anachronistic consideration that reflects the priorities of nineteenth- and twentieth-century observers rather than those of their seventeenth-century subjects (Scott 2000, 279).

Many contemporaries branded the Levellers as "democrats," invoking the word's associations with anarchy and common vice, in order to make them appear disreputable to respectable opinion. But those observers who focused on the notion of parallel forms of government in church and state deserve particular notice. Richard Baxter, for instance, reported that the soldiers in Whalley's regiment (among the first army units to get behind the Leveller reforms in 1647) were "talking for Church democracy or State democracy" (Gooch 1927, 116). Lilburne had indeed published a defense of what was often called a "popular" or "democratic" form of a particular church, according to which "by a free and voluntary Consent...a constituted or *Politic* Body or *Corporation*...hath power...to choose, elect, and ordain...and to reprove and admonish her own *Officers*" (Lilburne 1645a, 28). To the extent that the principles of a genuinely democratic ecclesiology (a subject to which I will return in a transatlantic context in Chapters 4 and 6) had been translated into civil government by the Levellers' political theory, the charge that they were democrats was plausible.

A second discursive context that is relevant to at least a few Leveller writings is classical republicanism. References to popular versus aristocratic kinds of republic, as well as allusions to ancient history and to modern commentators like Machiavelli, figure prominently in some early pamphlets associated with the Levellers, including *Englands Miserie and Remedie* (1645), *Vox Plebis* (1646), and *Londons Liberty* (1646) (Glover 1999, 64–70). The appearance of republican themes in Leveller writings centers around a brief partnership with Marchamont Nedham, the notorious publicist who wrote the parliamentarian newsbook *Mercurius Britannicus* before first switching to the king's side and then to Cromwell's (Worden 1995). Nedham appears to have helped the Levellers in their early publications (Scott 2003, 156–7, 243–7), particularly in the extended passages on ancient history in *Vox Plebis* (Worden 1995, 320–1). There the Roman republic is celebrated in Machiavellian terms, particularly stressing the Bodinian theme of the tribunes' dominance over the senate, and the English situation is described using Roman language. Thus the House of Commons is described as composed of those "whom we have chosen and entrusted for us to sit at *Westminster* as Guardians of our Birth-rights and most powerful Tribunes of the people's liberties" (Overton 1646, 58). Machiavelli is explicitly cited on a number of occasions, particularly for his praise of the various procedures by which influential men were held accountable for crimes against the Roman people; in this connection Athens's ostracism of Themistocles and Alcibiades is also held up as worthy of imitation (60–1). Democratic accountability of this classical sort is punctuated with the exhortation that a free state "must cherish impeachments and accusations of the people against those that, through ambition, avarice, pride, cruelty, or oppression, seek to destroy the liberty or property of the people" (61).

The classical allusion that closes *Vox Plebis* had already been printed, almost verbatim, in *Englands Miserie*, praising the Roman senator Flaminius for disregarding his "birth and degree" by acknowledging the people's supremacy over the senate (Wildman 1645, 4; Overton 1646, 68). This praise of self-denying elites frequently turned into a direct attack on "aristocracy" in Leveller writings. From the beginnings of their self-consciousness as a movement they accused the Presbyterian-dominated Long Parliament of seeking an "aristocratical government over the people in the state" (Sharp 1998, 43). Overton's appeal to the House of Commons in his *Arrow against All Tyrants* had two aristocratic targets, the House of Lords and the Presbyterian clergy (57). The first embodied inherited privilege and could claim no popular authorization for its considerable power; the second championed a model of church government in which the "elders" dominated the "brethren." When in 1649 the Levellers denounced Cromwell's Council of State as an "Aristocratical Tyranny," it was merely the culmination of a long-abiding concern (Dzelzainis 2005, 276–9). They never used "democracy" in favorable terms, but they did not hesitate to use "aristocracy" pejoratively.

Though the Levellers were at pains to dispel charges of communism and anarchism (that they wished to do away with property and magistracy, respectively) (Sharp 1998, 161; Overton 1647, 3–5), they never addressed the charge of democracy. It would have been a much harder point to rebut, at least according to Bodinian criteria of consent and control. The treatise on *Maxims of State* (1642) traditionally attributed to Raleigh (and therefore composed in the 1610s) illustrates how the Bodinian conception of democratic sovereignty included not only selection but also accountability. Raleigh there defined a "popular state" in patently Athenian terms: offices are filled by either lottery or election, incumbent re-eligibility is disallowed except for military commanders, and terms of office last only one year. Above all, this regime allows the people "to compel their magistrates, when their time expireth, to give an account of their behavior and government, and that publicly before the commons" (Raleigh 1829, 8:29). At the time of its publication this classical model would likely have been understood to endorse the calling to account of Charles I's ministers before the Long Parliament – Charles's deputy in Ireland had been impeached and executed the year before. Indeed no national institution but parliament resembled the Roman tribunes; perhaps a recognition of this fact underlay Charles's accusation that the parliamentarians were attempting to convert England to a "democracy" (Greenberg 2001, 198), if this charge was not just a polemic exaggeration. But the Levellers' turning of accountability from king-to-parliament to parliament-to-people presented an even more radical vision of a "popular state" – thus reflecting a key difference between their fiduciary model of accountability and the classical model of Nedham and Raleigh.

Something like Raleigh's parliamentarian approach to democracy may also have been behind Henry Parker's notable remark in *Jus Populi* (1644): "the truth is, both Monarchy and Aristocracy are derivative forms and owe a dependence upon Democracy, which though it be not the best and most exact form for all nations and Empires at all times, yet it is ever the most natural and primarily authentical, and for some times and places the most beneficial" (Parker 1644, 61). This was not the view of Bodin, for whom monarchic and aristocratic states need not "depend" on the whole people; but it resembled the modification of Bodinian sovereignty made previously by Althusius. Yet Althusius and Parker generally shunned popular control even as they held all states to be necessarily founded in popular consent. Thus the Levellers, in radicalizing conceptions of political trust to inject democratic accountability into representative, constitutional government, were at least as committed to a "democracy" or "popular state" as those like Parker who already admitted it as an acceptable regime type, if not more so.

Hobbes and Locke

The upshot of the Levellers' contributions to political discussion in the English Civil War was that for the first time the principle of accountability was not only (a) preferred to the discretionary conception of political trust but also (b) directed to genuinely popular agencies and (c) applied to the "pacified" constitutional processes of a modern state. In short, the prime elements of democracy's conceptual modernization were in place. The political theories of Thomas Hobbes and John Locke cannot be fully understood without reference to this powerful precedent. Whatever contributions they may have made to the history of democratic theory (see Tuck 2001, Shapiro 2003), they both stopped well short of the Leveller brand of democratic constitutionalism. In light of the recent history of radical trust and accountability these giants of political philosophy appear to have been, each in his own way, derivative and even backward-looking figures.

Commenting on "the Liberty of Subjects" in 1651, Hobbes attacked the pernicious habit, as he saw it, "of favoring tumults, and of licentious controlling the actions of their Sovereigns; and again of controlling those controllers" (Hobbes 1996, 149). Hobbes was referring not only to the gentlemen who had recently led England into civil war but more specifically to the radicals who had briefly threatened to win it: if "controlling the actions of their Sovereigns" had been the project of Parker and the parliamentarians, "controlling those controllers" was the distinctive Leveller agenda. Hobbes's own analysis of the concept of liberty began with a critique of those who "mistake that for their Private Inheritance, and Birth right, which is the right of the Public only" (150), and none of his contemporaries had trumpeted the "birthright" of an Englishman more loudly than Lilburne, the Leveller chief.

Thus some of the most important parts of Hobbes's multifaceted *magnum opus* were more or less direct polemic engagements with the democratic constitutionalism of the Levellers. If what was distinctive about the first two books of *Leviathan* (1651) compared with what Hobbes had previously written in *De Cive* (1642) was the later work's account of authorization and representation (see Tuck 1993, 326–7), that account might be profitably read in light of intervening developments. In particular, the Levellers had radicalized the role of authorization and representation in English debate; for a time they had even posed a credible threat of influencing the future of the English constitution.[1] Hobbes's engagement with the Levellers offered a dose of their own medicine: much as they had done to the parliamentarians, he turned his opponents' language against themselves. In the first place, he took pains to argue that principals are generally liable for their agents, including being bound by covenants made by "their Actors, Representers, or Procurators...so far-forth as is in their Commission, but no farther" (Hobbes 1996, 112). He went on to describe the formation of government precisely in terms of representation: everyone in society agrees to "*Authorize* all the Actions and Judgments" of the "Sovereign Representative" (121). In this way Hobbes used the language of representation and (harking back even to Roman law) *procuratio* to suggest that, if a prince abuses his people, it is the people's own act, and they have no one but themselves to blame. In short, Hobbes was arguing for a radically different notion of representation from what the radicals had brought to bear on both king and parliament: he sought to purge the notion of political representation precisely of the principle of accountability.

In order to achieve this aim, moreover, Hobbes cleverly deployed "trust" and its associated idioms. At times, in fact, he appeared to offer a conception of discretionary trusteeship different in elaboration rather than substance from that of James I half a century earlier: "the office of the Sovereign (be it a Monarch or an Assembly) consisteth in the end for which he was trusted with the Sovereign Power, namely the procuration of *the safety of the people*, to which he is obliged by the Law of Nature, and to render an account thereof to God, the Author of that Law, and to none but him" (Hobbes 1996, 231). Hobbes arrived at Bodin's and James I's conclusion about unaccountable sovereigns by a different route from theirs, of course, one resembling rather that of Suarez and Grotius: accepting an original democratic sovereignty and then explaining its alienation to supreme authority. Still, there can be little doubt that terms like "trust," "procuration," "safety" (as in *salus populi*), and "account" were deliberately employed in such a way as to mimic Parker and particularly the Levellers up to but no further than the final, cutting phrase: "and to none but him [God]." What Walwyn had called a "thread-bare doctrine" was being modified and reinforced in the new Cromwellian era.

Locke's deployment of "trust" could scarcely have been more different from Hobbes's. Yet in his own way he too was a throwback to a pre-Leveller

---

[1] Wootton has previously claimed that Hobbes was responding to "a revolution in political debate" inspired by the Levellers (Wootton 1986, 56–8), but his sense of this "revolution" revolves around substantive rather than formal democracy: elections rather than accountability, consent rather than control.

kind of political theory. In the 1680s, when civil war beckoned once again and reprints of Buchanan and the Huguenot tracts were again (as in the 1640s) made available to the English reading public, Locke's *Two Treatises of Government* (1689) gave further and dramatic point to the power of a century-old radical tradition. Locke is, after all, well known as a theorist of political trusteeship, for his analysis of political authority as a "Fiduciary Power to act for certain ends" (Locke 1988, 2.149)[2] lies at the center of the account of legitimate power and justified resistance in the second *Treatise*. But his place in the story of democracy's modern rehabilitation falls short of the Levellers', since he saw little need to turn democratic accountability from extraordinary to ordinary politics.

On Locke's account the authorization of government is "a delegated Power from the People," "derived from the People by a positive voluntary Grant and Institution," and a "trust reposed in them" (Locke 1988, 2.141, 2.149). High officers of government are "Protectors and Guardians" as well as "Trustees or Deputies" (2.222, 2.240). Following the Levellers, Locke's "certain ends" controlling the delegation of power always intimate *salus populi*: "the public Good and Safety," "*the common good*," and "the Peace, Safety, and public Good of the People" (2.110, 2.131). Also following the Levellers, breach of trust is the prime trigger of justified resistance: the people may "remove or *alter the Legislative*, when they find the *Legislative* act contrary to the trust reposed in them" (2.149). Locke's famous language of the "Dissolution of Government" (the title of his chapter 19) and of forfeiture even echoes Overton's claim that "while the *Betrusted* are *dischargers* of their *trust*, it remaineth in their hands, but no sooner the *Betrusted* betray and forfeit their *Trust*, but (as all things else in dissolution) it returneth from whence it came, even to the hands of the *Trusters*" (Overton 1647, 6; see Sharp 1988, 43n). Locke argued further that (in the absence of a neutral judge) the trustor has the right to judge the performance of his trustee (2.240); thus "the Body of the *People*" must decide for itself whether to resist a tyrant with arms (2.242). Locke's previous experience as secretary in the court of Chancery (Laslett 1988, 114), like the fact that Althusius wrote his dissertation on the law of inheritance (Carney 1995, 11), further suggests the importance of the specifically legal aspects of fiduciary agency for early-modern theories of constitutionlism.

Locke's second *Treatise* offered a defense of accountability in its extreme form: resistance to tyranny. But regular accountability of the sort which

---

[2] Citations of Locke's *Two Treatises* are given by book and paragraph.

the Levellers had novelly theorized was not on his agenda. He had no plan of constitutional reconstruction and took an aloof and stand-pat position during the heated debates surrounding the membership and activities of the Convention Parliament in 1689, in the wake of the Glorious Revolution (Schwoerer 1990, 536–7). All that Locke offered by way of constitutional reform was a vague and private suggestion that the "ancient constitution" be reinstated (540–1). If Hobbes's approach to the accountable trust looked back to James I, Locke's looked back to James's tutor Buchanan.

States of Nature

For Hobbes and Locke the state of nature was both a starting point for moral philosophy and an ending point for malfunctioning societies; for the Levellers it was the condition of their country for the better part of a decade (Zagorin 1954, 15–16). As Scott has lucidly explained, the "institutional absence" wrought in England by several years of wrenching civil war was a prime precondition of the radicals' proposals for constitutional reconstruction (Scott 2000, 244, 288). Even those institutions that continued in existence, principally the House of Commons, had been so ravaged by the fortunes of war that contemporaries lost the sense of their untouchability. The Levellers responded to this state of nature with a program of institutional innovation which was held together by pioneering arguments about accountability in a modern state: elections were occasions of deliberation and judgment, but judicial forms of accountability, including both special inquests and general liability, were sites of power and punishment. Whereas the classical model of accountability under-wrote parliamentarian efforts to check monarchic abuses, the fiduciary model employed by the Levellers managed to incorporate ancient institutions like audits and impeachments while orienting them toward more genuinely popular bodies: the local electorate or the local jury rather than centralized councils of elite or even representative composition.

Locke famously said that "in the beginning all the World was *America*" (Locke 1988, 2.49). For some Englishmen earlier in Locke's century, at least, America had indeed presented a new beginning, a condition of "institutional absence" even more complete than what the Civil War had thrust on the Levellers. Equipped with essentially the same conceptual tools, those Anglo-American colonists had undertaken projects of political construction earlier than the Civil War radicals, and they had developed theoretic techniques that were similar to the later ones in important respects but also distinctive in their own right. Whereas the Levellers proposed a battery of institutions and rationales for democratic accountability, electoral as well as non-electoral, the Anglo-American debates presented a stark alternative between anti-democratic elections and non-electoral mechanisms of democratic accountability.

3

Fidelity and Accountability in Virginia and Bermuda

> But admit that we could not enjoy the same long, but that the English there would aspire to government of themselves.
>
> Richard Hakluyt, ca. 1580 (Taylor 1935, 143)

In the descriptive, promotional, and polemic literature of the early Virginia and Bermuda colonies, the outstanding feature is moral critique – a discourse of virtue and corruption. Aside from the crucial minutiae of latitude and longitude or silkworms and sassafras, a sweeping moralism is what unifies most of the extant writings on the transatlantic activities of the Virginia Company during its short lifetime, from 1606 to 1625. This moralism, continuing certain tendencies from the previous generation of Elizabethan colonial literature, set a precedent for future colonies by conceiving England's American plantations as commonwealths in their own right. Capt. John Smith was the outstanding figure in this line of thought.

Moralism was joined by proceduralism among the political themes discussed in relation to Virginia and Bermuda. The interaction of these two, especially during debates around the dissolution of the Virginia Company in 1624, brought ideas of trust, and of discretion and accountability, to bear on the institutional-design phase of colonial discourse. Among the ways of joining trust to the common good which emerged from these debates, one led to the notion of a morally self-sufficient and practically self-governing colony featuring internal mechanisms of accountability. John Bargraves was the outstanding figure in this second phase of theoretic development.

A substantial historiography has established the prominent place of the moral philosophy of classical humanism in early English thinking about colonization generally (Jones 1946; Quinn 1976; Fitzmaurice 2003, ch. 2), and this basic insight applies to the Virginia discourse of virtue in particular

(Fitzmaurice 1999; Fitzmaurice 2003, ch. 3). This insight must be qualified by recognition of the importance of supplementary Christian categories, both for European colonial ideas generally (Pagden 1995, 27–30) and for the particular cases of Virginia and Bermuda, as we will see. Most importantly, however, the moral criticism surrounding the Virginia Company's activities must be understood in relation to the institutional criticism. Ideas about community walked hand in hand with ideas about agency. The widespread application of the commonwealth idea to American community – the recognition that the colonies counted as commonwealths in their own right – was joined by the widespread application of the fiduciary idea to American agency – the conception of colonial authority in terms of trust.

The most perceptive explorer of all these themes was Captain Smith. He was the outstanding moral and political critic of Jacobean colonization, much as Richard Hakluyt (the younger of two cousins of the same name) had been for the Elizabethan era. Smith has always been a controversial figure in American history generally, but his place in Anglo-American political thought more particularly has not been well understood. Accordingly, my analysis of his role in the Virginia discourse of virtue and corruption will focus more on how he developed his conception of colonial authority, revolving around a distinctive view of the virtue of fidelity, than on how far he inflated his own efforts to embody that conception.

Bargraves, by contrast, appears in the historical record as a somewhat ephemeral and obscure figure. Yet his diminutive stature in histories of colonial America is the result of a failure not only to find but also to understand the evidence. His opposition to the "democratic" joint-stock form of administration in the metropolis coexisted with proposals for intra-colonial government based on local elections and local accountability. Historians have judged Bargraves from either the mistaken presumption of a fundamental inconsistency between these two themes or else an ignorance of the latter. Thus they have been tempted into the misleading (and anachronistic) claim that Bargraves was the mortal enemy of a self-consciously democratic movement within company and colony (e.g. Brown 1969, 448). On the contrary, there was no political or ideological movement animated by definite ideas of democracy in Virginia; there was only Bargraves himself. Far from having "no sympathy with popular institutions" (Morton 1960, 108), he was the first to offer a theoretic defense of them in an intra-colonial context, and to recognize their dependence on concrete and specialized procedures of accountability. Like Captain Smith, Bargraves followed Hakluyt (see epigraph above) in recognizing not only the possibility but indeed the value and necessity of colonial self-government within a larger imperial order. Unlike most others involved in overseas colonization at the time, however, Bargraves imagined colonial self-government to include not merely popular consent but also popular control. Toward this end his proposed "Forme of Polisie" for reorganizing Virginia's government adopted a *classical*-republican model of accountability (see Chapter 1 above) in which a multitude of political bodies were counter-poised against one another, with a specialized accountability agency called the Syndex in charge of prosecuting state crimes.

Smith and Bargraves were united in condemnation of the self-serving, exploitive management of American affairs by factions within the Virginia Company, but they offered different remedies. Smith's solution was more substantive in nature, placing wide discretionary powers in colonial virtuosos possessing equal parts of honesty and competence; Bargraves's was more formal, creating an elaborate institutional framework of colonial government which rendered local officers locally accountable. Both theories of colonial politics embraced the commonwealth idea, but Smith championed the discretionary and Bargraves the accountable conception of political trust. Neither, however, ramified the commonwealth idea by appeal to the principle of popular sovereignty, so that the origin of political authority and the ultimate reference point of accountability always remained the crown not the colony. Thus Bargraves proves that democratic accountability could be imagined even in the absence of popular sovereignty, and that a colony could be considered internally democratic though externally dependent on another state.

Vices

The leading fact of early efforts at settlement in Virginia and Bermuda was practical failure, and the leading reason adduced for this failure was moral corruption. Founded in 1607, Jamestown almost met the fate of all the abortive Elizabethan projects. Food supplies went unprovided or unsecured, resulting in starvation and disease; labor was diverted from subsistence agriculture to fruitless efforts at mining and silk-works; Indian relations were mismanaged, meaning daily insecurity as well as evangelical failure. The form of government stipulated for the colony by the original Virginia Company charter (1606) featured a weak governor and several assistants. Almost immediately dissensions among the leading men broke out, and the basic tasks of building a new settlement languished in various stages of incompletion (Osgood 1907, 1:23–97; Craven 1949, ch. 3; Fitzmaurice 1999, 33).

The search for answers produced a catalog of vices. William Strachey sought to explain starvation, disease, and faction as the result of "sloth, riot, and vanity" (Wright 1964, 66). Captain Smith, speaking from his experience as one of the first assistants at Jamestown, added that "pride, covetousness, extortion, and oppression" were "defects sufficient to bring a well-settled Common-wealth to misery, much more Virginia" (Smith 1986, 2:329–30). As late as 1619, John Pory observed that "in these five months of my continuance here, there have come at one time or another eleven sail of ships into this river; but freighted more with ignorance than with any other merchandise" (Tyler 1907, 286). The conventional wisdom, then, was that bad colonists made bad colonies.

In Bermuda the natural abundance of the soil, by encouraging both physical and moral relaxation, only multiplied the fruits of vice: as Strachey queried, "what hath a more adamantine power to draw unto it the consent and attraction of the idle, untoward, and wretched number of the many than liberty and fulness of sensuality?" (Wright 1964, 41). This colony was begun in 1609 when an expedition to Jamestown, led by George Somers, was blown off-course and wrecked on the reefs around the Bermuda islands. Within months the expedition's crew had rebuilt its sailing vessels and moved on, but the new settlement surpassed Jamestown in its favorable soil, mild climate, and lack of a native population with which to compete for resources. Captain Smith recounted the tale of the ironically named "Three Lords of Bermuda" who insisted on staying behind to enjoy a life of ease when all the others sailed on to Jamestown. "They grew so proud and ambitious, contempt took such place, they fell out for superiority, though but three forlorn men"; in one of their many altercations "one of them was bitten with his own dog, as if the dumb beast would reprove them of their folly" (Smith 1986, 2:352).

Defying others' frequent and sneering references to "the multitude," Captain Smith found that the most damaging vices, such as avarice, resided not so much in the many as in "a few that engrosses all, then sells all again to the commonalty at what rate they please" (Smith 1986, 2:329). Whereas Thomas West, Lord Delaware, had criticized the low origins of the colonists he went to Jamestown to govern in 1610, on Smith's observation Delaware's own entourage – "this lewd company, wherein were many unruly Gallants packed thither by their friends to escape ill destinies" (2:220) – brought little improvement. Smith found these adventurous aristocrats "ten times more fit to spoil a Common-wealth than either begin one or help to maintain one" (2:225) and "tormented with pride and flattery, idleness and covetousness, as though they had vowed here to keep their Court with all the pestilent vices in the world for their attendants, enchanted with a conceited stateliness, even in the very bottom of miserable senselessness" (2:310).

The vices bedeviling Virginia and Bermuda were construed in opposition to the cardinal virtues of wisdom, justice, courage, and temperance drawn from humanist moral philosophy (Fitzmaurice 2003, 74–6), but they also included Christian derivatives and modifications of corresponding vices, pride and avarice in particular. The first put individuals above larger entities and was linked to terms like "vanity" and "ambition." As Samuel Purchas commented, "only by pride do men make contention, with blind-staring eyes of self-love abounding in their own sense...forgetting that...they are planting a Colony, not reaping a harvest, for a public and not (but in subordinate order) private wealth" (Purchas 1907, 19:236). The second, avarice, more narrowly involved taking for oneself what belongs to others and was associated with terms like "covetousness" and "injustice." In these terms Captain Smith charged Edward-Maria Wingfield, his early rival at Jamestown, with shirking the routine hardships of the fledgling colony and embezzling company provisions for his own use (Smith 1986, 1:33).

Both pride and avarice involved disregard of a higher purpose: the common good of the colonies. Promoting the general welfare of colonial society thus became the hallmark of virtuous colonial agency, as evidenced by the fact that at the extreme end of vicious colonial action was not merely the disregard but the active subversion of that welfare: conspiracy. For the Jacobean generation this was a prime factor in the failure of England's previous endeavors overseas. Purchas believed the fifteenth-century expedition of Robert Thorne and Hugh Eliot might have given England first claim to the New World "if the Mariners would have been ruled by their pilot"; instead, a mutiny led to the abandonment of the voyage, thus opening the door for Columbus's voyages on behalf of Spain (Purchas 1907, 19:225). Strachey advanced a similar diagnosis of later failures. When John White, head of the second Roanoke expedition in 1587, received instructions to relocate the island colony to Chesapeake Bay, he could not convince his stubborn colleagues to go along. On Strachey's view this project "miscarried by the wretchedness of unfaithful instruments" – not least White himself, who returned to England prematurely and devoted himself to privateering rather than securing provisions for those under his charge. The "Lost Colony," then, had not been lost so much as betrayed, leading adventurers like Raleigh to give up such noble expeditions, "wearied with so great an expense and abused with the unfaithfulness of the employed" (Strachey 1953, 15, 147, 149–50).

Soon a new generation of English adventurers found conspiracy in their own midst, at Jamestown. Wingfield saw himself toppled from power by a combination of Captain Smith, John Ratcliffe, and John Martin to share the governorship among themselves by rotation (Wingfield 1860, 84). Smith soon emerged as the de facto autocrat, and he was successful at least at stealing enough corn from the Indians to keep the colonists alive. In turn he decried a whole series of conspiracies forming around him, like the "confederacy" of Dutch and English colonists who supplied the native chief Powhatan with firearms in exchange for trading privileges for themselves (Smith 1986, 1:250–1). Bermuda also saw conspiracy; in fact Strachey, for whom colonial conspiracies were something of an obsession, recounted no fewer than three plots that were hatched after the wreck of Somers's expedition (Wright 1964, 41–7).

Commonwealths

The problems of the young colonies, then, were at bottom problems of trust. The lesson of these stories of conspiracy was not just the immorality of disobedience pure and simple but also the binding force of the greater good. The commonwealth idea was pervasive in the literature associated with the Virginia Company and expressed the consensus, formed in response to the colony's early problems, that Virginia must be a self-sufficient body politic, not just a province of the kingdom to be exploited for England's benefit. This important feature of Jacobean colonial thought has been underlined by recent research, and its corresponding denigration of profit-taking has been correctly identified as corrosive of received ideas in colonial historiography about commercial gain as a dominant motive or ideological impulse (see Fitzmaurice 2003, 6, 10, 71, 85–7, 98–9).

Richard Hakluyt was the intellectually eclectic figure looming over invocations of the commonwealth idea in a colonial context, but it would be a mistake to suppose that he relegated religious considerations to second place behind humanist glory (contra Armitage 2000, 61–81). When Purchas wrote in 1625 that "Godliness is the best gain" (Purchas 1907, 19:236), he was merely following the influential line of colonial criticism which Hakluyt had already developed under the motto, first penned in 1582, "Godliness is great riches" (Hakluyt 1850, 13). Hakluyt's partnership of Christian and classical moralism against private profit was also evident, for instance, in William Crashaw's sermon before the Virginia Company in 1610, which insisted that the evangelistic mission was "of a more noble and excellent nature, and of higher and worthier ends," than the pecuniary motives Crashaw feared were being pushed to the fore by "sows that still wallow in the mire of their profit and pleasure" (Crashaw 1610, C/2r). It was typical of the Virginia Company's promotional literature to lavish attention on economic considerations while nonetheless pointing out their subordination to religious ones (Miller 1948). A published sermon by Robert Gray in 1609, for instance, vigorously employed the language of classical rhetoric but also, as Hakluyt consistently had done, named the evangelistic before the civic kind of glory:

> Time, the devourer of his own brood, consumes both man and his memory. It is not brass nor marble that can perpetuate immortality of name upon the earth.... The name, memory, and actions of those men do only live in the records of eternity which have employed their best endeavors in such virtuous and honorable enterprises as have advanced the glory of God and enlarged the glory and wealth of their country. (Gray 1609, A/3r-v)

Captain Smith shared with Gray the humanist conviction that the New World was above all a proving-ground for virtuous men seeking honor and glory, but he distinguished himself on two counts: Smith's priorities inverted those of the Hakluytian tradition by placing the civic above the evangelistic, and the force of his expression of the civic-humanist attachment to the common good was simply unrivaled. Both points were nowhere more strikingly exemplified than in the sweeping address to those readers possessing "but the taste of virtue and magnanimity" in Smith's *Description of New England* (1616):

> What so truly suits with honor and honesty as the discovering things unknown, erecting Towns, peopling Countries, informing the ignorant, reforming things unjust, teaching virtue[?]... For example: Rome, What made her such a Monarchess, but only the adventures of her youth, not in riots at home, but in dangers abroad?... What was their ruin and hurt, but this: the excess of idleness, the fondness of Parents, the want of experience in Magistrates, the admiration of their undeserved honors, the contempt of true merit, their unjust jealousies, their politic incredulities, their hypocritical seeming goodness, and their deeds of secret lewdness? Finally, in fine, growing only formal temporists, all that their predecessors got in many years, they lost in few days. Those by their pains and virtues became Lords of the world; [these] by their ease and vices became slaves to their servants. This is the difference betwixt the use of Arms in the field and on the monuments of stones; the golden age and the leaden age, prosperity and misery, justice and corruption, substance and shadows, words and deeds, experience and imagination, making Commonwealths and marring Commonwealths, the fruits of virtue and the conclusions of vice. (Smith 1986, 1:343-4)

Smith's adherence to conventions about evangelism was not obviously insincere, but in his texts they pale in comparison to the humanist striving for an altogether more civic kind of glory. And he would become openly skeptical of the company's testimonials of religious motivation, accusing the chief officers under the leadership of Thomas Smythe in the 1610s of "such strange absurdities and impossibilities, making Religion their color, when all their aim was nothing but present profit, as most plainly appeared by sending us so many Refiners, Gold-smiths, Jewellers, Lapidaries, Stone-cutters, Tobacco-pipe-makers, Embroiderers, Perfumers, Silk-men... and all those had great sums out of the common stock" (Smith 1986, 3:272).

Not all forms of economic activity were considered vicious. Agriculture required hard labor, patience, and trust in God's bounty, while trade was often endorsed as a help to human fellowship; both were essential to "making Commonwealths." It was rather a third kind of activity, plunder, that undermined humanist values: piracy and mining were both regarded as a kind of theft – easy money, all extraction and no contribution, avarice at its height. "What... can be more pleasant," Smith asked of a prospective settler, "than planting and building a foundation for his Posterity, got from the rude earth, by God's blessing and his own industry, without prejudice to any?" (Smith 1986, 1:343). Virginians, however, had been setting the wrong example:

The worst mischief was, our gilded refiners with their golden promises made all men their slaves in hope of recompense; there was no talk, no hope, no work but dig gold, wash gold, refine gold, load gold; such a bruit of gold as one mad fellow desired to be buried in the sands, lest they should by their art make gold of his bones.... Never any thing did more torment him [Smith] than to see all necessary business neglected to freight such a drunken ship with so much gilded dirt. (Smith 1986, 1:218–19)

Captain Smith's application of the commonwealth idea to America was both unusually eloquent and also idiosyncratic in breaking from the evangelistic tradition of Hakluyt and Purchas which the mainstream of Virginia Company literature was following. But the civic and evangelistic strands of criticism both agreed on the basic point that England's colonies should be regarded not merely as exploitable resources but rather as bodies politic in their own right. This conception of colonial community not only guided the recurrent discussions of virtue and corruption in Virginia and Bermuda; it also conditioned discussions of colonial agency – of trust, accountability, and discretion.

Fidelity and Accountability

Applying the commonwealth idea to colonial community, it turned out, readily lent itself to conceiving colonial agency in terms of "trust" and the fiduciary idea. If short-term profits were not to undermine long-term evangelistic success or economic diversification, colonial leaders had to be found who would be faithful to the collective purposes of kingdom and colony over the interests of individuals or factions. Thus fidelity of a particular type came to be seen as the master key to Virginia virtue.

The virtue of fidelity in colonial agents could be promoted by either substantive or formal means. From the company's point of view, an obvious tactic for conquering vice was to select leaders of a certain character. On the other hand, the commissions by which governors and other officers in Virginia and Bermuda held their posts represented a more formal tactic for improving colonial leadership. These documents provided a concrete referent for agents' fidelity and a touchstone by which to try pride, avarice, and other vices. Whoever assumed the title of president at Jamestown, according to the oath drawn up by the royal Council for Virginia in 1606, would be made to "swear that I shall be a true and faithful servant unto the King's Majesty. . . . Of all matters of great importance or difficulty I shall make his Majesty's Council for Virginia acquainted therewith and follow their directions therein" (Brown 1890, 1:78). Delaware's 1610 commission likewise required that he govern "according to such directions, orders, and instructions as by his Majesty's said Council . . . be in that behalf made" (1:379).

Thus the ideal of colonial fidelity followed Englishmen's tendency to conceive power in terms of fiduciary authorization. As in the seventeenth century's broader European debates around sovereignty (see Chapter 2 above), authority in the colonies could be ramified by two concepts of trust, the *accountable* and the *discretionary*.

The accountable concept of trust fit the formal response to vicious colonial leadership, which revolved around written commissions. Thus faithful servants were expected not only to follow their principals' instructions but also, as was essential to enforcing this obligation, to render account of their actions. As the first council of the Jamestown colony wrote back to London, "we acknowledge ourselves accountable for our time here spent, were it but to give you satisfaction of our industries and affections to this most Honorable action" (Brown 1890, 1:106). Later, after the Jamestown council had splintered, Wingfield sent home a report defending his own conduct: "I do freely and truly anatomize the government and governors, that your experience may apply medicines accordingly; and upon the truth of this journal do pledge my faith and life" (Wingfield 1860, 76). Communication and information were the obligations attached to accountability in its discursive dimension. In that spirit the company complained, much later, to Gov. George Yeardley and his council that "we have many times found loss and interruption in our business through want of frequent relation from Virginia" and therefore "require [you] at least to make a quarterly dispatch to us" (Kingsbury 1935, 3:477).

The same plea for the discursive accountability of agents to their principals, as well as the anxiety that agents' personal ends would destroy the public welfare of the colony, marked the beginnings of neighboring Maryland in the 1630s (Hall 1910, 23, 155). This was a permanent feature of English colonization in the Chesapeake region and beyond (see Chapter 4 below), and it had important implications for the fate of the Virginia Company. Charges of infidelity by way of pecuniary corruption and corresponding demands for making good the losses suffered were especially salient in the 1620s, triggering the bitter fight that would lead ultimately to the company's demise.

When Edwin Sandys took over the leadership of the Virginia Company from Thomas Smythe in 1619, questions of accountability immediately assumed central importance. No sooner were Smythe and his comrades out of office than Sandys and his allies began pressing for audits of the old accounts (Craven 1932, 105–16). Sandys's conception of what fidelity required included a rigorous settling of accounts (106–12). The resultant atmosphere of division and enmity was intensified by the massacre of hundreds of English colonists in 1622 in a coordinated Indian assault, and again soon thereafter by negotiations with the crown over rules for the production and sale of tobacco, Virginia's most marketable commodity. The latter issue in particular drove the Smythe camp's decision to appeal for a royal investigation of the Sandys administration, as announced in a petition to the Privy Council delivered by Robert Johnson, Smythe's son-in-law, in 1623 (Andrews 1933, 48–9).

Ultimately Sandys's quest for strict accountability foundered because company accounts from Smythe's reign were either missing or in disarray. For a different set of reasons the implementation of strict accountability of agents to principals in a transatlantic setting, via formal procedures of scrutiny and sanction, proved equally difficult. Distance and time conspired to reduce control from across the ocean to a virtual nullity: at roughly three months per one-way voyage, the issuance of instructions, the discovery and report of disobedience, and the sending of a new commission or a new agent might take almost a year. The accountable concept of trust, it seemed to some observers, needed a less rigid alternative, and the principle of discretion proved congenial to humanist ideas about the substantive requirements of virtuous colonial leadership.

Discretion

Many colonial principals came to the conclusion that, once an agent was selected for his virtues, he had to be allowed scope for discretionary action. Already by 1609 the Virginia Company had put a proviso to this effect in the governor's commission issued to Thomas Gates:

> We do by these our letters [and] instructions bind you to nothing so strictly but that upon due consideration and good reason, and upon divers circumstances of time and place wherein we cannot here conclude, you may in your discretion depart and Dissent from them... and do all ordinances or acts whatsoever that may best conduct to the glory of god, the honor of our King and nation, to the good and perfect establishment of our Colony. (Kingsbury 1935, 3:24)

The next governor, Delaware, was similarly advised of a discretionary zone within his commission, which included the proviso that "in defect of such informations [company instructions] he the said Lord Governor and Captain General shall and may rule and govern by his own discretion or by such laws for the present as he... shall think fit to make" (Brown 1890, 1:379).

These gestures toward discretion embodied a recognition that local contingencies could overcome metropolitan directives to such an extent that *operational* fidelity (to specific instructions) might conflict with *purposive* fidelity (to the grand ends of colonization). Perhaps the company had learned a lesson from Captain Smith, who waged what amounted to a one-man pamphlet war against strict operational fidelity in colonial affairs. In his first published account of the Jamestown settlement, in 1608, Smith recounted how his proposals for military and exploratory exercises on the James River were frustrated by arguments from operational fidelity, "some alleging that, how profitable and to what good purpose soever our journey should portend, yet our commission commanding no certain design, we should be taxed for the most indiscreet men in the world" (Smith 1986, 1:85). But Smith steadfastly refused to be hamstrung by commissions and instructions. In a passage under the marginal heading "a strange mistake in wise men," Smith related how company principals "kindly writ to me... with such tedious Letters, directions, and instructions, and most contrary to that was fitting; we did admire how it was possible such wise men could so torment themselves and us with such strange absurdities and impossibilities" (3:272). Flouting instructions was perhaps Smith's most salient characteristic as a colonial leader, but it also received his close theoretic attention.

Smith's hostility toward operational fidelity derived from his privileging of the firsthand experience of agents over the directive intelligence of principals. It was in this vein that, with typical panache, he held up England's great Iberian rivals as models for emulation (as Raleigh had done previously):

It is not a work for every one to manage such an affair as makes a discovery and plants a Colony. It requires all the best parts of Art, Judgment, Courage, Honesty, Constancy, Diligence, and Industry to do but near well.... Columbus, Cortez, Pizarro, Soto, Magellan, and the rest *served more than an apprenticeship* to learn how to begin their most memorable attempts in the West Indies; which to the wonder of all ages successfully they effected, when many hundreds of others far above them in the world's opinion, *being instructed but by relation*, came to shame and confusion in acts of small moment, who doubtless in other matters were both wise, discreet, generous, and courageous. (Smith 1986, 1:327; emphases added)

Captain Smith was not the only company agent to defend a discretionary conception of colonial leadership after returning from America. Nathaniel Butler wrote his *Historye of the Bermudaes* after serving as governor of the island colony. In it he portrayed the first company-appointed governor of Bermuda, Richard Moore, as a kind of discretionary virtuoso, regularly departing from the London script in order to promote the colony's welfare. Soon after landing, for instance, Moore threatened two mutineers with hanging even though he had received no authority from the company to carry out summary executions: "although he well knew that his commission extended not so far, nor meant he to transcend it, yet to make a show, and breed terror, he caused twelve men to be empanelled upon them"; Moore's bluff had the desired effect of preventing further disturbances (Butler 1882, 25). Later, when the company sent out a surveyor to map the islands' choicest real estate, Moore refused to allot either manpower or provisions for the task because, he said, the Spanish threat required that all available resources be dedicated to the speedy completion of fortifications. On Butler's telling, Moore explained that "the company of adventurers must pardon him, therefore, if in this point he declined from this their injunction and command; for he had the advantage of them by ocular experience, and the lives of himself and his men lay at the stake; the adventurers indeed might lose some expense of coin, but he and his were to make it good upon the expense of blood" (36–7). The company replied by condemning Moore's "continual contempt...of their all-sufficient directions" (43), but Butler's account obviously favored Moore's side of the dispute: he acknowledged his accountability, but to the larger purpose of the colony's welfare as opposed to the minutiae of his principals' instructions.

Indian Policy

Butler and Captain Smith pioneered an influential vision of Virginia politics which saw accountability at the purposive level as requiring discretion at the operational level. Captain Smith's attempts to put this conception into practice are best illustrated by his policies toward the Indians around Jamestown.

Smith was sharply critical of the company's original injunction against engaging in any hostilities with native peoples because he believed that following it fostered their contempt and encouraged them to take advantage of the vulnerable English settlements. When some Indians offered corn to the starving colonists at prices which the English considered extortionate, Smith violated company instructions with a show of force. "Seeing by trade and courtesy there was nothing to be had, he made bold to try such conclusions as necessity enforced, though contrary to his Commission": Smith took a company of soldiers to invade a native village, captured one of their idols, and then ransomed it for food (Smith 1986, 2:144). He later bemoaned pacifistic strictures on Indian policy in the early New England charters as well (2:457–8).

Though Smith's defense of discretion in Indian policy was broadly compatible with a kind of Machiavellian statecraft, his Machiavellism had less to do with the permissibility of injustice (contra Fitzmaurice 2003, 179–85) than with the prudential question of when to abandon diplomacy in favor of conquest – and the latter point had already been discussed in relation to English colonies in Ireland in the 1590s (Peltonen 1995, 74, 81–5). Justice and the common good were for Smith precisely the constitutive values which form the ethical context of political action. Far from rejecting justice, Smith regarded it as essential to combat vices like pride and avarice: as we have seen in his bracing statement of the relation between civic virtue and American colonization, "justice and corruption" ran parallel with "making Commonwealths and marring Commonwealths, the fruits of virtue and the conclusions of vice" (Smith 1986, 1:343–4). Smith's defense of colonial discretion, then, sought liberation not so much from traditional ethical constraints like justice (purposive accountability) as from the narrower class of obligations emanating from the directives of principals (operational accountability). His Indian policy, accordingly, grew out of a novel configuration of a conventional trust-based framework of ethical analysis.

The company's instructions to Governor Gates in 1609 commended Captain Smith to a place on the new council. They also paid tribute, albeit unwittingly, to his Indian policy: "for Powhatan and his Weroances [deputies], it is Clear even to reason beside our experience that he loved not our neighborhood, and therefore you [Gates] may no way trust him, but if you find it not best to make him your prisoner yet you must make him your tributary" (Kingsbury 1935, 3:18). The company had ratified Smith's conduct after the fact but missed his theoretic point: not that they should command ruthlessness of their obedient servants from afar, but rather that they should allow flexibility to the discretion of a colonial virtuoso.

Smith's resolution of the dilemma of accountability and discretion was theoretically coherent, but practically it was no more comforting than the alternatives. The dictum that good men make good colonies was easy to grasp but difficult to implement. Something about not just the Atlantic Ocean but also human nature seemed to stand in the way – the immanence of pride and avarice, the human folly that embarrassed the dog at Bermuda. Smith's discretionary theory of colonial agency was never consistently implemented and probably could not have been consistently successful. Thus accountability and discretion remained, in this early stage of American colonization, equally frustrating as practical tools, though increasingly salient as ideological counters.

Trust and Ideology

Because empowering discretionary virtuosos was not a long-term institutional solution to recurring American problems, colonial managers and observers continued to search for formal structures of accountability to balance the chaotic tendencies of transatlantic reality. The question of institutional reform came to a head around the dissolution of the company by royal writ in 1624. The dichotomy of accountability and discretion figured heavily in these debates, with the former championed by those whom their opponents branded as "democrats" and the latter by those derided as "oligarchs."

We have seen that the conflicts resulting in the dissolution of the company began with the Sandys faction's insistence that Smythe and his associates be held strictly accountable for the company's debts and investors' losses. The Smythe faction countered this argument from accountability by appealing to the discretionary concept of trust, meanwhile shifting the moral burden of the discussion from honesty to competence. Only under the Smythe regime "were the Governors and Chief Officers men of known sufficiency and experience for those services," whereas under Sandys leaders reached their posts "out of favor, alliance, and affection" (Kingsbury 1935, 4:135). The pro-Smythe argument continued: "the officers in Virginia [appointed by Sandys] are applauded for their obedience in exercising the directions and desires of the Company here. We only wish that men had been employed in that service to whose advice and Counsels the Company might rather have harkened and received light and information for their proceedings" (4:146). This point about local knowledge echoed Captain Smith's arguments for allowing wide discretion to agents on the ground.

The Smythe party's campaign for dissolution prevailed in the court of King's Bench, which issued the writ of *quo warranto* against the Virginia Company in June 1624, but still the fight continued. The pro-Sandys group hoped for the creation of a new corporate organization and tried to shift the focus of the debate around trust. The king had sent a royal commission to Jamestown to reorder the colony's affairs, and the incumbent (pro-Sandys) council in the colony phrased their protests against this group precisely in terms of the accountable trust. The council viewed the company's old tobacco contract with the king as benefiting investors in England at the expense of planters in Virginia: "some whom his majesty hath appointed commissioners for those affairs are contrivers and favorers of this Contract, Contrary to their duties and the trust imposed upon them by his majesty," whereas the members of the council "have discharged their Consciences in his majesty's service with all integrity and fidelity" (Kingsbury 1935, 4:561). According to "The Discourse of the Old Company," a pro-Sandys document drafted in 1625 after King James's death and his son Charles's accession, the royal commission's "proceedings are kept in great secret, which breeds suspicion that they have not been good; else why do they fly the Light?" (Brown 1890, 1:299–300).

The coherence of the fiduciary framework within which the Sandys-Smythe debate took place suggests that something akin to a doctrinaire attachment to a particular conception of trust was operative on each side, with the Sandys camp committed to the accountable and the Smythe camp to the discretionary. In the context of the constitutional arguments regularly appearing in English politics in the early decades of the seventeenth century, these patterns of argument in 1623–5 should be regarded as ideologically colored rather than purely rhetorical and opportunistic. This is a very different claim from the "patriotic" or Whig-historical identification of Sandys and his allies as true-believing constitutionalists, or even republicans, who meant to use the entire Virginia enterprise as a vehicle of opposition to Stuart absolutism (e.g. Brown 1968); this interpretation of Sandys's plans for Virginia was long ago discredited (see Craven 1932, ch. 1). But the Sandys-Smythe conflict did, nonetheless, feature elements of a larger ideological rivalry: the accountable concept of trust was a key conceptual tool for those seeking to establish the English crown's obligation to work in consultation with Parliament and to redress its grievances, and denying the force and cogency of this concept was an important goal of those wishing to widen the Stuart monarchs' freedom of action. The debate over the dissolution of the Virginia Company in 1624 employed the same tools, albeit for a different task, as the debate leading to the Petition of Right in 1628 (see Chapter 2 above).

What was at stake for the colonies in the dissolution debate, then, was not the future of American independence and self-government, as the facile Whiggism would have it, but it was something of significance nonetheless. As we will soon see, the utopian reform projects coming out of this debate broached the idea of intra-American, intra-colonial accountability for the first time. For ideas of accountability and discretion were not only counters of ideological commitment and weapons of polemic struggle; they were also tools of institutional design.

Institutional Reform

The first Virginia charter, issued in 1606, had created a royal council for Virginia which selected and supervised the Virginia Company based in London; for the initial voyage to Jamestown, the company chose one governor and six assistants, vesting a veto power in the latter over the former (Craven 1949, 61–2). With the issue of a second charter in 1609, the company's structure became more democratic, with its leadership (the treasurer and his council) to be selected by the general assembly of the company rather than the royal council for Virginia, while government within the colony became more autocratic, with the colony governor now given "absolute" power and the colony assistants power of advice only (90–1). The third and final Virginia charter of 1612, in addition to enlarging the company's patent to include the Bermuda islands, formalized the transfer of powers from the royal council for Virginia to the company which had already taken place in practice (111–13).

Thus the Virginia Company, under Smythe's leadership, undertook several stages of revision of its organizational structure during the Jamestown colony's early troubles. The most famous case of institutional reform was the law code sent out with Governor Gates in 1609 but not implemented until Delaware replaced him the following year (Strachey 1947). Building on the new charter of 1609, the company granted Delaware a measure of authority unabridged by any veto power in the local council, including the right to rule by martial law (Brown 1890, 1:377–8). Harsh penalties and the rigorous regimentation of daily life – work, prayer, and little else – were the leading characteristics of this regime, and Delaware was instructed by the company to eschew "the niceness and letter of the law, which perplexeth in this tender body rather than dispatcheth Causes" (Kingsbury 1935, 3:28).

The combination of martial law and political absolutism at Jamestown was at first widely hailed for its beneficial results. Even John Rolfe, whose ties to the Sandys group were close, credited the "absolute" and "monarchical" government that replaced the original "aristocratical" regime for having driven out idleness and provided basic public works for the settlement (Rolfe 1971, 3). Smythe explained his decision to turn to an absolute governor as a response precisely to the problems of virtue and corruption which all acknowledged in the early years. Thus he cited the feedback of colony officials, who "did see such a necessity that the said laws should be made and published, in some cases *ad terrorem* and in some to be truly executed, as without which the Colony, consisting then of such debased and irregular persons, could not possibly continue" (Kingsbury 1935, 3:521).

But the many Jamestown settlers who chafed under this harsh system found sympathetic advocates in London. Though admitting that the draconian law code brought over by Delaware had been a salutary short-term expedient, *The New Life of Virginea* (1612) called for that regime to come to an end: "let them live as free English men, under the government of just and equal laws, and not as slaves after the will and lust of any superior" (Johnson 1947, 17). Later, in 1625, "The Discourse of the Old Company" kept the memory of martial law alive, charging that the Smythe regime had left colonists "without assurance of their Liberties, being violently detained as servants beyond their covenanted times" (Brown 1890, 1:158). The Sandys regime, according to its backers, liberated the colony from this oppression with a counter-vailing program of institutional reform: increasing population, shipping, women and children, subsistence agriculture, life expectancy, free trade, and dividends from land. These gains were put down specifically to Sandys's reforms of the colonial structures he inherited from Smythe: "the bloody Laws [of 1610] being silenced and the Government ordered like to that of this Kingdom... provisions being made for the maintenance of Officers that they should not need to prey upon the people... the liberty of a General Assembly being granted them, whereby they find out and execute those things as might best tend to their good" (1:159–60).

The House of Burgesses

"The liberty of a General Assembly," famously, involved the creation of the House of Burgesses in 1619 to meet with governor and council at Jamestown. A similar institution was set up in Bermuda the following year, and these were the first representative assemblies in the American colonies. Their genesis may have been pragmatic and promotional rather than ideological – as the company's summons for the Bermuda assembly noted, "every man will more willingly obey laws to which he hath yielded his consent" (Craven 1949, 136) – but their continued existence became a matter of potent symbolism. Though the idea of replacing the martial-law regime of 1610 with common-law and representative institutions was not opposed by Smythe and Robert Johnson when it was first mooted (Andrews 1933, 43–4), Sandys and his associates certainly made rhetorical hay of the institutional reforms they oversaw.

The Virginia House of Burgesses, which left better records of its early life than did its Bermuda counterpart, gathered two deputies chosen by the citizens of each of eleven plantations and together with the council was to advise the governor on local affairs; both the latter two bodies were technically chosen by the company in London, though in fact the governor had a large say over the composition of his council. The governor also had a veto over the other two bodies. Measures passed by the General Assembly (burgesses plus council) and confirmed by the governor were then subject to ratification by the company's quarterly general courts in London. The company was eager to exploit the promotional value of this kind of reform, but the assembly itself had no intention of languishing in tokenism. At its first meeting the assembly proposed that its own legislation take immediate effect, even before ratification in London; they undertook, furthermore, to review the new colony charter drawn up by the company, "not to the end to correct or control anything therein contained, but only in case we should find aught not perfectly squaring with the state of this Colony" (Tyler 1907, 255, 277–8).

In the issue these proposals were rejected by the company, but the spirit of local self-government continued to lead a healthy existence in Virginia. The "Ordinance and Constitution" promulgated by the Sandys regime in 1621 even held out hope that, provided the colony were "well-settled," at some future time the arrow of legislative dependence would be reversed and the company's resolutions would be subject to the assembly's ratification (Kingsbury 1935, 3:484). This might also have been a promotional gesture, but it reflected the same sense of the inevitability of colonial self-government which had been present since Elizabethan times, among the Hakluyt circle (see epigraph above). In a similar vein Captain Smith commented sympathetically on the assembly's proposal: "as they can make no Laws in Virginia till they be ratified here [in London]; so they think it but reason, none should be enacted here without their consents, because they only feel them and must live under them" (Smith 1986, 2:292).

There was a close relation, then, between the commonwealth idea and the establishment of representative political institutions in English colonies; indeed, in terms of public rationale, the former was at the heart of all Sandys's reforms. The Sandys group always claimed motivation by the same over-riding goal which earlier critiques of the company under Smythe had made their watchword: they "had an eye rather to the benefit of the plantation than the profit of the Adventurers" (Kingsbury 1935, 3:503). Sandys's ambitious roster of initiatives pointed toward a self-sufficient community as opposed to a mere trading post, and they had a utopian air about them: ironworks, glassworks, vineyards, a whole portfolio of economic and especially agricultural diversification; the migration of women and children; public schools for English and Indian children alike (Craven 1949, 144–5); not to mention an English-looking mixed constitution.

Interestingly, it was the political facet of Sandys's ambitious reform program rather than the social or economic which survived the dissolution of the company. An informal assembly of planters periodically met with governor and council from 1625 to 1629, and throughout the 1630s the House of Burgesses participated in regular legislation until, after repeated petitions from Jamestown, it finally obtained royal confirmation in 1639 (Andrews 1933, 56–7; Craven 1949, 160). Yet the house remained a weak institution (Craven 1969), one to which King Charles barely paid attention (Kukla 1989, 74), and it seems never to have been viewed as a viable vehicle of political accountability. The reality was that colonists with grievances against their local government had to find their remedy on the other side of the Atlantic.

Royalization

The commonwealth idea was if anything more self-consciously and coherently employed by the opposing side in the dissolution debate, an anti-Sandys coalition that included Captain Smith and others who would not normally have been the natural allies of the Smythe group. They cited the colonies' general welfare as bodies politic to advocate royalizing colonial affairs into the hands of the Stuart kings: placing the whole Virginia business under the control of crown rather than company. Ironically, perhaps, this line of thought produced in John Bargraves's proposals an offshoot that supplied not only a theoretic defense of representative colonial institutions but also the first formulation of intra-colonial political accountability.

The notion that colonization for the common good required a royal administration was as old as the Virginia venture itself. A manuscript drafted prior to the company's incorporation (1606), announcing "Reasons or Motives for the Raising of a Publique Stock," argued against the regime which in fact would soon be tried: "it is honorable for a state rather to back an exploit by a public consent than by a private monopoly.... Better men of [be]havior and quality will engage themselves in a public service, which carrieth more reputation with it, than a private, which is for the most part ignominious in the end, as being presumed to aim at a lucre, and is subject to emulation, fraud, and envy" (Brown 1890, 1:38).

This point of view was essentially the one later adopted by Captain Smith, Butler, and several others. Butler's famously cutting commentary on Jamestown affairs under Sandys blamed principals and agents all around: "unless the Confusions and private ends of some of the Company here [England], and the bad executions in seconding them of their Agents there, be redressed with speed by some divine and supreme hand... instead of a Plantation it will shortly get the name of a Slaughterhouse" (Tyler 1907, 418). Thus Butler became an advocate of the royalization of all colonial activity, "being a work, to speak truth, which to bring it to perfection requires the power and purse of a monarch" (Butler 1882, 11). Smith summed up the position he had taken in his testimony during the dissolution proceedings in the preface to his *Generall Historie* (1624): "the counsel of divers is confused; the general Stock is consumed; nothing but the touch of the King's sacred hand can erect a Monarchy" (Smith 1986, 2:43). John Martin, an old ally of Captain Smith at Jamestown, penned a manuscript in 1622, "How Virginia May Be Made a Royal Plantation" (Kingsbury 1935, 3:708–10). After dissolution, even the pro-Sandys "Discourse of the Old Company" imagined an acceptable course of royalization, urging that the colonies be supervised by a council strictly accountable to the king rather than by a relatively autonomous cadre of Smythe and his associates (Brown 1890, 1:304).

There was no inherent contradiction, then, between recognizing the moral status of a colony as a commonwealth in its own right and making it legally subordinate to royal sovereignty. Indeed it was already common for writers inspired by classical republicanism to conceive English towns in similar terms, even while supporting a national monarchy (Peltonen 1995, 56–62).

"Democracy"

The campaign for royalization was punctuated by condemnations of "democracy," as the joint-stock form of corporate organization was widely called, and it is in this context that the term's place in the Virginia Company's activities must be understood. "Democracy" applied to the metropolitan rather than the colonial arena. Votes were counted in the company's general courts according to persons (one man, one vote) rather than shares. The standard arguments about tumults and incompetence were used against this particular instance of "popular" government and had nothing to do with the conduct of affairs in the colony itself (contra Bruce 1910, 2:250–4).

Chief among the respondents to this charge against the company was William Cavendish, one of Sandys's staunchest allies, who put his name to a paper rebutting a number of the aspersions that had been cast on the Sandys regime; the last of these was the allegation that government by a numerous assembly in London (regardless of that body's relations with Virginia itself) made the company a "democracy." Cavendish first of all denied the fairness of the charge, since the king remained the supreme legal authority over the colonists (Kingsbury 1935, 2:358). But he also conceded that "it is true that according to your Majesty's Institution in their Letters Patents the Government hath some show of a Democratical form." He went on to justify this arrangement by observing that

> these plantations, though furthered much by your Majesty's grace, yet being not made at your Majesty's charge or expense, but chiefly by the private purses of the Adventurers, they would never have Adventured in such an Action, wherein they interest their own fortunes, if in the regulating and governing of their own business their own votes had been excluded. (2:359)

This had been precisely the rationale behind the expansion of the company under the third Virginia charter in 1612: in order to get more contributors to keep the enterprise afloat, the full privileges of membership, including voting for company officers and policies, had to be extended to all. A similar logic seems to have underlain the Sandys regime's reforms of colonial institutions, in order to encourage more colonists to emigrate there, as well as the pragmatic concessions to local self-government which Hakluyt and Captain Smith had countenanced. This, then, was an utterly conventional argument for corporate democracy.

Cavendish's secretary, Thomas Hobbes, was personally engaged in Virginia affairs at the time and may have been involved in the paper on democracy within the company. Cavendish had Hobbes inducted as a member of the company in order to add a reliable pro-Sandys vote to its proceedings, and Hobbes regularly attended meetings during the dissolution fight and voted in line with his employer's partisan interest (Malcolm 1981). Hobbes could well have written or advised the Cavendish paper defending company democracy in a manner consistent with his argument in *Leviathan* (1651) for the superiority of monarchic commonwealths on grounds of "convenience" (Hobbes 1996, 131). After all, the company was a "system subject" or "body politic": jurally subordinate to, but otherwise free to order its internal affairs without endangering or altering, the "Sovereign" (ch. 21). A similar thought underlay Cavendish's charge that "whereas they [Smythe et al.] cry out against Democracy and call for Oligarchy, they make not the Government thereby either of better form or more Monarchical" (Kingsbury 1935, 2:359). In short, there was no reason to think a joint-stock company necessarily threatened the English monarchy by its very existence. But, if this was true, the same logic would apply to democracy within an American colony.

Bargraves versus Smythe

One of the most articulate and persistent contributors to the dissolution debates was John Bargraves, who showed how the Cavendish/Hobbes line of thought might apply to democracy in not only company but also colony. He was the first and, for a few years at least, the only participant in American colonization to take this theoretic step. He made his key move in a visionary and torturously complicated plan of colonial administration which included procedures of accountability within the colonies' own representative institutions. Almost as complicated were the personal and polemic contexts out of which this plan emerged.

Bargraves was a member of the Virginia Company, had been employed in the colony as an agent for John Martin, and for a time was the bane of Thomas Smythe's existence. In 1622 he brought a complaint in the court of Chancery against Smythe and Robert Johnson which brought both the commonwealth idea and the fiduciary idea to bear on Virginia affairs. Bargraves alleged that martial law in the colony had been inextricably linked to conspiracy in the company. Echoing other critics of the absolute regime of 1610, Bargraves indicted Smythe for issuing "a certain book of Tyrannical government in Virginia... whereby many of the king's subjects there lost their lives, and were brought into slavery, and the petitioner and those he employed were thereby much damnified to their great loss" (Kingsbury 1935, 3:605). This was the result of a London-based faction's domination of the company, with Smythe "taking to himself absolute power of Governing both the Plantation and the Company according to his will, when no laws were made to prevent faction and packing of Courts, nor no order kept of managing business in public Courts lawfully assembled, but they were carried by private packings" (3:638).

Conspiracies, of course, troubled observers of colonial affairs precisely because they embodied infidelity on a grand scale. Accordingly, the burden of Bargraves's "Charge against Sir T. Smith" was that "Sir T. S. hath not performed the trust reposed in him by His Majesty, but contrariwise with great Reason it may be strongly presumed that both he first came to undertake this charge with sinister and private ends of his own and hath so continued therein" (Kingsbury 1935, 4:81). This way of combining trust and the common good, as we have seen, was a staple tactic of analyzing the metropolitan side of Virginia affairs during the dissolution fight.

Bargraves went further to argue that Smythe's abuses condemned the joint-stock form of organization altogether (Kingsbury 1935, 3:607). Smythe and Johnson "by practice and faction have framed a Company... able by most voices to carry the government as they list" (3:605): this was a complaint against tyranny of the majority. Bargraves considered himself one of the unfortunate minority who lost their investments through the embezzling connivance of a self-interested majority, and the goal of his petition was to get relief for these losses. Though he maintained that the Sandys regime was better than its predecessor, Bargraves still lamented that there was "no Course taken to prevent oppression of single Planters or small Bodies of Adventurers by plurality of voices of greater numbers interested in any differences" (3:638).

Smythe relied on considerable reserves of goodwill with King James and the Privy Council, and Bargraves's several petitions to the latter were all either deflected or ignored. Still, he was making trouble of a sort that could help the Sandys faction. But, given his arguments against the joint-stock form and his debts to the Sandys-led company, the Smythe faction saw an opportunity. Thus Smythe's ally Nathaniel Rich called on Bargraves for dirty laundry on Sandys in May 1623. According to Rich's "Note" on this meeting, Bargraves's story was that "by his long acquaintance with him... there was not any man in the world that carried a more *malicious* heart to the government of a Monarchy than Sir Edwin Sandys did; for Capt. Bargraves had heard him say, That if ever God from heaven did constitute and direct a form of Government it was that of Geneva" (Kingsbury 1935, 4:194). Sandys was further charged with maintaining a "popular" form of company government "because his intent was to erect a free state in Virginia," and with planning to send extreme, separatist puritans to Virginia, "those Brownists by their doctrine claiming a liberty to disagreeing to the Government of a Monarchy" (4:194).

Rich's "Note" has inspired the Whiggish condemnation of Bargraves as an enemy to Sandys and all he stood for. Since Sandys did indeed accept the proposal of the so-called Pilgrims to settle in Virginia (before they eventually settled farther north), and since he did institute the House of Burgesses in 1619, he has been touted as a prophet of religious toleration and political liberty (e.g. Brown 1969, 262-3). But the bigger picture includes the £500 debt that Bargraves owed to the Virginia Company, which his lawsuits against Smythe might have enabled him to pay off if Smythe's connections had not supplied insuperable obstacles. After defaming Sandys in Rich's hearing, however, Bargraves was granted the protection of the Privy Council, so that Sandys could take no legal steps to collect Bargraves's debt (Kingsbury 1935, 4:487-8). Circumstantial evidence, then, suggests that Smythe and Rich suborned Bargraves's slander on Sandys in exchange for legal and financial relief. Even more decisive, however, is the textual evidence that Bargraves did not long remain on Smythe's side of the dissolution debate.

In December 1623, six months after his conversation with Rich, Bargraves wrote to Lionel Cranfield, earl of Middlesex and Lord Treasurer to King James. Bargraves was again on Smythe's back, claiming that he and his allies ("the delinquents") were seeking the dissolution of the company merely in order to "conceal from the king the Iniquity of their former government." He went on to announce his change of mind on dissolution itself and to urge Middlesex against it: "the company and the government by voices must of necessity continue... for the giving of consent to laws that shall bind their estates [is] the right of all free subjects" (Bargraves 1922, 512). This was close to Cavendish's argument for corporate democracy. But Bargraves now went further by insisting that the real solution to Virginia's problems lay rather in reform on the other side of the Atlantic, for he recommended that the company should "transfer the government to the Planter (to whom of right it belongs)" (512-13). Still, he meant to deny neither crown nor company a role in colonial management: the former would retain ultimate sovereignty and exercise supervision through the Council for Virginia, while the latter's consent would still be required for grants of land and regulations affecting members' investments (513).

Bargraves's final position on the matter was little different from that of Sandys and Cavendish (and possibly Hobbes): acknowledge royal supervision but preserve the company and give the colony itself greater powers of self-government. Bargraves's hostility to "slavery" and tyrannical rule, and his use of the commonwealth idea and the fiduciary idea, were not unusual. Where he set himself apart was in channeling these idioms into the most sophisticated and articulate of the many utopian proposals advanced during the dissolution debates, in a remarkable paper that advocated political accountability within the colonies consistent with royal supremacy over them.

Bargraves's "Forme"

Bargraves's last letter to Middlesex introduced "A Forme of Polisie," a compilation of elements of five other treatises he said he had composed. This manuscript, as its title suggests, proposed a new kind of formalism – different from both Smythe's and Sandys's, though explicitly hostile to the former and implicitly friendly to the latter – to solve colonial problems in both London and Jamestown. Bearing the subtitle "to Plante and Governe Many Families in Virginea, Soe As It Shall Naturally Depend one [on] the Sovereigntye of England," Bargraves's tract was clearly not intended to confer legal independence on Virginia. Indeed the "Forme of Polisie" was patterned after a royal charter, adopting the first-person voice.

Bargraves perceived a simple set of alternatives for institutional reform:

> either to authorize one set form of government both here and in Virginia framed to the attaining of our end ["dependency on England"], and so leave the laws to be ordained according to that form; or else that the adventurers here should give laws and government by popular voices to the planters in Virginia as if they were their tenants or servants. The said planters being as well free subjects to the king, those that venture their lives as well as their goods. (Bargraves 1914, 561)

This formulation made it clear that the second option was unacceptable, consistently with Bargraves's suspicion of tyranny of the majority within the Virginia Company, and he proceeded to spell out the first option. Bargraves condemned (almost verbatim from his earlier petitions) Smythe's "certain tyrannical book of government" and the "slavery" he believed it had introduced to Virginia (Bargraves 1914, 564). Such measures had to be repudiated in the name of the colony's common good, since "the plantation is now so strong that it is able to defend itself and fit to put on the face of a commonwealth" (561). Echoing other pro-Sandys accounts, the commonwealth idea was thus taken to apply to the colony itself, and its welfare had to be a prime object of the king's "sovereignty... to benefit not to destroy our subjects" (564). If only the colonists' welfare were duly considered and promoted, England would have an empire united by "natural love and obedience" rather than force (562). In turn, "they will receive such content that they will strive to maintain [their government] in the same form we shall now settle it, [and] we may for these reasons give them the elections of their own governors, at which all free subjects do naturally desire" (567).

There was a constructive rather than conflictual relation, then, between the legal supremacy of the crown and the practice of local elections in the colony: Sandys's introduction of the House of Burgesses had royal approval in 1619, after all, and Bargraves was proposing a variation on the same theme. More importantly still, Bargraves's conception of colonial government included not only consent but also control, with popular rights of not only selection but also accountability and distinct procedures for each.

The powers of Bargraves's colonial "Council of Union" (including representatives from the several settlements, or "corporations") were simply stated and comprehensive: they included taxing and spending, making war and peace, instituting price controls, making commercial contracts with the metropolis, settling new plantations, and administering local justice (Bargraves 1914, 569). Though the precise relations among different institutions seem to drown in a swamp of procedural and psephological detail, there was to be in addition to the Council of Union a "General Parliament" (567, 574), perhaps corresponding to the existing House of Burgesses. It is clear, at least, that all American "officers, magistrates, and governors" were to be elected by franchises varying, and narrowing, from the local to the regional to the colony-wide level (566–7).

Compared to these elaborate mechanisms of consent, those of accountability were relatively straightforward. Meeting concurrently with the General Parliament was to be a "Syndex" of fifteen "Protectors of the Commonwealth," and this body's sole function was to effect accountability throughout the system. They had

> power to inquire, examine, try, and adjudge (as need shall require) all the great councillors... that shall have the administration of justice within any of our said provinces or colonies. And whichsoever of them shall be found guilty of oppression or the encroaching farther upon our [the king's] sovereign power than to him or them [is] limited by these our orders, or warranted by our council of state, they shall have power to punish them according to the laws, either with loss of life, goods, or banishment. (Bargraves 1914, 574)

In short, Bargraves's Syndex was to be a sort of representative jury for political crimes with functions of both audit ("inquire, examine") and impeachment ("try, adjudge").

Five aspects of this scheme of accountability are particularly noteworthy. First, it was motivated by the same hostility to tyranny, in defense of the commonwealth idea, which animated Bargraves's petitions against the Smythe regime: punishing "oppression" was meant to deter "the undoing of our obedient subjects" and to avert "the ruin of the commonwealth [Virginia]" (Bargraves 1914, 574). Second, the Syndex was meant as a representative body, three of whose members were to be annually elected from each of Virginia's five social ranks. Third, the trust of authority held by colonial officers was understood to originate in the crown (hence "limited by these our orders"), even though the colonists were to select officers from among themselves. Fourth, Bargraves was proposing for Virginia a mixed regime of counter-vailing agencies, in which the Syndex embodied the favored mechanics (special inquest), agency (representative), and rationale (public liberty) of what I have been calling the classical model of accountability (see Chapter 1 above). Finally, Bargraves evidently did not assume that officers' elective tenure was sufficient by itself to control them.

On Bargraves's scheme, then, Virginians were to be governed by officers not only selected by them but also held accountable by a body drawn from a broad range of colonial society. This was the only scheme of regular accountability, operable through ordinary constitutional processes, to have been proposed for any American colony at the time. The Syndex might be called "democratic" in the modern sense of being broadly representative but "aristocratic" or "ephoral" in the classical sense of being numerically small and elective. In any case what was still missing from a fully fledged conception of a modern democratic state, leaving no final appeal to an outside agency like the crown, was the formal principle of popular sovereignty.

Utopias

Bargraves's "Forme of Polisie" laid out a utopia for Virginia even more fantastic than the one Sandys had tried to realize there. Several other commentators produced colonial blueprints that were much less detailed and in any case more reminiscent of the Elizabethan military garrisons of their authors' early lives, including John Martin (Bargraves's former employer) and Capt. John Smith (Martin's friend and ally) (see Kingsbury 1935, 3:708–10; Smith 1986, 3:297–8). These plans were successors to those devised in the later sixteenth century for colonization in both America and Ireland, such as Humphrey Gilbert's feudalistic scheme for Newfoundland (Quinn 1976, 83). By comparison Bargraves's contribution was unusual in its elaboration, classical-republican in its inspiration, and exceptional in its concern with accountability.

The course of Virginia politics after the dissolution of the company vindicated Bargraves's concern with internal procedures of accountability. The famous "thrusting out" of Gov. John Harvey in 1635, for instance, dramatically illustrated the lengths to which Virginians had to go to settle major disputes within the colony. After refusing to recognize the legality of an impeachment proceeding against him in the House of Burgesses, Harvey was arrested by disgruntled members of his council and forced onto a ship bound for England, where the colonists' "petition of grievances" was heard by a royal commission (Thornton 1968; Hoffer and Hull 1978, 656-8). Harvey was reinstated by royal order, but his relations with the colony were never mended. King Charles's confirmation of the House of Burgesses in 1639 may have represented an attempt to shift internal power from the troublesome governor and council to the representative assembly (Kukla 1989, 81-96).

Bargraves's "Forme of Polisie," with its intra-colonial mechanism of accountability, might have averted events like the Harvey episode. In the issue Virginians could only pursue accountability on the other side of the ocean, and without the astute management of Gov. William Berkeley through the Civil War period (see Kukla 1989, 105-7, 113-15) the recurrence of similar episodes would have been likely. The case was the same in neighboring Maryland, over which Cecilius Calvert, Lord Baltimore, ruled as an absentee landlord. There a general assembly was allowed to propose laws and engage in discursive wrangling with the resident governor, but all resolutions taken in the colony were ultimately subject to Baltimore's veto from England (Scharf 1967, 1:130; Jordan 1987, 26-32, 42-5).

Bargraves had accepted the conventional wisdom of a number of commentators on Virginia affairs, most notably Captain Smith, which established the commonwealth and fiduciary ideas as the cardinal premises of colonial community, and he ramified the latter by making the accountable trust the guiding principle of colonial agency. He thereby showed how a New World colony with no established institutional traditions of its own might be conceptualized as a democratic state, one embodying the ancient criterion of popular control through accountability, even while remaining legally dependent on the English crown. But it would take the thought and practice of Englishmen in another part of the Americas to ramify the commonwealth idea by the principle of popular sovereignty – and thereby to establish the essential conceptual partnership of modern democratic theory, pairing popular sovereignty with accountability.

Even as Bargraves was submitting his last proposal for Virginia in 1623, another colonial movement had already introduced new traditions of discourse to another part of the New World, where classical humanism was supplemented by a particular ecclesiology and a particular jurisprudence.

Radical Calvinist theories of church government took the whole congregation to possess ultimate authority: in the language that New Englanders had learned from the sixteenth-century French jurist Bodin (Bodin 1962, bk. 2, ch. 2), the "state" (or sovereignty) of a true church must be "popular," whatever form the "government" (or administration) might take. In the process of working out their theories of church politics, they prioritized two of the leading principles that had been present in Bargraves's utopia: consent and accountability. It is to the influence on early New England politics of congregational ecclesiology and Bodinian jurisprudence that we now turn.

4

Politics and Ecclesiastics in Plymouth and Massachusetts

> It seems most agreeable with the light of nature that, if there be any regular government settled in the church of God, it must needs be a democracy.
>
> John Wise, 1717 (Wise 1958, 60)

In the 1590s the separatist martyr-to-be Henry Barrow developed his ideas on church government by dint of an attack on the "constitution" of the Church of England, thereby supplying one of the first known instances in which that word was used to refer not just generically to laws or ordinances but more specifically to a systemic configuration of authority (Stourzh 1988, 39). In the next couple of decades Henry Ainsworth, another English Calvinist known for his separatism, would use the term "constitution" in a similar fashion as he developed his own ecclesiology (40). The colonists who founded New Plymouth in 1620 owned and read books by Barrow and had known and worshiped with Ainsworth in their years of Dutch exile. It is therefore a fact of some interest for the origins of democratic constitutionalism that the so-called Pilgrims and their pastor, John Robinson, subscribed to a radically populist theory of church government, in defense of which they had backed Ainsworth in an important intramural dispute in the English exile church at Amsterdam.

One reason for the relative lack of scholarly interest in the political ideas of the early New England colonies may be a failure to appreciate that, in the minds of seventeenth-century puritans, theories of ecclesiastics were theories of politics. New Englanders recognized important differences between spiritual and temporal forms of power, but they also acknowledged the essential unity of their organizational principles. For this reason it was possible for ideas of democracy in the church to be transferred to democracy in the state, as I will argue the Pilgrims exemplified in their Plymouth colony. More generally the political ideas of early New England illustrate the construction of an ecclesiastical model of accountability – primarily from Calvinist materials but with classical and Bodinian influences.

Yet the novel developments in politics and ecclesiastics in New England took place against a background of continuity with the intellectual furniture of previous English colonization. The mixture of classical humanism and Christian evangelism which typified Elizabethan and Jacobean colonial discourses was fully inherited by the puritans of New Plymouth and Massachusetts Bay. To be sure, the quest for a haven for religious conscience would supply an unusually strong sense of communal solidarity and a unique determination to obtain de facto independence from English control, but the commonwealth idea and the associated virtue of fidelity continued to operate much as they had in Virginia and Bermuda (see Chapter 3 above), thanks in part to New Englanders' reliance on the writings of Capt. John Smith. What was new in the political ideas of New England had to do with the addition of the principle of popular sovereignty and its joining, by some, with the principle of accountability operating through unapologetically popular bodies.

Famously, English colonization in the regions to the north of Virginia made its first strides toward stability and permanence at Plymouth Rock in 1620. By the end of the English Civil War, some thirty years later, five colonies or "commonwealths" in New England presided over upwards of forty distinct towns or "plantations": New Plymouth was centered on the town of Plymouth, Massachusetts Bay on Boston, Connecticut on Hartford, New Haven on the town of the same name, and Rhode Island and Providence Plantations on the town of Providence (see Figure 4.1). Most of these settlements revolved around gathered churches departing in varying degrees from the forms and procedures of the Church of England, and ecclesiology was the leading literary product of the region. But, contrary to the presumptions of much contemporary publicity and subsequent scholarship, there were significant ideological cleavages within the so-called New England Way in ecclesiastics.

Confining popular power within the church to selection or consent while excluding accountability or control was, generally speaking, the tactic adopted by Massachusetts writers like John Cotton and Richard Mather. In this way they made themselves appear more biblically correct and less politically disruptive, both to themselves and to their Calvinist brethren around Europe, than the separatists and "schismatics" whom they were often accused of imitating. Yet the populist tendencies of the more radical theories of church power at times overcame the forces of moderation

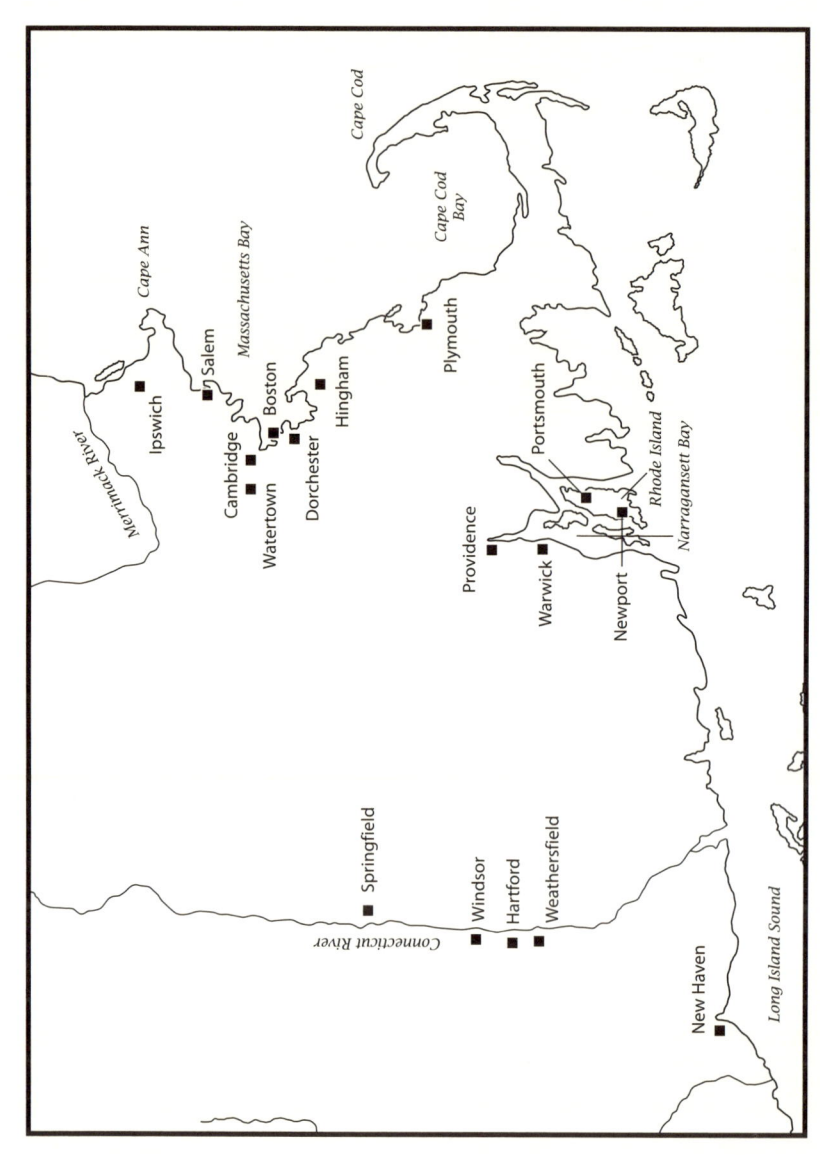

FIGURE 4.1. New England towns, ca. 1640.

and firmly established ideas of democratic accountability. The key figures in this development were Robinson, the "Pilgrim Pastor," and Bodin, the sixteenth-century French jurist whose ideas on sovereignty and the classification of regimes were absorbed into the New Englanders' ecclesiastic debates. Robinson was exceptional in the subtlety of his understanding of Bodin's protocols of classification and their application to ecclesiastic regimes; even more remarkably, he revalued the Bodinian "popular state," from the worst form of government to the true form of a Christian church. This claim and the language used to make it were equivalent in their radical import to those of John Wise early in the next century (see epigraph above). In Wise's time the writings of Cotton and Mather were being retrieved from Massachusetts's founding period to argue that ecclesiastic populists were fundamentally mistaken about the New England Way (see Mather 1712, pref.; Miller 1958, ix–x).

Thus the Pilgrims were the immediate heirs, as Wise was a mediate heir, to an alternative New England way based on Robinsonian populism. Ecclesiastic debates in the international Calvinist press constituted a school of political theory for many English puritans, and the Pilgrims had as their mentor a protagonist of distinction in those debates. By the later 1640s mainstream divines like Cotton and Mather would make a concession to Robinson's legacy by allowing accountability in the form of extraordinary deselection: the deposition and replacement of a corrupt minister. Still, their favored Aristotelian "mixed" regime was meant generally to disempower the congregation except in the last resort, much as in the resistance theories for civil government of the Huguenots and Althusius (see Chapter 2 above). The Bodinian "popular state," by contrast, was supposed to keep the people undivided and supreme by subjecting officers to regular accountability.

Moreover, the political principles of the church were frequently regarded as commensurate with those of the state – notwithstanding polemically prudent assertions to the contrary. In Plymouth's civil affairs ecclesiastic populism was echoed by constitutional developments that reposed ultimate control not only in a unicameral assembly over the magistrates but also in the freemen over the assembly. On this evidence the Pilgrims were the first American colonists not only to conceive a "popular state" for the church but also to construct one for civil government. Moreover, since Robinson himself never set foot in America, the theoretic foundations for Pilgrim democracy were laid independently of the mythic influences of the American wilderness. Yet, as we will see, the Pilgrims' unmistakable commitment to the general principle of accountability was not matched by an articulate attachment to its specific non-electoral forms.

Colonial Continuities

The colonization of New England exhibited striking and substantial continuities with previous English colonial activity, especially with Virginia and Bermuda. The very name of the region came from *A Description of New England* (1616), written by none other than Captain Smith, whose extensive writings on American colonization, covering not only his years in Virginia but also his later explorations northward, served as an important guide for the puritans who settled there. What in time made New England distinctive, in both institutional and ideological terms, can only be appreciated by reference to how conventionally it began.

The Pilgrims began their venture fully within the established institutional framework of English colonization, obtaining an indenture for a "particular plantation" in 1619 from the Virginia Company, then under the leadership of Edwin Sandys (Morison 1951). The Massachusetts settlement began in similar fashion in 1628, when John White and his associates joined with prominent gentlemen and merchants from London to seek a patent from Ferdinando Gorges's Council for New England. It was on this basis that John Endecott led the establishment of Naumkeag (a.k.a. Salem), but in 1629 the Salem project was absorbed into a larger effort that succeeded in getting its own royal charter, under the name of the Massachusetts Bay Company (Osgood 1907, 1:119–28; Andrews 1934, 1:355–9).

Even the Mayflower Compact (see Bradford 1952, 75–6), the mythic symbol of puritan (and eventually American) independence from English control, in fact merely underlines New England's utterly conventional beginnings within the usual structure of royal authority and chartered companies. Just as in Bermuda eight years before, a voluntary compact of settlers was published for an English audience at a time when the Plymouth colony's legal status was in doubt. The Pilgrims' indenture from the Virginia Company authorized them to settle west of the Hudson River, but in the issue the *Mayflower* proved unable to round the shoals off Cape Cod's southern flank. On their way to a legal no-man's-land, the Pilgrims feared the sort of mutinies seen at Bermuda when the expedition of Somers and Gates had made landfall outside the Virginia Company's jurisdiction (see Chapter 3 above). The Bermuda Compact of 1612 was subsequently administered by Gov. Richard Moore at a time when the enlargement of the Virginia Company's jurisdiction to include the Bermuda islands still had not passed the royal seals. Its basic form and intent were similar to those of the Pilgrims' later version: a voluntary "subscription" promising mutual faith and obedience to King James as well as local governors (Jourdain 1947, 23–4).

What distinguished the New Englanders' from previous Anglo-American settlements was not their beginnings but rather their subsequent movements toward de facto independence, albeit Plymouth and Massachusetts took different routes to this end. In the former, William Bradford and a few other "Undertakers" negotiated with the colony's English creditors to assume the entire debt to themselves and to pay it back in fixed installments; those colonists thereby relieved of their obligations surrendered a six-year fur-trade monopoly to the Undertakers (Langdon 1966, 30–2). Then, in 1630, Bradford obtained a new indenture from Robert Rich, earl of Warwick, the former Virginia Company principal to whom Charles I had recently granted portions of southern New England, and the puritan earl had no intention of meddling in colony affairs. As a result of these dealings the Pilgrims achieved the freedom to manage their business with no strings attached. Massachusetts took an altogether more direct route to the same end, at around the same time, when the Massachusetts Bay Company managed to move in its entirety from London to Boston. Before sailing on the *Arbella* John Winthrop was elected governor of the company; before his election the company voted in 1630 to transfer the whole corporation to Massachusetts Bay (Shurtleff 1854, 1:55, 59), taking advantage of their royal charter's omission of the usual proviso that the corporation reside in England. All members of the company not intending to emigrate resigned their places, and they were replaced by new members intent on going (Osgood 1907, 1:146–7). These maneuvers amounted to "a most pronounced declaration of independence" (1:221–2), but one made within the conventional framework of English law.

If the New England colonies' de facto independence resulted from a few deliberate variations on the established institutional themes, their conceptual tools and public justifications remained more continuous than discontinuous with the main currents of Anglo-American settlement. Both the Plymouth and Massachusetts colonists adduced the standard laundry list of motives for colonization in their promotional literature. *A Relation or Journall of . . . Plimoth in New England* (1622), or "Mourt's Relation," summed up the anticipated results as "the furtherance of the kingdom of Christ, the enlarging of the bounds of our Sovereign Lord King *James*, and the good and profit of those, who either by purse, or person, or both, are agents in the same" (Winslow 1974, pref.). This was the usual tripartite formula of English colonization in its usual order of priorities – evangelism, civic glory, private profit – and one also invoked by accounts of subsequent New England settlement. John White, writing on behalf of Massachusetts in *The Planters Plea* (1630), broke no new ground by citing the divine command to "be fruitful and multiply," the social and economic imperative of relieving over-population in England, and the honorable Christian mission of evangelism (White 1947, 1–4).

In particular, these notorious refugees of conscience were no less inclined to cite commercial motives than others had been. In 1630 John Cotton gave a sermon in which he took it as his first task to assure his audience that it was lawful under God that "some remove for merchandise and gain-sake" (Cotton n.d., 8). Winthrop's "Conclusions for the Plantation in New England" (1629) also lavished attention on economic considerations while, as the Virginia Company's literature had often done (see Chapter 3 above), keeping them subordinate to missionary ones, suggesting, for instance, that the pathways to the East and West Indies first opened by commerce could then be exploited for proselytization. The standard line, which harked back to the Elizabethan colonial projects, was that the English could obtain material goods from heathen peoples in exchange for the spiritual goods of Christianity (Winthrop n.d., 1).

But both the Pilgrims and the Bay puritans were keenly aware of the lessons that had been drawn from the Virginia experience about the dangers of the profit motive, and they were sympathetic to the analysis of colonial virtue advanced by commentators on Virginia affairs like Captain Smith (see Chapter 3 above). Indeed they saw their own efforts as answering that critique in a constructive way. Captain Smith's *Description of New England* is mentioned on the first page of Robert Cushman's 1621 sermon to the Pilgrims "Self-Love" (Cushman 1846, 7), and a copy of the work was still in William Brewster's library at Plymouth when he died in 1644 (Dexter 1890, 39). The New Englanders first of all shared Smith's general depreciation of plunder in favor of husbandry. Thus Cushman warned that the nature of the country would not at all suit those who "look after great riches, ease, pleasures, dainties, and jollities in this world": New England offered only barren ground in need of hard labor and heathen souls in need of salvation (Cushman 1846, 7). Of the Virginia settlers Cushman had heard that they "have now lost even the sap of grace and edge to all goodness, and are become mere worldlings" (24). Winthrop shared Cushman's sense that Virginia provided a negative example: the southern colonies, he believed, had encountered troubles "through their own sloth," for "they used unfit instruments, a multitude of rude and misgoverned persons, the very scum of the people" (Winthrop n.d., 8).

In this vein Brewster and John Robinson wrote to Sandys in 1617 to reassure the Virginia Company that the Pilgrims would make good colonial servants because they were "industrious and frugal." But they went further to distinguish themselves from the usual run of Virginia colonist by stressing something like fidelity: "we are knit together as a body in a more strict and sacred bond and covenant of the Lord, of the violation whereof we make great conscience; and by virtue whereof we do hold ourselves straightly tied to all care of each other's good, and of the whole by every, and so mutual" (Ashton 1852, 135). In similar terms the Bay puritans exhibited their sense of solidarity in the "Cambridge Agreement," by which the plan to remove the corporation to America was first concluded: "this whole adventure grows upon the joint confidence we have in each other's fidelity and resolution herein, so as no man of us would have adventured it without assurance of the rest" (Kavanagh 1973, 1:293). This was a purely internal kind of fidelity, not a trans-oceanic one between colonial servants and their metropolitan masters – thus foreshadowing the New Englanders' use of ideas of not only personal but also political trust.

The Fiduciary Idea

The well-known sense of unique communal purpose around the idea of religious refuge, and the exaltation of public welfare over private interest, defined the New England version of the commonwealth idea – the notion of colonies as self-sufficient bodies politic with purposes particular to themselves and common to their members. As in Virginia and everywhere else in English America, the notion that authorized agents were obliged to pursue those purposes took hold, and the contrast between discretion and accountability entered the thoughts of colonists on a daily basis in the ordinary course of business. Thus the language of trust figured in what was perhaps the most important area of conceptual continuity from New English to previous English settlement: the persistence of the fiduciary idea in discourses of colonial agency.

The defense of discretion seemed to resonate particularly strongly in the Massachusetts settlement. To this effect Winthrop perceived the relevance of the analogy between the exigencies of commercial agency in transatlantic colonization and the problems of government more generally: "there is no wisdom of any State can so provide, but that in many things of greatest concernment, they must confide in some men; and so it is in all human Affairs: the wisest merchants, and the most wary, are forced to repose great trust in the wisdom and faithfulness of their servants, factors, masters of their Ships, etc." (Winthrop 1971, 2:454). At Salem the New England Company seemed to have learned a lesson from Captain Smith's writings on Virginia. As at Jamestown, initially a "temperate course" was desired of

Governor Endecott in Indian relations; but Endecott's original instructions also included the proviso that "if necessity require a more severe course, when fair means will not prevail, we pray you to deal as in your discretions you shall think fittest for the general good and safety of the plantation and preservation of our privileges" (Shurtleff 1854, 1:389–90).

The Pilgrim project exhibited in especially pronounced form the dilemmas of transatlantic agency, and their reflections on their experiences led them, quite contrary to the Bay tendency, to affirm the value of strict accountability. The Pilgrims were beset by unfaithful agents from the beginning. Their first attempt to get out of England in 1608 was foiled by the captain they had hired to transport them, who after accepting their payment turned them over to the local constable (Bradford 1952, 12). Christopher Martin, deputed governor of the *Mayflower* before its departure in 1620, squandered seven hundred pounds given for outfitting the ship and, according to a contemporary letter, "neither can nor will give any account of it" (55). Most spectacular was the case of Isaac Allerton, the colony's principal business agent in England for most of the 1620s. Allerton embezzled the colony's funds for his own failed commercial schemes, and by the early 1630s, when Bradford finally obtained an account, it was found that Allerton's secret dealings had set the Pilgrims back by twenty-three hundred pounds (241–3). James Sherley, the London adventurer whom the Pilgrims then engaged in Allerton's place, also incurred their suspicion and was cashiered in 1637 after repeatedly refusing to render his accounts (297–8).

The Pilgrims' experiences with the trials of transatlantic agency are especially vivid and minutely recounted, but not different in kind from those of colonists and investors involved in Virginia and Bermuda. They left Bradford in particular with a bitter taste in the mouth and, evidently, a settled commitment to strict accountability. "Even amongst friends, men had need be careful whom they trust, and not let things of this nature lie long unrecalled" (Bradford 1952, 237). Bradford even echoed the epigraph of John Ponet's *Shorte Treatise of Politike Power* (1556) (see Chapter 2 above), citing Psalms 118 – "it is better to trust in the Lord than have confidence in man" – and 146 – "put not your trust in princes," which Bradford glossed, parenthetically, "much less merchants" (101).

Bodin's Regimes

The fiduciary idea featured not only in ideas of private relations of authority but also in theories of both state and church – of politics and ecclesiastics. The latter was the subject of far more analysis than the former in early New

England, but it was widely accepted that similar principles applied to both. Moreover, both kinds of regime were understood in the terms set by Bodin's classification of different kinds of "commonwealth," in the idiom favored by Richard Knolles's 1606 English translation.

The puritans who emigrated to America came from an intellectual world in which Bodin figured as one of the most familiar authorities on politics. His *Six Books of the Republic* (available in French, Latin, and English) could be found in many private libraries in England (Salmon 1959, 24) and was a standard text for instruction at the University of Cambridge (Greenleaf 1964, 125), where the most prominent New England ministers received their theological training. These included John Cotton, Thomas Hooker, John Norton, Hugh Peter, Thomas Shepard, and John Wilson; leading civil officers like Roger Williams and John Winthrop were also Cambridge products. The English vogue for keeping Bodin's *magnum opus* in private libraries crossed the Atlantic, and both Bradford and Brewster owned their own copies in New Plymouth (Anderson 2003, 41); likewise John Winthrop Jr. (Morison 1956, 135), whose lending practices were so promiscuous as to make his private library "almost circulating" (Wright 1920, 54–7).

New Englanders used Bodin as, among other things, a source of lessons from the history of political thought and practice. Bradford, for example, alluded to Bodin's critical remarks on Plato for the impracticality of communal property (Bradford 1952, 120–1; Anderson 2003, 108). But equally significant were Bodin's more general ideas on classifying different regimes. Many New Englanders were interested in showing that the way they organized their churches was not "popular" or "democratic," as I will explain shortly, and also (especially in Massachusetts) in determining what sort of civil regime was desirable, as we will see in Chapter 5 below. The key passages of Bodin's *Six Books* which bore on these concerns were found in Book 2, Chapters 2 and 7. Bodin claimed to be the first to distinguish "state" from "government": the former referred to the location of ultimate authority in a commonwealth, or to sovereignty; the latter, to the distribution of powers of regular administration (Bodin 1962, 199). Bodin held that the classic tripartite classification of regimes (monarchy, aristocracy, democracy) could be used to describe the subject of either state or government (one, few, many) (183–4, 249); he further stipulated that it was possible for the state and the government of any given commonwealth to rest on different bases and therefore to receive different names (233, 235, 240, 250). But, since the ultimate right to determine how the regular powers of government are distributed lay always with the sovereign power, the proper name for a commonwealth's regime type was always to be settled according to the form of its state (249).

This scheme of classification undermined the conventional and widely acclaimed conception of the mixed regime drawn ultimately from Aristotle but also found in Polybius and Machiavelli. As Salmon and Franklin have both suggested, Bodin's state/government distinction replaced the old idea of shared power among different bodies with a new sort of "mixture": a discrepancy in the compositions of sovereign and administrative bodies (Salmon 1959, 22; Franklin 1973, 34–5). It also made admissible the term "mixed government" but not "mixed state," since Bodin insisted that sovereignty was indivisible (Bodin 1962, 193–4). One important consequence of this view was that it was impossible for officers of government holding delegated power to wield complete discretion, for they must always be accountable to whichever agency bears sovereignty. Much as Hobbes would do later (Hobbes 1996, ch. 19), Bodin offered arguments for the superiority of a monarchic sovereign but admitted the possibility of an aristocratic or democratic one (see Bodin 1962, bk. 2, passim). In the case of a "popular state" – a term that Bodin used synonymously with "democracy" (e.g. 183) – any monarchic or aristocratic agencies of government must be under the complete and ultimate control of the sovereign people, with the result that a Bodinian kind of democracy would have been more radical than an Aristotelian mixed regime in which the democratic element was merely the "prevailing part," as Althusius would have said (see Chapter 2 above).

It is a fact of some significance, then, not only that New England puritans' writings on ecclesiology frequently employed the Bodinian state/government distinction for analyzing regime types but also that some of them endorsed a Bodinian "popular state" in the church. The key distinction was often reproduced with new terminology. Thus the Cambridge Platform, ratified by a convention of ministers from around New England in 1648, declared power of "privilege" to be in the brethren but of "office" to be in the elders (Walker 1960, 210). Yet the colonists' use of Bodin's protocols was often selective and incomplete, for many of them refused to name their churches' regime type "popular" or "democratic," as Bodin would have done, despite their own admission that "privilege" lay with the whole church. Instead they preferred the less precise but also less controversial language of mixture. By making this strategic departure from Bodin they were also departing from the populist legacy of John Robinson, revealing their analysis of church regimes to be an Aristotelian body clothed in Bodinian garb. The Pilgrim Pastor was a consistent Bodinian, albeit one with more populist sympathies than the French jurist. And there is good reason to think that Robinson's legacy was continued in both the spiritual and civil arenas in New Plymouth, as we will shortly see, as well as the politics and ecclesiastics of Thomas Hooker and the Connecticut colony, as we will see in Chapter 6 below.

Calvinist Ecclesiastics

The Pilgrims' vision of church government represented one of many variants of Calvinist ecclesiology in the later sixteenth and early seventeenth centuries, and their pastor occupied a distinctive place in this context. Within the subject of "discipline" as distinct from "doctrine" – that is, of formal organizational questions as distinct from substantive theological ones – there were two broad problems: how to structure government within one church and how to structure relations among several churches. The more orthodox theorists, taking their cues from Calvin himself, tended to give an aristocratic answer to the first question and a hierarchal answer to the second. The latter was a special focus of intramural debate: some Calvinists came to doubt the propriety and biblical authenticity of any national hierarchy of churches, and among Englishmen this "independent" or "congregational" persuasion relied heavily on idioms of covenant and compact to explain and legitimize the gathering of particular churches (Miller 1939, ch. 15). Yet the first question, about distributing power within a particular church, was generally less contentious, since the pre-eminence of socially and spiritually superior elites found broad acceptance.

Robinson and the Pilgrims distinguished themselves by not only adopting the congregational position on inter-ecclesiastic power but also challenging the aristocratic position on intra-ecclesiastic power. The theory behind both these positions can be traced to the practice of the Marian exiles in the 1550s. The English church at Frankfurt, for instance, vested the power of admitting new members in the whole congregation rather than in the ministers, and the exile church at Wittenberg used a covenant that made joining comparable to signing a legal contract (Burrage 1912, 1:75–8). Perhaps even more influential was the example of the separatist congregations in London which refused to accept the restored Catholic establishment under Mary I. These churches survived persecution (though of course many of their members did not) thanks to an elaborate underground organization (White 1971, ch. 2), while John Ponet and others called for her overthrow from their continental sanctuaries (see Chapter 2 above). Later, under Elizabeth I, some of those who were disenchanted with the moderate course pursued in her return to a Protestant national church turned back to the idea of separatism. Thus Robert Browne and Henry Barrow, for instance, argued that the godly must separate from the Elizabethan Church of England as the Marian dissidents had done from its Catholic predecessor, and in consequence they too endured harassment, imprisonment, and execution. The Pilgrims were among the exponents of the congregational idea who would be dogged by the disreputable labels of "Brownist" and "Barrowist" for decades to come (Sargent 1992, 398, 408). This invective came even from fellow Calvinists who were firmly committed to reforming the Anglican system but were unwilling to do so at the price of the social and spiritual order promised by a national ecclesiastic hierarchy.

The conventional wisdom on questions of power within a particular church was if anything even more entrenched. Thomas Cartwright and Walter Travers, two of the most prominent English Calvinists in the Elizabethan period, spent time in Geneva in the early 1570s at the invitation of Theodore Beza, Calvin's successor. In 1574 Cartwright made an English translation of Travers's *Ecclesiastica Disciplinae*, a work that attempted to chart a third way between "tyrannical" and "democratical" ecclesiastics (Hall 1972, 32–3), and this sort of ideological positioning would appeal to many later English Calvinists, including New England puritans. Travers was willing to allow "the judgment and consent of many" a limited role in church government as long as the few, the elders, retained sole initiative and ultimate control (Travers 1617, 23). For instance, he admitted that the book of Acts described popular elections for certain purposes but denied that majoritarian voting could be "referred to the ordinary and perpetual government of the Church," holding that in the church, as in the commonwealth, the people's power was spent after "they had once given the helm into the hands of certain chosen men" (28). Popular consent, that is, excluded popular control.

But even this conventional wisdom on power within the church came under challenge by the first migrants to New England. The clearest picture of the Pilgrims' ideas on ecclesiology comes from the writings of Robinson, their pastor, who relied heavily on ideas of fiduciary agency to claim that the whole congregation of brethren is superior to the elders or officers of the church – a kind of ecclesiastic popular sovereignty which rejected, often implicitly but sometimes explicitly, the aristocratic third way of mainstream Calvinism.

Robinsonian Populism

Robinson accompanied the Pilgrims when they fled to Amsterdam from Yorkshire, and then again to Leiden, and served as their minister while in exile. Though he died in 1625, before his anticipated migration to American soil could occur, his books remained in New Plymouth's libraries and some of his ideas survived in its institutions. Robinson was an internationally renowned Calvinist theoretician whose works would be cited for several decades after his death, especially in disputes on church government between ministers in England and Massachusetts in the 1640s. His *Justification of Separation* (1610), a seminal work on congregational ecclesiology, not only made the author's name during his lifetime but also kept it alive when the work was reprinted in England in 1639 and 1644 (Burgess 1920, 110).

Robinson's populist ecclesiology began with the premise that any "company" of men can be a "church" even without church officers: the congregation is prior and superior to the eldership, since it is the former that ordains the latter (Robinson 1851, 2:132–3). He went on to argue that "the order of servants is inferior to the order of those whose servants they are"; thus the elders are "of" and "for" the church, not vice versa (2:228). Robinson offered an ancient Greek rationale behind this reposing of primary power in the church itself rather than "the church representative," explaining that the Greek term *ekklesia* had originally referred to "a convention of citizens called from their houses" to attend to public business, not "the assembly of sole governors in the act of their government" (Robinson 1625, 30). Thus, on Robinson's view, the controversial passage from Matthew 18:17, "tell it to the church" – which was widely taken to give Jesus' view of how members should be held accountable for their sins – referred authority over church censure to all the brethren, not just the eldership. Robinson also cited the ancient Greeks in connection with the exercise of popular consent, which followed as a leading principle of church government from the notion of popular sovereignty; thus he likened the election of church officers to voting by show of hands in Demosthenes' Athens (34).

Robinson's *Justification* repeated the Calvinist commonplace that a true church is a "mixed" regime, with Christ as monarch and the elders and brethren as aristocracy and democracy, respectively (Robinson 1851, 2:140), but this was only a rhetorical salve to the wounding label of Brownism, with its overtones of "schism" and "popularity" (2:139). For what he meant to show was merely that separatist churches had not evacuated the elders' authority entirely, as some critics had alleged. Indeed Robinson went on to give a forceful defense of the primacy of the brethren within the congregational scheme: Christ as monarch was considered to have transferred his "whole power" to the congregation, so that they held it within a particular church by "free and full title" (2:138). This comprehensive transfer of spiritual authority to the people entailed, in the fiduciary language common to discourses of sovereignty and resistance in the civil sphere (see Chapter 2 above), that the elders were "servants" and the brethren "masters." It even followed that the brethren had a right to depose the elders, by a ship-of-state analogy: "the pilot is to guide the ship... but if he either ignorantly or desperately will run upon the sands, he may be displaced by his passengers, and the fittest put in his room" (2:223–4). Thus the democratic element in the church was without question the major partner: whereas church officers may come and go, and in any case are needed merely to lend order to proceedings, "the assembly is constant" (2:140–1).

Robinson anticipated objections to this ecclesiastic populism precisely by denying the usual assumptions about the disruptive and unrighteous consequences of popular participation in political settings. His own church's experience, he suggested, had shown that recognizing the legitimate powers of the brethren could produce surpassing levels of harmony, modesty, and sobriety (Robinson 1851, 2:223). Indeed Robinson's break from the Church of England was ultimately bound up with his commitment to a radically populist interpretation of Matthew 18:17, which he believed to require that "the things which concerned the whole Church were to be declared publicly to the whole Church and not to some part only" (Burgess 1920, 69). This reading recalled the Roman-law maxim *quod omnes tangit ab omnibus comprobetur*, "what touches all should be approved by all." Robinson also approved the dictum of Proverbs 11:14 that "in the multitude of counsellors there is safety" (Robinson 1851, 3:392) and condemned those who rejected his populist reading of Matthew 18:17 as "heavy friends to the people's liberty" (Robinson 1625, 31).

Yet Robinson's uniqueness as an ecclesiologist was down to more than tone or emphasis. Unmistakably, and among Calvinist writers exceptionally, Robinson's mixed regime was of the Bodinian rather than Aristotelian sort. His favored ecclesiastic regime, that is, was mixed not as to ultimate sovereignty but rather as to regular administration. His language of "whole power" in *A Justification* had already suggested as much, but his later *Just and Necessarie Apologie* (1625) made it still more explicit. Thus he specifically denied that the church's "government" should be "democratic" while nonetheless affirming that its "state" should be "popular," even citing Bodin's *Six Books* for the significance of this distinction (Robinson 1625, 38).[1] As we will shortly see, other New England congregationalists employed

---

[1] Robinson specifically cited the last chapter of Bodin's first book (Bodin 1962, bk. 1, ch. 10), but this appears to have been an error. The distinction that Robinson was in fact making appears rather in Chapters 2 and 7 of Book 2.

something like Bodin's distinction but failed to follow his protocol that a regime ought to be named after its state not its government. Unlike Travers and his many theoretic heirs, then, Robinson found no third way between tyranny and democracy in the church; he simply preferred the latter. As he wrote in the *Apologie*, when elders usurp the power of excommunication, "neither are her governors to be reputed as servants, but Lords unto her; neither do they *exercise their office popularly* in the church, as they ought, but *tyrannically*" (Robinson 1625, 37).

Ecclesiastic Accountability

Consistently with his Bodinian view of the ecclesiastic "popular state," Robinson concerned himself not only with the selection of elders but also with their accountability – with popular control in addition to popular consent. In the *Apologie* he referred to the primary activities of the brethren in "communion," or acting as a unity, as election and "censure" (Robinson 1625, 11), the latter being a generic term for admonishing, punishing, or expelling members of the church. Robinson also cited the fourth-century theologian Chrysostom's definition of a tyrant as one who, even though ruling by popular consent, "yet will presume to do things as himself liketh, and as if he were to give account to none other" (38). The implication was that in a true, "popular" church the elders' powers should remain accountable to their superiors, the brethren. Yet posthumous uses of Robinson's name for strategic, polemic purposes often obscured the robust presence of ideas of democratic accountability in his writings, and modern scholars of colonial New England have followed this lead. Admittedly, Robinson was keen to emphasize that, far from excluding the elders from church government, he and his followers made them "the only ordinary governors in the church"; but where he differed from his intramural rivals was in rejecting the notion of elders as "controlling all, but to be controlled by none" (Robinson 1851, 2:7). This was the language of democratic accountability, foreshadowing (albeit on the opposite side of the question) Hobbes's sneer that Civil War radicals in England advocated the "licentious controlling the actions of their Sovereigns, and again ... controlling those controllers" (Hobbes 1996, 149; see Chapter 2 above).

Robinson first had occasion to formulate his radical combination of Bodinian jurisprudence and populist sensibility soon after the Pilgrims' arrival in Amsterdam in 1608. A division arose within the "Ancient Church" of English exiles there when John Smyth published two pamphlets opposing the baptism of infants. Francis Johnson, the church's minister, responded to this threat from within his congregation with several published works of his own, and the ensuing controversy eventuated in Smyth's expulsion (Ashton 1851, 3:460–1). But this debate over doctrine sowed the seeds of further division over discipline, for Smyth had advanced, as an adjunct to his case against pedo-baptism, a forthrightly populist ecclesiology based on the same interpretation of Matthew 18:17 which had animated Robinson. Smyth went so far as to claim that the whole church "reserv[es] power to correct her officers" by "censures," including the excommunication of elders themselves (Smyth 1609, 39). Henry Ainsworth took Smyth's side on discipline, though not on doctrine, and in this controversy Robinson and his followers naturally took Ainsworth's side. This debate was the immediate impetus behind Robinson's ecclesiastic polemics.

Recognizing the prestige of the Ainsworth-Robinson alliance, Johnson brought the Pilgrims within his polemic purview, accusing them of treating "the people as kings" (Burgess 1920, 191). He further charged that their "popular" view of church government was bound to lead, as in the case of Smyth, to the dangerous heresy of anabaptism (Dexter 1880, 325–32; White 1971, 144–9). Johnson even adopted a more aristocratic, elder-centered view of church government since, on the "popular" view, such horrendous errors might triumph through the will of a deluded people. He did not change the Pilgrims' minds, but his successful stand in his own church did induce them to leave Amsterdam for Leiden.

Robinson's manuscript "Answer" to Johnson a few years later, responding at the same time to critics of his *Justification*, used the Bodinian protocols of regime classification to explicate positions that he shared with Smyth, resulting in a defense of a kind of extraordinary accountability. Robinson relied on the distinction he had called attention to in the *Apologie*, though with a slightly modified terminology. Now he distinguished "power" – "the whole dispensation of Christ's kingly office" – and "government" – "the guidance and ordering of the church in her public affairs" – assigning the former to the congregation and the latter to the eldership (Robinson 1851, 3:476). Robinson charged that Johnson was wrong, on the one hand, to give "power" to the eldership but also, on the other, to accuse the Pilgrims of giving "government" to the congregation. This distinction, Robinson now reiterated, entailed a power in the people to depose their officers (3:477), since the elders were merely "betrusted with government in a special manner" (3:483): they played *servus* (slave) to the whole congregation's *dominus* (master) (3:484).

This controversy and its protagonists would make a lasting impression on congregationalism in general and New England in particular. Robinson and

Ainsworth were later cited by Richard Mather to prove the anti-democratic credentials of congregational theory against the likes of John Wise (Mather 1712, 18–20). Mather quoted Ainsworth's *Counterpoyson* (1608): "so for *popular government*... we hold it not, we approve it not; for if the multitude govern, then who shall be governed? Christian liberty (which all have) is one thing, the reins of government (which some have) is another thing. Now, how far the people's right and liberty and benefit thereby extendeth, would require a large discourse to show; which is not my purpose here" (Ainsworth 1608, 177). But Mather's reference was missing Ainsworth's point: the radical claim was in favor of a popular "state" not "government." Mather and his heirs should have been aware that Robinson's and Ainsworth's affirmations of this claim had been associated with the defense of Smyth, and that the sort of "large discourse" mentioned in the excerpt from Ainsworth had in fact been provided by Robinson. To be fair, however, even Smyth had misunderstood Ainsworth to have upheld the view of the "Puritans" that ecclesiastic sovereignty is "in the presbytery" (Smyth 1609, 68–9). The common source of Smyth's and Mather's error was their inability to appreciate the Bodinian terms of Ainsworth's and Robinson's analysis, by which power of "government" was in the elders but of "state" in the brethren. This mistake has been repeated by successive generations of modern scholarship.

Despite their formal Bodinian radicalism, Robinson and Ainsworth offered no equivalent to Smyth's clarion call for "correct[ing]" church officers by regular censures. Since the Pilgrims normally elected elders for lifetime terms (Robinson 1625, 25–7; Walker 1960, 91), they had all the more need for regular procedures of accountability. But Robinson's notion of ecclesiastic power, in the final analysis, was more discursive than authoritative or punitive, more to do with scrutiny than sanction – a fact that suggests an important tendency within the ecclesiastical model of accountability more generally. In his last published work, the *Apologie*, Robinson was making more and more concessions to the importance of elders' powers of "government." Accordingly, his defense of popular participation gravitated toward two discursive imperatives, truth and conscience. Thus, on the one hand, he wrote that doctrinal purity is "far more easily corrupted when some one or two alone speak all, and all the rest have deep and perpetual silence enjoined them," so that "disputations" among several speakers were needed to generate light, as from the sparks of clashing stones (Robinson 1625, 53). On the other, he urged members of the congregation to follow their elders' determinations, yet not *"for the authority of the commander, but for the reason of the commandment,* which the ministers are also bound in duty to manifest and approve unto the consciences of them over whom they are set" (56). In short, open debate and something like "reason-giving" were needed to approach truth and satisfy the demands of what democratic theorists today would call "public reason" (e.g. Gutmann and Thompson 1996). Robinson was most interested in emphasizing deliberation, that is, when he was least interested in emphasizing popular control.

The New England Way

Robinson's books and ideas made their way to New England though his person did not. Bradford's comment on the Johnson-Ainsworth controversy, written from New Plymouth three decades later, indicates both that the Pilgrims kept alive the memory of their pastor's intervention and that they still adhered to his populist ecclesiastics: whereas Johnson "came after many years to alter his judgment about the government of the church, and his practice thereupon, which caused a division amongst them," Ainsworth "continued constant in his judgment and practice... about the church-government, from which Mr. Johnson swerved and fell" (Young 1844, 445, 448).

Robinsonian populism as a general sensibility suited the Pilgrims, who were relatively equal among one another in their low social status (Lovejoy 1990). Robinson advised that they would therefore have to empower the "less skillful multitude" in civil government: "you are to become a body politic... and are not furnished with any persons of special eminency above the rest to be chosen by you into office of government" (Ashton 1852, 143). This advice might just as well have applied to ecclesiastic affairs. With Robinson himself staying with the majority of his congregation, which chose to remain in Leiden, the new church at Plymouth had to do without the leadership of a university-trained minister (Dexter 1880, 414–15). Plymouth's early proof of the viability of a congregational church in the New World would serve as an example for later churches, beginning with the first one in Massachusetts, at Salem. Famously, the Plymouth church elder Samuel Fuller visited Salem in its early days and persuaded the settlers there that the gathering of a church by covenant and the lay ordination of ministers were approved godly procedures in the wilderness (Andrews 1934, 1:378–81; Morison 1964, 37–40). As a result Salem's conforming Church of England minister returned home, and a separatist one took his place (Gildrie 1975, 14–15). In practice many churches in Massachusetts subsequently evolved in a Robinsonian direction, with the brethren exercising not only rights of consent to all major church decisions but also powers of accountability over elders (Cooper 1999, 27, 32, 39–42).

Yet the recognized ecclesiologists of New England tended to be self-consciously anti-democratic, especially after 1637, when the Antinomian controversy at Boston concluded with the banishment of Anne Hutchinson and her followers from Massachusetts (Hall 1972, 110–11). This episode was perceived as not only a grave threat to the colonies' very existence, having coincided with and disrupted preparations for war with the Indians, but also an indication that too much popular participation in church affairs could lead to heresy – the same connection made by Francis Johnson in Amsterdam in 1608–9. Following this shock, and in the later context of transatlantic debate, New England divines tended to cite Robinson as a champion of a mixed church regime like themselves. John Cotton, as we have already seen with Mather, claimed that Robinson was not as radical as was usually supposed, and that transplanted to New England his teachings had been moderated (Cotton 1648, 9–10). Scholars of seventeenth-century American intellectual history have tended to accept this reading of Robinson, and it fits nicely with the revisionist assumption of broad ideological consensus across early New England (see Chapter 1 above). But there were in fact significant differences between the official ecclesiology of Massachusetts and the Robinsonian version. Of course writers such as Cotton and Mather always endorsed the formula of a church regime mixed with Christ's monarchy, the elders' aristocracy, and the brethren's democracy, as indeed Robinson himself had done. But partisans of the so-called New England Way departed from Robinson in two respects: they understood the mixture in an Aristotelian rather than Bodinian sense and, in consequence, diminished the power of the brethren to hold the elders accountable.

The mixed-regime formula was in wide circulation but, in the New Englanders' case, may have owed its currency particularly to William Ames's *Medulla Theologiae* (1627). Ames spent many years in Dutch exile and had engaged in a running debate with Robinson over how far the "saints" should separate from the Church of England (Sprunger 1972, 29–44). Though Ames has been credited with having moderated Robinson's separatism (43), there was no comparable rapprochement on internal church government. Henry Jacob, a close ally of Ames in his Dutch exile, described the best regime as "not simply and plainly Democratical, but partly Aristocratical and partly Monarchical.... It is that mixed government which the learned do judge to be the best government of all" (Jacob 1610, A/3b). Ames's *Medulla* held that, putting Christ's other-worldly sovereignty to one side, the "visible system of administration" ought to be a mixture of aristocracy and democracy (Ames 1968, 1.33.20). Whereas the *Medulla* was the principal text in divinity at Harvard College from its founding in 1636 (Morison 1956, 42), it did not figure among the dozens of titles in theology held in the Pilgrim Brewster's library (see Dexter 1890).

The Aristotelianism of Ames's and Jacob's mixed regime, in contrast to Robinson's Bodinian revision, was even more explicit in the New England divines and their allies in England. In the 1640s it became common for defenders of congregational or "Independent" churches to couch their ecclesiastics in terms of a third way between Brownism and Presbyterianism, and the mixed regime fit this polemic need nicely. Thus Mather claimed that neither "a Government merely Popular or Democratical" nor one "merely Aristocratical" would do (Mather 1643b, 47–8). But the most elaborate version of this gambit appeared in Thomas Goodwin and Philip Nye's preface to Cotton's *Keyes of the Kingdom of Heaven* (1644). Goodwin and Nye were two of the renowned "dissenting brethren" who spoke up against a national Presbyterian church as members of the Westminster Assembly, which the Long Parliament called to reform the Anglican establishment amid civil war in 1643. The two dissenters condemned the error that found church power to be "radically and originally" in the people (Cotton 1644, A/2b) – referring to the sort of claim made by the Pilgrims' ally Smyth that the "delegated power" from Christ had been seated "in the body of the Church primarily and fundamentally" (Smyth 1609, 41). Goodwin and Nye also characterized the proper church regime as lying "in such a just balancing of power and privileges... according unto the several concernments and interests that each rank in the Church may have, rather than in an entire and sole trust committed" to one body (Cotton 1644, A/2b-3a). Goodwin and Nye's language thus followed the Aristotelian notion of distributive justice, with power shared or balanced among different social ranks, while rejecting the fiduciary-legal and Bodinian assumption of unitary sovereignty.

What makes the Massachusetts congregationalists' departure from Robinson all the more significant is the fact that they appeared to be familiar with Bodin's analytic protocols and frequently to use similar distinctions to his. Where Robinson had distinguished "power" and "government," Mather referred to a distinction between "power" and "the dispensing of power" (Mather 1643b, 65) and later called them "privilege" and "government" (Mather 1712, 21); John Norton described two kinds of "jurisdiction," "popular and extraordinary" and "ordinary and administrative" (Norton 1958, 86). With varying levels of clarity the congregationalists all admitted that the people have some fundamental authority within the church, but the matter was complicated by the universal conviction that ultimate spiritual sovereignty must reside with Christ (e.g. Mather 1712, 9). If the Bodinian "state" of the church must have some divine locus, that seemed to leave the "government" to be shared between elders and brethren on earth; hence the importance of the question of how much power Christ had transferred to the brethren, and of Goodwin and Nye's contradiction of Smyth on this point. Among the supposed fathers of the New England Way, only Robinson joined Smyth in putting the brethren on a par with Christ, juristically speaking, by calling the church a "popular state" with specific reference to Bodin.

Not surprisingly, given the desire of Cotton, Mather, and others to temper democracy with aristocracy in the church, they tended to admit the necessity of popular consent while denying democratic accountability. Mather made clear that popular consent in general constituted the "democratical" part of the mixed regime (Mather 1643b, 53, 54), and Norton confirmed the conventional wisdom that the election of church officers was its standard institutional expression (Norton 1958, 115). Cotton explicitly confined the power of the whole congregation to the admission of members and the election of officers (Cotton 1648, 22). But the popular control of church officers through regular procedures of accountability was entirely off the table, and extraordinary accountability was an inevitable but touchy subject of inquiry. Writing about affairs among English exiles in the Dutch provinces, Goodwin scolded a church that had deposed its minister for "having proceeded in a matter of so great moment without consulting their sister churches" (Goodwin et al. 1963, 16) and then narrated, with evident satisfaction, the story of the brethren's repentance and the pastor's restoration after the arbitration of other churches was finally allowed (20–1). In a similar vein the New Englanders adopted a neo-Thomist, substantive approach to resistance (see Chapter 2 above) in ecclesiastics, admitting its legitimacy only by vague references to "weighty cause" (Mather 1643a, 77) or "incorrigible maladministration" (Norton 1958, 125); Norton, while denying that church officers are mere "servants" and therefore revocable at the people's pleasure (94), would allow the deposition of a minister only, like Goodwin, by a council of sister churches (126).

By the later 1640s, however, the New Englanders joined Robinson's more formalistic position on the deposition of church officers. In 1648 the Cambridge Platform officially recognized the brethren's right to replace those in authority over them. Without any reference to the arbitration of sister churches, the platform declared that "if the church have power to *choose* their officers and ministers, then in case of manifest unworthiness and delinquency they have power also to *depose* them. For to open and shut, to choose and refuse, to constitute in office and remove from office, are acts belonging unto the same power" (Walker 1960, 215). Though the proviso about "unworthiness and delinquency" would still require interpretation, this statement of extraordinary accountability was formal and juristic in character, not substantive as in previous iterations, implying that the congregation's right to unmake elders was a logical correlative to its right to make them, not just a last resort to save their souls.

By 1648, then, the clear and significant theoretic difference between Robinson and the theorists of the New England Way – based on contrasting Bodinian and Aristotelian understandings of popular power in the church – was reduced to a practical equivalence – based on their shared willingness to countenance extraordinary moments of deposition but little else in the way of popular control. Thus the ecclesiastical model of accountability, despite its radical potential, harbored strong tendencies toward purely discursive forms of participation by ordinary people: ratification and selection. But Robinsonian radicalism would find another arena in civil procedures of accountability in the Pilgrim colony.

Pilgrim Politics

Ecclesiastical theory was an important vehicle for political ideas generally, and Robinson's ecclesiology in particular introduced the Pilgrims to the conjunction of the principles of popular sovereignty and accountability. Moreover, the predominant assumptions of congregational theorists allowed the transfer of basic principles from the spiritual to the civil arena. Though the intellectual life of the New England colonies has often seemed to modern students predominantly theological and hardly at all political, the puritans themselves had no doubts about the essentially political character of inquiries into church government. As Robinson remarked, "the visible church, being a polity ecclesiastical, and the perfection of all polities, doth comprehend in it whatsoever is excellent in all other bodies political" (Robinson 1851, 2:140).

In this vein, too, *A Discourse about Civil Government* (variously attributed to Cotton and to John Davenport, the founding pastor of the New Haven colony) referred to "two Administrations or Polities, *Ecclesiastical* and *Civil*," as two species of the same genus (Davenport 1663, 5). Accordingly, the gathered church was frequently compared to various civil bodies. Goodwin and Nye used the extended analogy of a municipal corporation, composed of aldermen and council, to explain their view of church relations between elders and brethren (Cotton 1644, A/5a, 6a). Norton admitted that the legitimacy of deposing a corrupt minister by the judgment of a synodal council was derived by analogy with principles of resistance in civil affairs (Norton 1958, 126), and indeed his argument's similarity to sixteenth-century theories of ephoral resistance would have been obvious to contemporaries. As Hugh Peter put it in the epistle dedicatory of Mather's *Church-Government and Church-Covenant* (1643), "we need not tell the wise whence Tyranny grew in Churches, and how commonwealths got their pressure in the like kind" (Mather 1643b, ep. ded.). This analogy recalled John Ponet's claim that the right of resistance belonged equally to "the body of the whole congregation or commonwealth" (Ponet 1972, G/5b).

Not only was ecclesiastics often considered analogous to politics; sometimes it was the stuff of politics, as the Pilgrims well knew. The most controversial item to come out of Brewster's press at Leiden (see Harris and Jones 1987) was David Calderwood's *Perth Assembly* (1619); indeed its publication was possibly the event that precipitated the Pilgrims' long-meditated migration to America (Sprunger 1994, 140–1). James I had called a special meeting of the Scottish kirk in 1618 with the aim of introducing elements of episcopal church government in Scotland, and he dispatched John Spottiswood, archbishop of Glasgow, to preside over the passing of an affirmative vote for the proposals in Perth. Calderwood's critique of this "null-assembly," unlike the other products of the Pilgrim press, was no mere theological treatise but in fact one of the most politically incendiary tracts of James's reign, and Brewster and his associates in Leiden were pursued by royal agents for their suspected role in its publication (Plooij 1932, 62–80). The reported rage of the monarch and the subsequent investigation opened by his ambassador to the Dutch provinces may have convinced the Pilgrims that their removal to America could wait no longer.

Perth Assembly used ideas of accountability to attack not only the conduct of the representatives in attendance but also the procedures by which this important public decision had been taken. In the first place, Calderwood argued that the Scottish ministers who supported James's design had sold out the kirk and thereby violated their trust.

> They were ordained to be [ac]countable to the general Assemblies for the manner of their entry and behavior in this new office. But like bankrupts, not being able to render account, they labored that no account should be made at all: that is, that there should be no ordinary general assembly to take account.... They have broken the caveats made with their own consent, violated their promises, and have sought pre-eminence both in Church and Common-wealth, with the ruin of others and the rending of their mother's belly. (Calderwood 1619, A/2a-b)

Calderwood further alleged that James and his agents had gained their political victory by setting up an illegitimate procedure. James commanded and Spottiswood intimidated: threatening that recalcitrant ministers would lose their posts, refusing to allow amendments to or debate on James's proposals, failing to count all the votes of their opponents, and allowing some to vote without the customary presentation of their commissions from their constituencies (Calderwood 1619, 1–3, 10). Calderwood's remarkable commentary on the Perth Assembly not only charged the occupant of the English and Scottish thrones with tyrannical innovation and manipulation; it also spelled out seven criteria that procedures of deliberation and voting in parliamentary bodies must meet if they are to count as "free and lawful assemblies" (13).

Calderwood's analysis of ecclesiastical politics doubtless appealed to the Pilgrims because of their conviction of the tyrannical and unbiblical character of the Anglican hierarchy, but they appear also to have been sympathetic to his more general ideas of political accountability. So much is suggested by the conduct of public affairs in the colony they founded the year after publishing *Perth Assembly*. Though the documentary record is patchy, and though historians have always been much more interested in substantive questions of the franchise than in details of constitutional structure and political procedure, it appears that the government of Plymouth in its first few decades revolved around the objective of popular control.

In its early years the Plymouth colony conducted its affairs by something like a town meeting, with all members assembled as a "general court" presided over by a governor and his "assistants" (King 1994, 147). Elections of officers were held annually, as was typical of English corporations. Just as debates were getting under way in London over whether the "democratic" joint-stock regime in the Virginia Company should be discontinued (see Chapter 3 above), the Pilgrims' financial backers wrote to Governor Bradford complaining of rumors that Plymouth had a democratic government; the governor's reply prudently accentuated his own discretion in directing affairs (Langdon 1966, 91). The prominence of the governor and assistants, at least in judicial proceedings, is suggested by Bradford's recollection that the expansion of the magisterial body from two to six in 1624 was necessitated by an increase in "the number of their people ... and their troubles and occasions therewith" (Bradford 1952, 140).

But the Pilgrims placed ultimate control over their magistrates in the hands of the freemen as a body. A law-reform commission set up in 1636 mostly confirmed previous practices, such as the annual election of governor and assistants and the making of laws by vote in the general court, or "by the freemen of the Corporation and no other" (Shurtleff and Pulsifer 1968, 11:6). That this formula implied unicameralism is suggested by a later resolution that the magistrates and deputies vote as one body "for the future as formerly" (11:55–7). The governor had no veto or other legislative powers apart from summoning special sessions of the general court and holding a casting vote when necessary to break a tie (Langdon 1966, 95). Indeed in 1646 the governor and all the magistrates were stripped of all but judicial duties (Shurtleff and Pulsifer 1968, 11:54). This move was evidently a response to a sharp clash in the previous year's court, when Bradford and the assistants first delayed the effort of the October court to repeal an unspecified measure of the June court (Langdon 1966, 95–6) and later suppressed a petition to institute a colony-wide policy of religious toleration which had considerable support among the deputies (65, 96). Whether Bradford and associates had relied on formal or informal powers in defeating the 1645 petition for toleration, the governor himself was re-elected the following year – but only after all the magistrates' constitutional powers had been reduced. This was a case of the general court's assertion of superiority over its chief officers, much as a gathered church might admonish without deposing its pastor, and it was made possible by the unicameral voting structure of the court.

Equally central to Plymouth politics was the control of the general court itself by the freemen. Reforms enacted in 1638 allowed freemen to avoid the usual fine for non-attendance at the general court by sending deputies to all but one court per year (a court of election still required personal attendance); the new towns farther up Cape Cod were thereby incorporated into the Plymouth colony (Langdon 1966, 85). At the same time the freemen's control over their representatives was secured by the provision that any act done by a court of deputies might be undone by the succeeding court of election, and this power was regularly exercised (Shurtleff and Pulsifer 1968, 11:31ff.). An amendment to this order two years later added another weapon to the freemen's arsenal, requiring that town "committees" (as representatives were often called) call a meeting to receive instructions from their constituents before attending court (11:36).

Consistently with the tradition of construing fidelity in terms of strict accountability in which they began their American adventure, the Pilgrims attempted to reconcile the convenience of representative government with the democratic desideratum of popular control. Yet their institutional vehicles for democratic sovereignty included procedures of ratification and selection without traditional, articulated mechanisms of accountability such as special inquests. Their best shot at popular control, apart from unicameral legal supremacy pure and simple, was deselection: the periodic opportunity to cast out their officers in a court of election. Thus Robinson's ecclesiology and New Plymouth's early constitutional development both suggest that the ecclesiastical model of accountability would struggle to supply regular, non-electoral vehicles of control without supplementation by the classical and fiduciary models. That supply would only come in other New England contexts.

Popular States

In 1643 John Norton defined a "commonwealth" as "a multitude of freemen considered as an homogenous body united by a Civil bond" (Norton 1913, 280). The notion that the New England colonies were self-sufficient bodies politic had been firmly established from their beginnings. The Pilgrims and the Bay colonists adopted the commonwealth idea that had already been broached in Virginia affairs (see Chapter 3 above), by way of the humanist ideal of the common good as a superior purpose to private profit. The New Englanders, of course, also possessed a peculiar sense of solidarity based on the idea of a religious haven and a correspondingly fierce spirit of independence from English control.

To these notions of communal self-sufficiency the Pilgrims in particular added conceptual tools derived from two intellectual traditions that were largely inactive in the literature dealing with Virginia and Bermuda: Bodinian jurisprudence and Calvinist ecclesiology. The principle of popular sovereignty, which could not have been squared with the legal status of the Virginia Company's plantations, achieved greater prominence in the New England colonies partly from their de facto independence of metropolitan control but mostly from their fondness for analogous notions of church covenant – in short, of a kind of popular sovereignty in ecclesiastics. Yet popular sovereignty could not guarantee democratic accountability unless it assumed a strongly Bodinian character, according to which the right not only to select governors but also to hold them accountable is taken to be inherent in an undivided sovereignty. Alongside its radical potential – so uncertainly realized in Robinson – the ecclesiastical model of accountability also bore a mitigating aristocratic force – so triumphant in Robinson's posthumous interpreters.

It is unclear whether, in "the New England mind," the ecclesiastical covenant preceded and informed the political or vice versa (Miller 1939, 412–13). In any case the Robinsonian "popular state" in the church was realized in some respects by the Pilgrims' civil state. Robinson's theory of the church was too democratic for the divines in Massachusetts Bay to admit without modification. Even in the bowels of the New England Way, however, there is reason to believe that democratic ideas and practices in ecclesiastics had theoretic ramifications for politics: as Cooper has summed them up, "limitation on authority, higher law, accountability, and popular consent" (Cooper 1999, 45). It is to the recurrent and eventful debates within Massachusetts politics that we now turn.

5

Constitutional Conflict and Political Argument at Boston

> It is particularly essential that [the United States House of Representatives] should have an immediate dependence on and an intimate sympathy with the people. Frequent elections are unquestionably the only policy by which this dependence and sympathy can be effectually secured.
>
> *The Federalist*, no. 52, 1788 (Hamilton et al. 2005, 286)

Against the conventional wisdom derived from studies of the revolutionary period, Riley long ago showed that bicameralism in America originated not in imitation of the British parliament but rather, in the seventeenth-century New England context, as the result of developments within the typical structure of the English trading companies under which the colonies were begun (Riley 1896, 161–3). More specifically, the division of legislative power between two chambers arose from the evolving independence of the governor and his assistants as a body from the company courts to which they had been originally attached. This is precisely what happened at Boston after the Massachusetts Bay Company was removed in its entirety from London to New England in 1630. There the advocates of non-electoral procedures of accountability of magistrates to freemen were the same constitutional reformers who resisted this bicameral development, though in the end they accommodated themselves to it. They failed in their quest for unicameralism, which their critics on both sides of the Atlantic derided as "democratic," but they succeeded at least in articulating and institutionalizing robust means of subjecting governing elites to popular control.

Among the anti-democratic critics was John Winthrop, who seems to tower over the early political history of Massachusetts – partly because for over half of that period he was the colony's governor but largely because his writings are the most detailed extant records of the colony's first two decades. With a few notable exceptions, Winthrop's journal does not hide the frequent and sometimes severe conflicts within Massachusetts political society, but the paucity of records from hands other than his often makes it difficult to understand the true theoretic grounds of the divisions. In the context of seventeenth-century political and ecclesiastical theories, however, it is clear that those conflicts were implicated in the development of an ideology of democratic accountability. Though Winthrop was a valued and necessary figure in early New England affairs, he was far from untouchable. In fact he was audited in 1634 and impeached in 1645: these two attempts at non-electoral accountability are the bookends of Massachusetts's brief movement for democratic constitutionalism.

Yet the best modern studies of the politics of Massachusetts's early years heavily discount ideological rivalry as a component of constitutional conflict, in favor of regional animosities, material gain, and simple lust for power. Most notably, Wall has expanded a suggestion originally made by Andrews by arguing that the conflicts of the 1640s in particular were motivated not by ideas but by a hunger for power nourished by cross-cutting socio-economic and geographic differences (Wall 1972, chs. 1–2; cf. Andrews 1933, 82). Unfortunately, this interpretive diminution of ideological conflict in Massachusetts has obscured an important feature of colonial American intellectual history and has encouraged the widespread assumption of consensus in political values across New England.

In fact ideological rivalry at Boston gave rise to novel forms of political argument which would, much later, lead rather significant second and third lives. Granted, the reformers' prime mechanisms of accountability, audit and impeachment, were old-fashioned borrowings from the ancient Greeks, as was the principle of rotation in office which they invoked to resist the formation of a permanent ruling clique. Unlike the ancients, however, New Englanders like Israel Stoughton and Nathaniel Ward favored rotation in a context in which all officers attained their posts by election not lottery. Thus they recognized a truth about politics which both ancient Greek and Renaissance Italian experience might also have suggested (see Manin 1997, chs. 1–2): a stable oligarchy can result from elective just as surely as from hereditary or co-optative succession. The reformers also showed a special exuberance for written codes of legal limitation, suggesting a theoretic alliance between accountability to the people and accountability to the law.

The other side of the debate was equally significant for modern democratic thought (see epigraph above). Like Bodin and James I (see Chapter 2 above), Winthrop regarded authoritative discretion as normative in politics; unlike them, he attempted to offer a tangible, practical concession to his rivals' contrary commitment to the accountable conception of trust. He and other opponents of the leading reform measures – unicameralism, rotation, legal limitation, and non-electoral procedures of accountability – devised the proposition that regular elections in and of themselves are sufficient to effect popular control. They emphasized the electoral mechanism precisely in order to displace all the others and thereby to stave off "democracy." Thus the first two decades of constitutional conflict at Boston showed how the anti-democratic tendencies of the *ecclesiastical* model of accountability, with its reliance on the mechanism of deselection, were used to counter the reformist reliance on elements of the *classical* and *fiduciary* models (see Chapter 1 above).

Bay Establishment

The Massachusetts Bay colony, by contrast with New Plymouth, included professionally and intellectually distinguished individuals eager to assume their rightful places atop a new social and political hierarchy. Winthrop, the kingpin of the Bay establishment, was elected governor of the Massachusetts Bay Company prior to the removal of the first wave of colonists, and of the company charter, to America. Winthrop would continue to serve as governor of the colony for twelve of his remaining nineteen years; when not in the top post he was always on the board of assistants. That body of twelve magistrates sitting with the governor also had a relatively stable composition, since only twenty-seven different men served during the colony's first seventeen years; almost half of these would be removed from office only by death (Wall 1990, 22–3).

As a group the magistrates constituted an organic Massachusetts elite, and they regarded themselves as their brothers' keepers, obligated to devote their efforts to the welfare of the whole community. Winthrop's "Modell of Christian Charity," a sermon delivered aboard the *Arbella* en route to America in 1630, stressed the moral necessity of both social inequality and mutual help among the various divinely ordained social ranks (Morgan 2003, 75–93). This notion of noblesse oblige was the natural companion of discretionary rule, and the prevailing political ideas of the magistrates generally reflected suspicion of the accountable conception of political trust and commitment to its discretionary alternative. Reflecting the fiduciary idea's ease of transfer from private to public affairs, Winthrop even used analogies drawn from transatlantic commercial agency to illustrate the necessity of political discretion. "The wisest merchants, and the most wary," he wrote, "are forced to repose great trust in the wisdom and faithfulness of their servants, factors, masters of their Ships, etc." (Winthrop 1971, 2:454). Somewhat like Capt. John Smith (see Chapter 3 above), Winthrop believed that governors must be similarly discretionary figures.

On arriving in America, Winthrop and his fellow magistrates immediately used their discretion to depart from Massachusetts's royal patent. The charter provided that the governor, deputy governor, and assistants all be "constituted, elected, and chosen out of the freemen" on an annual basis (Shurtleff 1854, 1:10, 12). But Winthrop was elected governor by the assistants rather than by the freemen (Osgood 1907, 1:154–5), and his first term of office in America lasted not one but two years. As a body the magistrates handled the colony's public business by themselves, including the imposition of a special tax in 1631 to which the inhabitants of Watertown took exception. Thus the first challenge to the Bay establishment began with what must appear in hindsight an utterly conventional American exercise: a tax revolt.

Realignment

The Watertown protesters' displeasure with the prospect of material loss led them to question the structure of policy-making in the new colony: the decision taken in Boston was one with which they had had nothing to do. Thus they alleged that "it was not safe to pay moneys after that sort, for fear of bringing themselves and posterity into bondage" (Winthrop 1972, 1:70). But, after consulting with the magistrates, the Watertowners ultimately acquiesced in the payment of the tax. Winthrop mollified the protesters with the observation that their power of election would allow them "to remove" the assistants they disliked and "put in others" (1:70), and the apparent success of this argument would encourage Winthrop and others to identify elections as mechanisms of accountability throughout the next decade and a half. But that notion had not yet been applicable to the governor himself, and the next meeting of the general court brought constitutional reform within the freemen's purview for the first time in 1632. The court passed an order requiring that the governor be elected by all the freemen rather than by the assistants alone (Shurtleff 1854, 1:95).

The Watertown protest was the first of many episodes of political dispute and constitutional change. For the next two decades the politics of Massachusetts would feature repeated contests over the substance of law and policy as well as the structure of law- and policy-making. These contests usually reflected stable patterns of ideological conflict between, in the terms of some contemporaries, "liberty" and "arbitrary government"; or, as others characterized it, "mere democracy" and "mixed" government. More precisely, the theoretic disagreements underlying this conflict involved "discretionary" versus "delegated" power (Breen 1970, 59) – in the terms of Chapter 2 above, the discretionary versus the accountable conception of political trust. The watershed moment in the history of political thought in early New England was the reform movement of 1634, which not only brought these ideological cleavages into full view but also, briefly, realigned Massachusetts politics.

The freemen who amended the procedure for electing the governor in 1632 may or may not have known that they were merely bringing the colony into line with its legal patent. In 1634 a group of deputies from out-lying towns traveled to Boston to request of Governor Winthrop that the patent be displayed for public examination. One of these deputies was Israel Stoughton, who described in a letter to his brother John (a well-known puritan minister in England) how this request had originated in the 1632 tax protest:

When I came into the Country [1630], for one whole year after, the government was solely in the hands of the assistants. The people chose them Magistrates, and then they made laws, disposed lands, raised moneys, punished offenders, etc., at their discretion; neither did the people know the patent nor what prerogative and liberty they had by the same. But there being some sums of money raised, and a speech of more, it made some inquisitive into matters, and particularly after the patent. (Emerson 1976, 146)

Winthrop and the magistrates yielded to this request. Apart from confirming that the annual election of the governor by the freemen was not just permitted but indeed required by the patent, the deputies determined that further work of codification was needed to limit the discretion of the magistrates. In the following year, 1635, they formed a committee to review the colony's laws and to frame a "Magna Carta" for Massachusetts (Winthrop 1972, 1:160). Winthrop arranged for John Cotton to submit a biblically inspired law code called "Moses His Judicialls," but it failed to garner broad support. Subsequently the magistrates resisted calls for a new attempt at law reform and defused the issue by appointing committees to study it.

The reform movement of 1634 had more immediate success with a second broad agenda, that of structural change, than with legal limitation. In response to the deputies' concerns about discretionary rule, Winthrop suggested that a small committee be elected by the general court and convoked once a year by the governor, with limited powers to revise laws, present grievances, and ratify proposed taxes (Winthrop 1972, 1:128–9). But that year's court ignored this advice and opted for a number of more sweeping changes: giving "none but the General Court" broad powers "to make and establish laws...to elect and appoint officers...to set out the duties and powers of the said officers...to raise moneys and taxes" (Shurtleff 1854, 1:117–18). Moreover, ad hoc representative arrangements were codified when towns were allowed to appoint two or three deputies "to deal in their behalf in the public affairs of the commonwealth" with "the full power and voices of all the said freemen" (1:118). Finally, in the annual elections the freemen reshuffled the personnel of the magistracy, relegating Winthrop to the place of assistant and putting Thomas Dudley in his place as governor, with Roger Ludlow as deputy governor.

The regime constructed by Winthrop and his associates had been thoroughly repudiated and partially reconstructed. The annual court of all the freemen had asserted its authority over colony affairs and created a body of representatives to act in its stead for all but one of the annual sessions of court. Moreover, Winthrop had been displaced from the top post for the first time since his election as governor of the Massachusetts Bay Company in England in 1629, and he would not return to that position until 1637. Israel Stoughton wrote to his brother in England that Winthrop "hath lost much of the applause that he hath had (for indeed he was highly magnified).... He is indeed a man of men, but he is but a man; and some say they have idolized him, and do now confess their error" (Emerson 1976, 151). In 1634 and 1635 the freemen not only excluded Winthrop from the governor's office but included in the top two posts four men who had previously opposed him on some important issue: Dudley and John Haynes as governors, Ludlow and Richard Bellingham as deputy governors. Thus 1634 was a year of significant realignment in Massachusetts politics, but the changes in personnel would prove to be short-lived compared to those in structure.

The Negative Voice

Winthrop and his allies on the board of assistants fought back using the chief procedural weapon guaranteed to them by the patent: the "negative voice," or magisterial veto. Later in 1634, for instance, Winthrop led the magistrates in blocking the request of Thomas Hooker and his Newtown (a.k.a. Cambridge) congregation to move to the Connecticut River valley, thereby nullifying the affirmative vote of the General Court as a whole (Shurtleff 1854, 1:119; Winthrop 1972, 1:140–1). The negative voice of the magistrates now became the target of the reformers, Stoughton chief among them, who attacked it in fiduciary terms.

Stoughton wrote a paper listing twelve reasons against the magisterial veto, and his prime argumentative tactic was to pose as the defender of the accountable against the discretionary conception of political trust. Predictably, this tactic aroused Winthrop's and others' ire. "The main accusation which they stuck to," Stoughton wrote, "was that I denied the Assistants to be Magistrates, and made them but Ministers of Justice, etc., which charge I denied... though I also did say they were Ministers of justice and might without dishonor be called Ministers as well as Magistrates" (Emerson 1976, 149). Stoughton clarified his point by observing that "the patent makes their power Ministerial according to the greater vote of the general courts, and not Magisterial according to their own discretion" (149). In short, the governor and assistants were to use their power only to further the purposes of the general court, not to obstruct them by an independent veto: "their power, call it ministerial, or magisterial, or magistratical (which you will), was not so great that they could do aught or hinder aught simply according to their own wills, but they must eye and respect general courts, which by patent consist of the whole company of freemen" (149). Much the same could have been said about magistrates in ancient Athens, whose subordination to the assembly was enforced through various mechanisms of accountability. Indeed, in a gesture reminiscent of the Athenian *euthynai*, or annual audits (see Chapter 2 above), the General Court even appointed Stoughton and Ludlow – the spokesman for the opposition and the new deputy governor, respectively – to examine Winthrop's financial accounts from the previous five years (Shurtleff 1854, 1:120).

Still, Winthrop and his allies maintained stern opposition to the proposal to abolish their veto power. Stoughton offered a counter-proposal in these terms: "that there shall be power of suspension on either party in cases where they agree not, until the mind of the whole body of the Country may conveniently be known; and then the issue to be on the Major part's side according to the patent" (Emerson 1976, 146). Thus the deputies were proposing both that the negative voice be reduced to a temporary power of suspension and also that they should have it as well as the magistrates; ultimately deadlocks were to be broken by majority vote either of all the freemen (if "the Major part's side" referred to the once-yearly courts of election) or of the deputies attending a regular session of the General Court. If Winthrop and the magistrates had been generally confident of popular support, as historians have often assumed they were, this proposal should have been acceptable to them. But, on Stoughton's account, "this was at first proposed and approved by Ministers and country; but not by Magistrates" (146): in short, the magisterial veto was used to preserve itself.

The magistrates' own counter-proposal, which was eventually passed by the 1636 General Court, gave the veto to both deputies and magistrates, as Stoughton had previously moved, but referred cases of deadlock not to "the Country" but rather to a committee composed of equal numbers of deputies and magistrates. In short, the numerically inferior magistrates were given parity both in the veto itself and in the subsequent resolution thereof.

In response to his rival's list of twelve reasons (no longer extant) against the magisterial veto, Winthrop charged Stoughton as "the troubler of Israel ... a worm ... and an underminer of the state." Stoughton, "for peace' sake," offered his proposals to be burned; the offer was accepted. But at the next court, in March 1635, the magistrates pressed Stoughton about a private conversation in which he was reported to have said that "the Assistants were not magistrates." These remarks, as we have seen above in Stoughton's own explication, recalled the broader early-modern association of the accountable trust with the juristic language of *ministerium non dominium* (see Chapter 2 above). Winthrop, the defender of discretion, sharply reproved Stoughton, and the General Court responded by banning Stoughton from all colony offices for three years (Emerson 1976, 150; Shurtleff 1854, 1:135–6). For Stoughton, it seems, the taking of Winthrop's accounts had amounted to a massive political miscalculation, since the results of his and Ludlow's investigation revealed that Winthrop had in fact incurred debts of twelve hundred pounds on the colony's behalf, only a fraction of which had been reimbursed to Winthrop (Winthrop 1972, 1:396–7).

Winthrop and his allies also proposed institutional reforms of their own to recover some of the power they had lost, chiefly the "standing council" (Brennan 1931, 57–62). This body was created in 1636 for managing colony affairs between meetings of the deputies and was composed of prominent men elected for lifetime terms. Together with the negative voice, the standing council would become one of the dominant concerns of deputies advancing ideas of democratic accountability in defense of further constitutional reform in the 1640s. But the fact that these struggles continued unresolved into the next decade indicated that the realignment of 1634 had been partial and short-lived.

Dealignment

The political significance of the so-called Antinomian controversy (see Battis 1962) which began in the churches lies in the dealignment in 1637 of the realigned civil regime of 1634. Not only was Winthrop returned to the governor's office in that year; more to the point, the Massachusetts colony temporarily overcame cleavages over its constitutional balance of power in order to unite in defense of doctrinal orthodoxy and military security. But this dealignment, while returning Winthrop to the highest political prominence, would eventually be seen in some ways to have stoked rather than extinguished the ideological fires around democratic accountability.

The Antinomian affair was begun by theology, ended by politics, and ramified by constitutional considerations (see Shuffelton 1977, 242–9). Henry Vane arrived at Boston in 1635 with a potent combination of noble blood and pious reputation, and he was elected governor of the colony the following year. Vane joined the Boston church and was sympathetic to Anne Hutchinson and others there who openly criticized ministers who they believed exalted a "covenant of works" over a "covenant of grace." During the colony-wide dispute over this fine point of Calvinist theology, Antinomians outside Boston adopted vocal and disruptive tactics of protest, sometimes interrupting sermons with questions for the minister and even abandoning public services in favor of conventicles in private homes. The affair took on an overtly political aspect when the assistants passed, over Governor Vane's dissent, an order giving themselves authority to expel new migrants who might swell the ranks of heresy. One minister, John Wilson, even defended this measure in terms of *arcana imperii*, or "secrets of state" (Winthrop 1972, 1:214). Meanwhile the General Court was raising an army against the native Pequots, and the fact that soldiers sympathetic to the Antinomians were refusing to fight because Wilson had been named military chaplain doubtless deepened the disgust that many New Englanders felt for the heresy. By the end of 1637 Vane, having been replaced by Winthrop in the governor's chair, was back in England, and Hutchinson and other Antinomian principals were banished out of Massachusetts's jurisdiction (Shurtleff 1854, 1:205–8).

In political terms the Antinomian controversy resulted in a more unified governing class. Occasional rivals of Winthrop's like Thomas Dudley and John Endecott were zealous against the Antinomians and assumed prominent places in the restored regime. Most dramatically, perhaps, Israel Stoughton, the erstwhile "troubler of Israel," was in 1637 elected to a place on the board of assistants for the first time. His suspension from officeholding had been cut short the previous year (Shurtleff 1854, 1:175), and late in 1636 he was again representing Dorchester in the General Court (1:185). He was also an important figure in the Pequot campaign, having been preferred in command to the heretical John Underhill (Wall 1990, 544), and the same court that formally banished the Antinomians also passed an order that Stoughton "hath liberty to take his 150 acres of meadow formerly granted him on both sides of Neponset River" (Shurtleff 1854, 1:207). The records do not indicate who took the lead in Stoughton's rehabilitation, but there was a clear motive for Winthrop to dissuade him from joining Hooker's party in their move to Connecticut (Wall 1990, 520), as Ludlow and Haynes, Stoughton's allies in the reforms of 1634, had already done.

The Antinomian affair, then, dissolved the fault-lines of prior constitutional dispute. In some measure it even inspired an exclusionary backlash, especially within the churches. The populist influence of the Pilgrim ecclesiology was seen to ebb from the teachings of Cotton and Richard Mather after 1637 (Hall 1972, 109–12), and most churches adopted more restrictive admissions practices, especially with regard to servants (Rutman 1965, 146–7). But the appeal of formal principles of democratic accountability survived well intact among many colonists. The Antinomians themselves had at times resorted to the language of the reform movement of 1634. Winthrop recalled that after Hutchinson's banishment her friends in the Boston church "were earnest with the elders to have him [Winthrop] called to account for it" (Winthrop 1972, 1:249), presumably by a process of internal censure. Winthrop's response was to invoke the principle of magisterial discretion which had always guided his conduct in office. That this invocation would not prove acceptable on a durable basis is attested by the fact that the campaign for legal limitation was revived and carried on with some success in the later 1630s and early 1640s. Success in the Antinomian affair, ironically, sowed the seeds of Winthrop's most difficult political battles of the next decade.

Legal Limitation

Written legal limitations on magistrates' authority had been proposed as early as 1634, when the reformist deputies demanded a view of the patent and subsequently moved the drafting of a new law code. The motive behind these proposals was to rein in magistrates' discretion, not the General Court's freedom of action. Thus Winthrop perceived the motive behind the first movement for law reform, in 1635, as the fear "that our magistrates, for want of positive laws, in many cases might proceed according to their discretions" (Winthrop 1972, 1:160). Having arrived in Massachusetts hard on the heels of this first, unsuccessful initiative, Vane sustained its momentum by staking the political claims of the Antinomians on an indictment of "so unlimited and unsafe a rule as the will and discretion of men" (Hutchinson 1865, 86). Thus he complained that the order allowing magistrates to expel newcomers "sets down no rule for the magistrate to walk by... but leaves it to their illimited consent or dissent" (91).

Winthrop's reply to Vane – characteristically – was conciliatory in style but uncompromising in substance. Magistrates' discretion, he claimed, was "regulated to direct all their ways by the rule of the gospel, and if they fail in any thing, they are subject to the church's correction" (Hutchinson 1865, 100). But this was precisely the claim he denied in response to Hutchinson's supporters within his own church. In his journal, moreover, Winthrop confided that "magistrates, as they are church members, are accountable to the church for their failings, but that is when they are out of their calling.... But if he doth thus in pursuing a course of justice, though the thing be unjust, yet he is not accountable" (Winthrop 1972, 1:249–50). Thus "to speak of discerning Christ's authority in church or common wealth, otherwise than as it is dispensed in the ministry of men, is a mere idea or fantasy" (Hutchinson 1865, 103). The job of the magistrate was quite simply to perform that task of discernment, a job that could not be done without full discretion vis-à-vis other human agencies. "Whatsoever sentence the magistrate gives... the judgment is the Lord's" and therefore must be obeyed (111). On Winthrop's account, then, the accountability to which a member might be subject in a gathered church had no parallel application to persons of civil authority.

Vane's attack on unlimited discretion was practically unsuccessful in the short term, but its logic was consistent with the renewed push for legal codification which followed the Antinomian affair. Stoughton and others believed that the disruptive Antinomian threat had to be put down but worried about the procedures by which this had been done (Breen 2001, 21–2). As before, Winthrop tried to stall efforts at reform, but in 1639 two different law-code prototypes were sent around the colony for comment and revision, one by Cotton (presumably based on his earlier effort, "Moses His Judicialls") and one by Nathaniel Ward (the Ipswich minister with some legal training) (Winthrop 1972, 1:322–3). It was not until 1641, availing themselves of Winthrop's absence from the governor's chair, that law-reform advocates got Ward's version ratified as the colony's new law code (Andrews 1934, 1:455–6). Article 1 of this "Body of Liberties" protected a laundry list of goods – ranging from life to reputation to property to family – from damage except "by virtue or equity of some express law." The next seven articles continued in the now familiar bill-of-rights vein, many of them prohibiting governmental action "but by the General Court" (Eliot 1910, 70–89).

The upshot of Ward's law code was to hold in check the powers of the magistracy not the General Court. In fact, in case of dispute among the magistrates about its provisions' meaning, "the General Court only shall have power to interpret them" (Eliot 1910, 89). Moreover, the Body of Liberties reaffirmed the freemen's right not only to remove magistrates at the annual court of election without showing any cause but also to do so between elections with cause shown (80) – in short, by episodic trials of impeachment. This written code of legal limitation was meant specifically to assist in making the assistants accountable to and controllable by the deputies.

Structural Reform

Law reform, then, was one of the issues around which Massachusetts politics gradually realigned again in the wake of the dealignment effected by the Antinomian controversy. Though the likes of Ludlow and Haynes were gone, while Stoughton eventually returned to England after the outbreak of civil war there, Richard Bellingham and Richard Saltonstall remained and were regularly elected to the board of assistants. They led a stable coalition of Essex County men which included William Hathorne, a prominent leader among the deputies. The same basic program of not only legal limitation but also structural reform that had animated the opposition of 1634 would also animate this new round of political opposition to Winthrop and his allies in the early 1640s. The success of legal limitation in the Body of Liberties in 1641 was followed by new efforts to shift structures of authority in favor of the deputies, whose main targets were the standing council and, again, the negative voice.

From the deputies' point of view the standing council, quite apart from the length of its members' tenure, represented an attempt to free magisterial discretion from the scrutiny and sanction of the General Court. The question was agitated at regular intervals from 1639 until 1644, when the deputies succeeded in getting acts of the standing council distinguished as something other (and presumably less) than magisterial acts but not in getting the council itself abolished (Brennan 1931, 67–8). The debate made clear that the deputies wanted the council to function as a fully accountable executive agency of the General Court, while the magistrates justified their independent discretion by reference to their having been annually elected (71ff.).

The same pattern of conflict and compromise held for the magistrates' negative voice during the same period. Though the deputies could also veto the assistants, as the numerically smaller body the latter were simply more likely to find themselves at odds with a majority vote of the whole court, and there is no record of any order favored by a majority of the magistrates having been nullified by a majority of the deputies. The mutual veto made the general court functionally bicameral even while the two bodies sat physically together, and everyone understood that the magistrates remained the great gainers from the arrangement.

A confluence of circumstances drove reformist deputies to intensify their efforts against the negative voice in 1643, in tandem with their opposition to the standing council. While that year's General Court was in adjournment Winthrop had offered assistance to one of two rival claimants to the governor's post in the French colony of Acadia to the north. The deputies objected that the General Court should have been consulted (Winthrop 1972, 2:112, 118–19), but they must also have reflected that, even if they had been able to assemble to deal with the situation, the governor and assistants could have vetoed whatever they resolved to do. The magistrates did in fact use their veto in an unrelated case, the celebrated judicial proceeding around "Goody Sherman's sow," and this was the proximate cause of the debate on the negative voice which was spearheaded by the Essex men (who also resided nearest to any potential danger from Acadia). As with the standing council sharp ideological conflict, with the exchange of position papers from both sides, resulted in modest changes. Early in 1644 an order was passed by the General Court requiring the deputies and magistrates to sit separately, with the agreement of both bodies still required to enact laws and orders (Shurtleff 1854, 2:58; Winthrop 1972, 2:160). The resort to a joint committee for breaking deadlocks was abandoned altogether (Howe and Eaton 1947, 294). Bicameralism had gone from a functional to a physical fact, while the magisterial veto remained intact.

The supreme unicameral assembly that the reformist deputies sought but failed to obtain was called "democracy" not by themselves but by their opponents. The regime-based critique of the deputies' agenda of structural reform would follow the same lines as ecclesiastic defenses of the "mixed" regime. In the very year of the resolution of the negative voice, Thomas Goodwin and Philip Nye saw John Cotton's *Keyes of the Kingdom of Heaven* (1644) into print in London. Their preface to the work defended an ecclesiastic "balancing of power and privileges" between elders and brethren (Cotton 1644, A/3b) in terms peculiarly relevant to the Massachusetts debate over the magisterial veto in civil affairs. Thus they condemned the radical democracy of Brownism because it "doth in effect put the chief (if not the whole) of the rule and government into the hands of the people, and drowns the *Elders'* votes (who are but a few) in the major part of theirs" (A/4a). Perhaps Goodwin and Nye were bearing in mind the plea for "popularity in the church" which had been made by John Smyth, the Pilgrims' old ally (see Chapter 4 above): "the definitive sentence, the determining power, the negative voice is in the body of the church, not in the Elders" (Smyth 1609, 55). In any case their preface was a patent attack on the same sort of straight majority voting on a unicameral basis which Winthrop and his allies feared would result from abolishing the magistrates' negative voice in the civil sphere. Thus Goodwin and Nye appeared to worry that the democratic virus might cross the ocean from America.

Indeed Winthrop and his allies, in addition to standing firm on the magisterial veto, were always looking to take precautions to prevent the "drowning" of their votes in the event that unicameralism prevailed. In 1639 the General Court passed an order, over some protest, reducing the number of deputies from three per town to two (Winthrop 1972, 1:300). In 1645, after the formalization of physically bicameral arrangements, the magistrates offered to return to a unicameral assembly with no vetoes on either side on condition that the deputies be elected by shire rather than town, "so as the deputies might not exceed them in number." Of course reasons of economy were always advanced for these proposals, but in private Winthrop recorded his hope that selecting deputies from larger districts would make them "the prime men of the country" (2:214). The towns themselves rejected this offer, perhaps recognizing that a numeric equality of magistrates with deputies in a single chamber was simply another way of achieving the same goal as bicameralism: to make quality count for more than quantity.

Historical Models

Winthrop's defense of the magistrates' senatorial role in government was not justified by reference to the modern notion of checks and balances; it was even more straightforwardly inegalitarian and anti-democratic. According to a "Replye" to opponents of the negative voice drafted by Winthrop in 1643, the loss of the magisterial veto would mean "our Government would be a mere Democracy, whereas now it is mixed" (Winthrop 1971, 2:429). He had in mind specifically the negative example of Athens, the "meanest and worst" regime, in which a magistrate voted as an individual equal to every other member of the assembly (2:430). His arguments were hardly different from those put to him in 1640 by a puritan nobleman writing from England, who decried a regime of "popularity... where wise men propound and fools determine, as it was said of the cities of Greece" (possibly a gloss on Bodin's *Six Books*; see Bodin 1962, 157); the "best form of government," rather, structured the power of few and many in a way "so fitly limiting each other, and thereby preventing the evils of either, [and] being equally poised one by the other" (Winthrop 1971, 2:426).

These invocations of ancient Athens in some respects did capture the spirit of the Massachusetts opposition's agenda. As we have already seen, in 1634 Winthrop himself had been required to submit his accounts for "moneys or other goods committed to me in trust for the commonwealth" from the beginning of his reign in 1629 (Winthrop 1972, 1:395). This kind of audit exemplified democratic accountability in the Athenian style; the other general method of calling officers to account, impeachment, had also been dear to the Massachusetts deputies. In that same year of reform John Cotton, newly arrived and giving his first sermon before the General Court, must have anticipated what lay in store for Winthrop, for he "delivered this doctrine, that a magistrate ought not to be turned into the condition of a private man without just cause, and to be publicly convict" (1:132). Eventually a modification of this principle was made the law of the colony when Article 67 of the Body of Liberties provided that the freemen may remove a magistrate at any meeting of court with cause shown. In short, the 1641 law code introduced Athenian-style impeachments to Massachusetts.

Reformist deputies appear to have perceived and endorsed the ancient Greek provenance of their proposals; so much was abundantly clear, at least, of the principle of rotation in office. Stoughton wrote to his brother in 1635 that the opposition deputies "desire to change year by year the governorship; but the assistants more rarely, yet sometimes, lest it be esteemed hereditary" (Emerson 1976, 151). This principle was informally observed for three consecutive years in the 1630s, when six different men were elected to the top two posts of governor and deputy, until the dealignment following the Antinomian affair. Later, after Winthrop voluntarily stepped down from the governorship in 1640 to attend to private business, the reformists seized the occasion to revive the idea and practice of rotation. Nathaniel Ward and Ezekiel Rogers, ministers from Essex County, defended it in their election sermons. In 1641 Ward gave "a moral and political discourse, grounding his propositions much upon the old Roman and Grecian governments," which "advised the people to keep all their magistrates in an equal rank" (Winthrop 1972, 2:35). Rogers gave the 1643 election sermon (over Winthrop's objection) and repeated Ward's attack on consecutive terms (2:99). The auditing of Winthrop and the regular declaration and occasional practice of rotation in office, together with the frequently expressed horror on the other side of "mere democracy," serve as reminders of how powerful an example ancient Athens was taken to be in the seventeenth century.

That the political imagination of early New England was generally oriented toward historical models is explained in part by the prevalence of works in their libraries like Machiavelli's *Prince*, Guicciardini's *History of Italy*, Bodin's *Six Books of the Republic*, and Raleigh's *History of the World* (Morison 1956, 134–9). Texts of the Italian Renaissance would have held a special appeal for English colonists. Like the Italian cities of the fifteenth and sixteenth centuries, the New England colonies were small and vulnerable; as Florence had fought against French and Spanish armies, for instance, Massachusetts lived in fear of attack by forces from French Acadia to the north, and Virginia had feared Spanish Florida to the south. Moreover, New England puritans would have read with sympathy of Florence's struggles against the political and military power of the pope; and, famously, both Machiavelli and Guicciardini could be savagely critical of papal corruption. To the extent that New Englanders saw similar corruption at work in the English court of Charles I – and they did fear invasion by an English viceroy every bit as much as by French or Spanish Catholics – they would have readily identified their plight with the Florentine republicans'.

In particular, Guicciardini's account of the constitutional debate in Florence after the expulsion of the ruling Medici family in 1494 may have been a model for some of his colonial American readers. On his telling, advocates of a popular regime stipulated three criteria for the new Florentine republic: that magistrates be rotated in office, that a "universal council" possess basic legislative powers, and that the deliberations of elite councils be subject to "universal consent" (Guicciardini 1969, 78) – so that Massachusetts's General Court as of 1634 would have looked like the successor of Florence's Great Council. Florentine opponents of this scheme raised the usual specter of democratic ignorance and confusion, as Winthrop and others would do, citing the turbulent deaths suffered by the Athenian and Roman republics (80–2).

An interesting feature of this Florentine debate was the wide appeal of the Venetian model of republican government revolving around elections, thus illustrating the limitations of the Florentines' conception of "popular government." Girolamo Savonarola, the charismatic friar at the head of the popular party, exhorted his fellow citizens to imitate Venice (minus the monarchic figure of the doge) by opening up the selection of magistrates to balloting by the Great Council (Guicciardini 1969, 83–5; Savonarola 2006, 161). This historical model approximated the voting of Massachusetts's freemen for their governor and assistants, but further mechanisms of accountability and control were not up for discussion – not, at least, on the account of Guicciardini, who was himself generally opposed to the popular party in Florence (Gilbert 1965, 27, 85–8). Regular elections, then, might have appeared to men like Winthrop and Cotton as the absolute limit of democratization which the classical-republican frame of reference provided by their Renaissance Italian sources would permit. The fact that their opponents pressed beyond these limits suggests, furthermore, that for some New Englanders the classical model of accountability was being supplemented by fiduciary influences.

Possibly the opposition deputies were drawn less to Guicciardini than to Machiavelli, who offered a much stronger endorsement of democratic accountability within the classical-republican tradition (see McCormick 2001, 2003). But the stronger evidence of New Englanders' literary acquaintance points to Raleigh, himself a Machiavellian of sorts (and author of an essay of his own called *The Prince*). On his account of the rule of the Four Hundred in Athens after the disastrous Sicilian expedition, in his *History of the World*, the ruling oligarchs "did cause all matters to be propounded unto the people, and concluded upon by the greater part of voices: but the things propounded were only such as were first allowed in private among themselves; neither had the commonalty any other liberty, than only to approve and give consent" (Raleigh 1829, 5:180). This derisory picture of "aristocracy" (5:182) resembled Guicciardini's "popular government" but undermined its appeal by implying that popular ratifications were insufficient conditions of genuine democratic politics; the same logic would have held for regular elections as the other main avenue of popular consent. Raleigh was no radical democrat, but he did couch his account of Athens's tyranny of "the Thirty" in terms of their failure at the "faithful execution of that which was committed to them in trust" (5:192). This fiduciary language, naturally invoking ideas of accountability in the minds of seventeenth-century Englishmen (see Chapter 2 above), combined with Bodinian influences to produce a theoretic framework of accountability which transcended the classical-republican model.

"Democracy"

No record survives in which reformist deputies used the term "democracy" as a banner of aspiration; but, as we have seen, written arguments on Winthrop's side of the debates at Boston were less likely to be destroyed by official order than those on the other side. Even so, the frequency with which extant documents raise the question of terminology and the classification of regimes indicates that these were points of debate. The insistent condemnations of "democracy" in the early 1640s were doubtless responding to, among other things, the declaration in favor of that regime type which had recently been made in neighboring Rhode Island by notorious heretics, including Anne Hutchinson and her associates (see Chapter 6 below). At times these condemnations appeared barely related to the usual issues of institutional structure or social class. The "Answers of the Reverend Elders" in 1643, for instance, endorsed all the main theoretic propositions behind the deputies' opposition to the standing council: the General Court is the supreme power in the state, the standing council must observe any instructions laid down by the General Court, and more generally judges should not be allowed to pass sentence wholly at their discretion (Hutchinson 1865, 205–13). But at the same time, without explicitly defending magistrates' independent powers, the ministers concluded that the Massachusetts regime was "mixed" between aristocracy and democracy (212). Their reasons may have been as straightforwardly rhetorical as those of Stoughton a decade before, when he felt compelled to protest what he saw as constitutional errors yet wanted to avoid appearing "anabaptistical" (Emerson 1976, 152).

The terminology of regimes employed by Winthrop and his allies shows the same uses of but also departures from Bodinian protocols of classification as were evident in defenses of an Aristotelian "mixed" regime in ecclesiastics. Cotton had in 1636 described Massachusetts as a "popular state" (specifically citing Bodin) because the "people choose their own governors," but not a "democratic government" because public affairs are "administered not by the people but by the governors" (Emerson 1976, 193). Formally this was the same claim that John Robinson had made for the church (see Chapter 4 above), but substantively, of course, rendering this definition in terms of consent but not accountability amounted to a significant omission from the usual Bodinian repertoire.

A similar analysis was later offered by John Norton, pastor at Ipswich, who supported Winthrop's defense of the negative voice as the dyke to democracy, which history had proved to be less durable than a mixed regime (Norton 1913, 281). "Democracy" for him was that regime "where the supreme civil power is by the people committed or betrusted for the execution thereof according to fundamental Laws, with such a number of the people though of any inferior condition among them" (280). This phrasing echoed Bodin's definition of a democratic state as one in which "such power given unto the magistrates belonged unto the people, and ... is not given but as in trust unto the magistrates" (Bodin 1962, 185), but Norton had no interest in the regular means of popular control which figured in Bodin's analysis of historical regimes like Rome and Geneva. Interestingly, Norton went on to define "aristocracy" as equally involving popular authorization, but here the recipients of authority were the "chiefer sort," whether "nobility" or "gentry" (Norton 1913, 280). Both democracy and aristocracy, on this account, were implicitly unicameral, and their only difference had to do with the class composition of the governing body. But Norton's argument for the functional bicameralism associated with the negative voice was that Massachusetts was meant to be neither of these; rather "our magistracy is but a Democratical, though Aristocratically administered" (280). Institutionally speaking, Norton's sense of this mixture required not only functional but also physical bicameralism, since separate sittings and deliberations of assistants and deputies supplied "more strength of reason" (281) – implicitly, of reason as reposed in the quantitatively inferior but qualitatively superior assistants. This was precisely the arrangement of separation that won out in 1644, and as pastor to some of the Essex County men who were agitating against bicameralism Norton may have played a significant part in the eventual compromise.

Accountability and Elections

Cotton and Norton were both Cambridge graduates and published authors in defense of the "New England Way" in ecclesiastics (see Chapter 4 above). Though they both appeared to observe the Bodinian distinction between "state" and "government" (this is less clear in Norton), they both departed from Bodin's "popular state" by giving the people regular powers of consent but not accountability. At the same time they reposed sovereignty in a bicameral assembly, thereby showing their notions of "mixture" to be of the Aristotelian rather than Bodinian sort. Just as they had done with respect to church government, Cotton and Norton used arguments for civil affairs which stressed the irrevocable transfer of popular sovereignty to officers. In tandem with Winthrop they developed the novel argument that elections themselves represent a kind of "calling to account" in order to make their essentially discretionary conception of political trust more palatable to their fellow colonists.

Winthrop evidently pioneered this new argument when he assured the Watertown protesters in 1632 that annual elections would give them control over the imposition of colony taxes. Yet Winthrop and the magistrates had little to fear from regular elections because they realized that prominent men such as they would be the freemen's favored objects of choice (Wall 1972, 7). Indeed the lessons from ancient Greek theory down to Renaissance Italian history indicated that elections tended to produce a stable governing elite (see Manin 1997, chs. 1–2). Cotton's advice to the 1634 General Court against removing magistrates from office indicated some sympathy with

Winthrop's position, and soon their correspondence with puritan noblemen in England would confirm the two Bostonians in their agreement on the theoretic relation between elections and accountability.

William Fiennes, Lord Saye and Sele, and Robert Greville, Lord Brooke, were two of the leading promoters of Anglo-American colonization, and their puritan sympathies made New England particularly interesting to them. Their personal interest in emigration, in fact, may have prompted the letters that Saye exchanged with both Cotton and Winthrop in the later 1630s and early 1640s. Though no dabbler in democracy, Saye made proposals to Cotton and Winthrop for reforming colonial government which included the ability of the colony "parliament" to "call the governor and all public officers to account, to create new officers, and to determine [terminate] them already set up" (Morgan 2003, 163). Though Saye's idea of a parliament included a hereditary rather than elective upper chamber, he suggested that a hereditary nobility in the colonies would not be dangerous "so long as they are always accountable to parliaments consisting of all the united estates yearly" (Winthrop 1971, 2:426).

Thus Saye was proposing for New England what Henry Parker and others would later be attempting to construct in old England (see Chapter 2 above): a kingless mixed regime with executive officers accountable to a broadly representative parliament. The Massachusetts elite's prime worry about this proposal was its dubious assumption that godliness and hereditary privilege could coexist (Morgan 2003, 166; Winthrop 1971, 2:434). The process of election, which figured so prominently in Calvinist ecclesiastics, seemed to them the correct method of selection for civil officers as well. But they did not directly challenge Saye's somewhat vague notion of regular accountability for such officers; instead they advanced annual elections to satisfy it. Thus Cotton's point-by-point reply to Saye's proposals held that "this power to call governors and all officers to account... is settled already [in Massachusetts] in the general court or parliament, only it is not put forth but once in the year, viz. at the great and general court in May, when the governor is chosen" (Morgan 2003, 163).

Later, during the disputes over the standing council and the negative voice, Winthrop and Norton returned to the identification of regular elections as mechanisms of accountability. Winthrop claimed that the supreme power that is "originally and virtually" in the freemen is, after election day, "actually in those to whom they have committed it" (Winthrop 1971, 2:437). As a result, there could be no popular control between moments of selection: the job of accountability was absorbed into the process of annual elections, at which notoriously unfit officers "would be soon removed and called to account" (2:438). Thus Winthrop attempted to avert open conflict between the discretionary and accountable conceptions of political trust by abandoning his previous reliance on the language of discretion and assuring his opponents that the means of popular control were already at their disposal, coexistent with the magisterial veto. For his part Norton admitted that there were inconveniences involved in Massachusetts's "mixed" government but alleged that "fundamental laws and annual elections," devices already in place by 1643, were sufficient to remedy them (Norton 1913, 282). He went on to claim that magisterial abuse "is curable within the year when at the election offending and incurable magistrates may be removed" (283).

At every turn, then, Winthrop and his ideological allies used the electoral thesis of accountability to dissuade reformers from their goals. That many deputies and freemen must have accepted this new argument is hardly to be doubted, since the reformist impulse in the 1640s stopped well short of its 1630s goals. But the ideological alternatives had at least been pretty clear: whereas the reformist deputies had advanced end-of-term audits and inter-electoral impeachments as the mechanisms of regular accountability appropriate to a supreme unicameral assembly, Winthrop and his allies offered annual elections alone as sufficient guarantees of popular control to compensate for the magisterial veto. By the middle 1640s the latter had won the day.

The parliamentarian kind of control advanced by Saye, of the executive by a representative assembly, followed the classical model of accountability, but the Massachusetts reformers had already been employing Bodinian and fiduciary resources to imagine the freemen as a unitary trustor controlling its trustees in colony government. As Winthrop caustically observed in 1635, under the previous year's reform program "the people would exercise their absolute power" (Winthrop 1972, 1:158). But the reformers appear to have had less to say about democratic accountability at the local level, between deputy and constituency, than at the central level, between magistrates and freemen. Locally practice spoke louder than theory. Town meetings regularly instructed their deputies about the introduction of legislation at the general court and occasionally even issued mandates on how to proceed on specific measures already on the colony's agenda. The Plymouth colony, as a matter of law, required its towns to send instructions with their representatives, while Massachusetts towns nearly always "required the deputy upon his return from Boston to make a report concerning the business which had been transacted at the General Court" (Colegrove 1920, 414, 423–4, 432). The Body of Liberties of 1641 codified the practice of instructions with respect to town officers, but with no mention of representatives in the General Court (Eliot 1910, 81). Indeed recent research on politics within Massachusetts towns has challenged the revisionist finding of municipal "oligarchy" (e.g. Waters 1968) precisely by uncovering the processes of formal accountability by which citizens attempted to control their town magistrates (Thompson 2001, 37–8). Still, unlike the Levellers a few years later, the Massachusetts reformers never proposed formalized audits or impeachments of court deputies by their local constituencies, relying instead on informal practices of instruction or mandate.

The electoral thesis of accountability was intended to prevent the attainment of a similar level of control over colony magistrates. It was a polemically successful gambit that made a departure of convenience from the discretionary conception of political trust. For Winthrop, Cotton, and Norton were normally unwilling to contemplate regular accountability to popular agencies; they did so only in irony, as part of a rhetorical appeal to mollify their opponents' concerns. Their true feeling about accountability is reflected in the fact that, at the same time, their political followed their ecclesiastical theories in rejecting the Bodinian version of structural mixture in favor of a more traditional Aristotelian one. Aristotle's own views on democratic accountability, though often quite favorable, were less relevant in this connection than his ideas of a just distribution of power according to geometric rather than arithmetic equality – that is, according to quality not quantity. Most New Englanders were firmly committed to the notion of popular consent, but positing an Aristotelian mixture of powers and social ranks allowed Winthrop and his allies to jettison another key component of Bodinian sovereignty: popular control via democratic accountability. Yet some New Englanders remained true to Bodin's analytic conception of democracy in politics as John Robinson had done in ecclesiastics (see Chapter 4 above).

The Hingham Impeachment

The reformist deputies rejected Cotton's suggestion in 1634 that magistrates not be turned out of office, on election day, without a full public trial, but in 1641 the Body of Liberties codified Cotton's suggestion that a trial of impeachment might be a legitimate form of accountability after election day. This idea, reminiscent of ancient Athens's *eisangelia* (see Chapter 2 above), was implemented in 1645 against none other than John Winthrop.

In that year the town of Hingham was split over the appointment of a new militia captain. A large contingent of the militia was opposed to the town council's choice and held a vote to choose their own captain; in the meantime they organized their own military exercises. At the behest of the council Winthrop arrested and jailed the rebellious militiamen's leaders. At the 1645 General Court nearly one hundred townsmen from Hingham presented a petition moving a public trial of Winthrop, and the court passed the motion (Winthrop 1972, 2:222-4). This dispute involved one of the most vital institutions of frontier life, and one in which ordinary colonists had a special stake. As we have seen, some Antinomians had refused to serve in the Pequot war because of their dislike of the military chaplain. According to Winthrop, one of the Hingham militiamen now "professeth he will die at the sword's point if he might not have the choice of his own officers" (2:221). In the issue, Winthrop was acquitted by a divided court, winning overwhelmingly among the magistrates but narrowly among the deputies. After his exoneration Winthrop gave his now famous "Little Speech on Liberty."

The simple message of Winthrop's valedictory was discretion over accountability, as expressed through a variety of fiduciary metaphors. First, economic agency: "When you agree with a workman to build you a ship or house, etc., he undertakes as well for his skill as for his faithfulness.... But when you call one to be a magistrate, he doth not profess nor undertake to have sufficient skill for that office, nor can you furnish him with gifts, etc., therefore you must run the hazard of his skill and ability" (Winthrop 1972, 2:229). Second, marriage: "The woman's own choice makes such a man her husband; yet being so chosen, he is her lord, and she is to be subject to him.... And whether her lord smiles upon her, and embraceth her in his arms, or whether he frowns, or rebukes, or smites her, she apprehends the sweetness of his love in all, and is refreshed, supported, and instructed by every dispensation of his authority over her" (2:230). The political relation of a magistrate to his subjects followed the same logic: "If he fail in faithfulness, which by his oath he is bound unto, that he must answer for.... [But] if the case be doubtful, or the rule doubtful, to men of such understanding and parts as your magistrates are, if your magistrate should err here, yourselves must bear it" (2:228-9).

Not surprisingly, Winthrop perceived the events of 1645 as continuous with those of 1634, invoking Stoughton's language of fiduciary power from the first ever conflict over the negative voice. Thus he accused those who moved his impeachment as holding "that magistracy must be no other, in effect, than a ministerial office, and all authority, both legislative, consultative, and judicial, must be exercised by the people in their body representative" (Winthrop 1972, 2:231). In fact he interpreted all the constitutional debates of the 1640s as little more than attacks on his own position – whether against the negative voice or the standing council, or for law reform. The reformist movement was no less than "the workings of satan to ruin the colonies and Churches of Christ in New England" (2:230). Unlike modern historians, however, Winthrop also perceived a coherent ideological motive in his opponents, not mere personal animosity or lust for power. It did not escape him that the nexus of *salus populi*, trust, and accountability echoed contemporary debates in war-torn England (see Chapter 2 above), and he feared that reformers in Massachusetts might "bring the like miseries upon ourselves" (2:233).

Democratic Constitutionalism

In theoretic terms "the workings of satan" contrived principles of democratic accountability that were oriented toward two sorts of criteria, not only popular will but also written law. The latter was not presumed to embody the former purely and simply, but it was no accident that the advocates of unicameralism, rotation, and non-electoral accountability also campaigned for legal limitation. The law was viewed as a potential instrument of popular power, both consolidating procedures of accountability and clarifying standards of judgment. This ideological partnership of accountability to the people and accountability to the law met its end, at least in New England, in the last major political fight of Winthrop's lifetime.

The year after Winthrop's impeachment and acquittal, Robert Child and several others presented a "Remonstrance and Petition" to the 1646 General Court advocating further legal reform according to English law and seeking civil and religious accommodation for Presbyterians. The first part of this proposal was vaguer than and ultimately subservient to the second, and it may have been simply a rhetorical appeal to the contingent of the court most suspicious of Winthrop and the magistrates. Since some of the leading Hingham protesters had been Presbyterians, and since the Presbyterian William Vassall was thought to be behind both the Hingham affair and now this petition as well (Wall 1990, 549), the Remonstrants would have been well advised to seek political arguments to overcome ecclesiastical prejudices. Thus Child invoked the language of accountability in demanding that the court fix "a settled rule for them [magistrates] to walk by in all cases of judicature, from which if they swerve there may be some power settled, according to the laws of England, that may call them to account for their delinquencies" (Hutchinson 1865, 217). The Hingham case had been pressed on behalf of the notion that delegated authorities ought to be kept under the control of the freemen; the Child petition, conversely, contained no such explicitly populist element but rather insisted that magistrates be held accountable to settled principles of law. These successive protests, then, represented the dissolution or disaggregation of what had been an integral, two-pronged agenda of democratic accountability from 1634 to 1645.

In fact the Remonstrance controversy indicated that the age of democratic reform in Massachusetts had expired with Winthrop's impeachment and acquittal. In the issue the Remonstrance garnered some support within the court but less than Winthrop's impeachment had done: the petition was denied and the petitioners jailed and fined (Andrews 1934, 1:487–90). The whole episode did result in minor adjustments to voting rules within the towns and to the colony's law code, which was brought out in a new edition (see Kavenagh 1973, 1:302–4). But the Massachusetts establishment, having survived the challenges of fundamental constitutional reform, was in good condition as the home country headed into the final years of civil war. Now the agenda of unicameralism, rotation, legal limitation, and non-electoral accountability would pass from the new side of the Atlantic to the old. Ironically, the Levellers in England were, with some sectarian and Independent support, invoking democratic accountability and legal limitation against the Presbyterians in the Long Parliament just as the Presbyterians in New England were doing the same against the broadly Independent leadership there. As has happened so often in the history of political thought, political arguments were being wielded as weapons of ideological conflict by multiple hands, sometimes on opposite sides of the battle lines.

In time one of the Massachusetts anti-democrats' favored weapons of struggle would also cross the lines: the proposition that regular elections are a sufficient mechanism of accountability would become the staple explanation and rationale not of aristocracy but indeed of modern "democracy." Hence the irony of John Winthrop's legacy to American political thought: whereas in 1773 his "Little Speech on Liberty" was reprinted in Boston to quiet the noises of rebellion (Breen 1970, 274), only fifteen years later the rebels-turned-victors used his electoral thesis of accountability to quiet the noises of resistance to the new United States Constitution (see epigraph above). Madison's emphasis on periodic elections as "the only policy" for democratic accountability attempted to satisfy the Anti-Federalists' desire for "sympathy" between representatives and constituents (see Dry and Storing, 1985, 340–2) while excluding some of their favored means of popular control, including rotation in office and inter-electoral recall (219, 347–9). This was another instance of anti-democratic irony: in this sense, at least, Winthrop is indeed a "forgotten founding father" (cf. Bremer 2003).

But that moniker may apply in yet another sense, since Winthrop had helped to push not only theological but also ideological dissent into the hinterlands of New England, where a more integral version of the Massachusetts opposition's democratic constitutionalism was realized. We turn now to the first flight to the frontier of this marginal but recurrently reviving tradition of American political thought.

6

Democratic Constitutionalism in Connecticut and Rhode Island

> In order to gain a clear and just idea of the design and end of government, let us suppose a small number of persons settled in some sequestered part of the earth.... They will then represent the first peopling of any country.... As the colony increases... the distance at which the members may be separated will render it too inconvenient for all of them to meet.... This will point out the convenience of their consenting to leave the legislative part to be managed by a select number chosen from the whole body.... And that the *elected* might never form to themselves an interest separate from the *electors*, prudence will point out the propriety of having elections often; because as the *elected* might by that means return and mix again with the general body of the *electors*... their fidelity to the public will be secured by the prudent reflection of not making a rod for themselves.... Here then is the origin and rise of government.
>
> Thomas Paine, 1776 (Paine 1987, 67–8)

By the time their agents in the Continental Congress had put their signatures to the Declaration of Independence in July 1776, several of the American colonies had already begun to revise their constitutions; most of the rest would soon follow suit. Thanks in part to recent experience with the exercise of executive power by George III and his various colonial deputies, and in part to the rhetorical purchase of anti-monarchic polemics like Paine's *Common Sense* (published in January of that year), the new constitutions shifted power away from governors and executive councils toward elected legislatures. These populist constitutions made a new revolutionary status quo, against which the United States Constitution of 1787 and its polemic defense in *The Federalist* were to launch an ultimately successful theoretical as well as practical coup.

There were only two exceptions to this trend of populist constitution-making by the new American states in 1776: Connecticut and Rhode Island.

These two states added bills of rights to their colonial charters and removed all references to the British monarch; otherwise they left their existing governmental structures intact (Riley 1896, 130; Wood 1969, 133–4). The reason is that the pre-revolutionary governments of these two jurisdictions were already the most democratic on offer in English America, and they had been so since their inception in the middle seventeenth century. First formed during the 1630s and 1640s, the constitutions of Connecticut and Rhode Island were barely altered by royal charters obtained in the 1660s and remained unchanged in their fundamentals down to the Revolution. Both were born as popular unicameral regimes and, though by the Restoration both had become functionally bicameral, retained key procedures making officers accountable to the whole citizen body. For this reason, among others, Connecticut and Rhode Island have long been recognized as exceptionally populist in politics and ideology relative to the other Anglo-American colonies (see Main 1966, 397; Hamilton et al. 2005, 265). An examination of the seventeenth-century origins of Connecticut and Rhode Island, then, will show why they were the first modern democratic states: they resulted from the conceptual partnership of popular sovereignty and the accountable trust, and from their application to representative and federal political systems through written constitutions.

The democratic exceptionalism of Connecticut and Rhode Island can be seen in terms of practice as well as theory and explained by circumstance as well as ideology. These two settlements were part of a wave of secondary migration out of Massachusetts which Andrews euphemized as "an overflow of population" (Andrews 1934, 2:3); in fact this wave was swelled and propelled by not only economic and theological but also ideological conflicts at Boston. Many of these hinterland communities – including in their geographic purview not only Connecticut and Rhode Island but also present-day New Hampshire, Maine, and Long Island, New York – were organized by plantation covenants under the assumption of a legal state of nature.

"One part of a community, seeking some new place for their habitation, becomes a distinct community of themselves" – this is how George Lawson, writing in England in the 1650s, illustrated the principle of "voluntary consent" in the formation of new societies (Lawson 1992, 28). The New England towns were recent examples of this kind of founding, and Lawson's interest in the colonies extended to the writings of Thomas Hooker, the pastor of the Hartford church, whom he took as one of the two chief exemplars of the congregational theory of church government (13, 155–6, 186, 191–2, 208). In turn, Lawson's *Politica Sacra et Civilis* (1660) anticipated and may have influenced Locke's ideas on sovereignty, resistance, and constitutional change as developed in the *Two Treatises of Government* (1689) (Franklin 1978, 88–9, 93–4). As my analysis of Hooker's writings will show, not only did he uphold the principle of consent and employ the distinction between fundamental and ordinary power ("real" and "personal majesty," in Lawson's terms) in proto-Lockean fashion; he also insisted on the principle of democratic accountability. If Hooker's colony exemplified the mythic account of political origins adumbrated by Lawson and elaborated by Paine (see epigraph above), his political theory went beyond Paine's electoral thesis of accountability to include non-electoral forms of popular control.

The instrument of the foundings of both Connecticut and Rhode Island was a written constitution uniting several towns in a unicameral assembly made accountable to the "freemen." In the case of the former, the ideological impetus came straight from the Massachusetts opposition's quest for accountable government (see Chapter 5 above). Hooker presided over the constitutional achievement *ab initio* in Connecticut of the reform program that had achieved mixed results in the Bay colony. As a theoretician he followed John Robinson, "the Pilgrim Pastor," in expounding a populist version of congregational ecclesiastics (see Chapter 4 above), but he went further in articulating parallel principles for civil government.

If the sources of Rhode Islanders' evident ideological commitments are more obscure, their twinning of the principles of popular sovereignty and accountability under the rubric of "democracy" was terminologically unique. Roger Williams wrote little about questions of constitutional structure in developing the arguments for religious toleration for which he was and is famous (Simpson 1956). Thus I will argue that, despite his opposition to toleration, Hooker was the stronger democratic theorist. But Williams was significant in not only describing the origins of government in terms conventional to the tradition of radical constitutionalism – drawing on commonwealth values, the fiduciary idea, and the principle of popular sovereignty – but also instituting, together with his neighbors, non-electoral procedures of accountability in practice. The basic conceptual toolbox of modern democracy, then, was fully in use in the constitutional development of a colony that actualized, in just over a decade, the mythic progress of liberal or contractarian accounts of political origins. Not only did Rhode Island pass from natural anarchy to primitive town democracy to a federal, representative system; Williams and his colleagues also explicitly made "democracy" the proper name for the regime type resulting from this development, all of whose various phases were united by the regular accountability of political agents to the citizen body.

Connecticut versus Massachusetts

The significance of the Connecticut settlement for democratic thought arises in part from the ideological context of its genesis. Modern histories have tended to regard the motives behind the founders' departure from Massachusetts as of a personal and economic sort (e.g. Jones 1968, 19), but these factors were neither exhaustive nor even primary. Equally if not more important was the fact that the Connecticut project was a direct offshoot of the democratic opposition to the Winthrop establishment at Boston.

Among the orders made by the Massachusetts General Court in the year of reform, 1634, was a grant of permission to some inhabitants of Cambridge to explore sites for a new settlement on the Connecticut River (Shurtleff 1854, 1:119). But when, several months later, the question of permission actually to move there came up, Winthrop led the assistants in vetoing the deputies' passage of the measure, thus prompting Boston's first public fight over the "negative voice" (Winthrop 1972, 1:140–1). This veto was momentous in the history of early New England. Not only did it begin one of the great constitutional debates of the Bay colony's early history, one not to be resolved for practical purposes for another ten years; not only did it prompt Israel Stoughton's protests against magisterial discretion in open court (see Chapter 5 above); it also resulted in the Connecticut colony's commencement under color of political and ideological rivalry.

The leading men of the new settlement included many of eminence, education, and declared discomfort with Winthrop's administration. In fact most of the reform impulse of 1634 had come from the three Massachusetts towns – Cambridge, Dorchester, and Watertown – which supplied the bulk of Connecticut's initial settlers (Johnston 1887, 67). John Haynes (of Cambridge) was a stalwart of the early opposition movement and had been elected as Winthrop's replacement as governor in 1635. Roger Ludlow (like Stoughton, of Dorchester) had been elected deputy governor in 1634. Richard Saltonstall (of Watertown) was meant to join the settlement on the Connecticut but was beaten to the choicest sites by Ludlow's associates (Andrews 1934, 2:74); in the issue Saltonstall remained in Massachusetts and became one of the leaders of the Essex County group which carried on the struggle for the reform agenda at Boston.

Above all the rest in reputation and influence was Thomas Hooker, a puritan preacher well known in England before his emigration. He had suffered and then fled the adverse attentions of Archbishop William Laud and was highly regarded on both sides of the Atlantic. Hooker settled in Cambridge and entered into a close relationship with Haynes, and he joined the Connecticut movement after only two years under Massachusetts jurisdiction. Though Hooker was not on record as having taken sides in the debates of 1634-5, circumstances surrounding his new colony soon drew him into a private correspondence with Winthrop in which he defended the principle of accountability against the Boston regime's norm of discretionary rule – thus revealing Hooker's political ideas to be in substantial agreement with those of the Massachusetts opposition.

Hooker versus Winthrop

Having stretched the western frontier of New England, Connecticut immediately faced war with the native Pequots, their successful conduct of which gave the new colony instant legitimacy in the eyes of Massachusetts. But the hardships associated with the war convinced Hooker and Haynes to seek in 1638 a formal alliance for purposes of defense (Osgood 1907, 1:306-7, 312; Andrews 1934, 2:98). Early negotiations were abortive, partly because of disagreements over the ground-rules for inter-colonial negotiation, especially how best to entrust power to envoys. The Bay favored "absolute power" in their commissioners; Hooker and his associates, power of "advice" only, requiring their agents to return to the whole colony for the ratification of terms (Winthrop 1972, 1:284). It is no surprise, in light of the Pilgrims' strong feeling for strict fidelity (see Chapter 4 above), that Plymouth later followed a similar manner of delegating power to their envoys, which Winthrop criticized as giving a "power only to treat but not to determine" – requiring them to submit all agreements back to their constituents for confirmation (2:100).

In fact Winthrop tried to draw Haynes, Connecticut's chief negotiator, away from this attachment to accountable delegation, but to no avail (Shuffelton 1977, 274-5). Winthrop complained that Connecticut "chose divers scores men, who had no learning or judgment which fit them for those affairs, though otherwise men holy and religious" (Winthrop 1972, 1:286). Hooker replied in Connecticut's defense, contrasting two kinds of consent, that of "the State" (required by Massachusetts) with that of "the magistrates and people" (required by Connecticut) (Hooker 1860b, 9). Hooker's choice of language reflected the view, common among the Bay opposition, that Winthrop and the other assistants managed affairs as if they alone represented "the State," whereas properly the General Court ought to hold supreme power as a single body inclusive of both "the magistrates and people."

Hooker defended his colony's practice by first stipulating, uncontroversially, that "judges" and "counsellors" must be elected by the people to hold office and exercise power; "only, the question here grows – what rule the judge must have to judge by; secondly, who those counsellors must be." Reflecting the same motives for legal limitation which had most recently been voiced by Henry Vane during the Antinomian controversy (see Chapter 5 above), Hooker argued that it "wants both safety and warrant" to allow public affairs to be entirely "left to his [the magistrate's] discretion" (Hooker 1860b, 11). In place of discretion Hooker required accountability, but particularly accountability to law. During that same year of 1638, Hooker preached an election sermon exhorting the freemen "to set the bounds and limitations of the power and place unto which they [people] call them [magistrates]" (Hooker 1860a, 20). In his letter to Winthrop, Hooker cited the ancients to elaborate the virtues of written law: "You will know what the Heathen man said, by candle-light of common sense: The law is not subject to passion, nor to be taken aside with self-seeking ends, and therefore ought to have chief rule over rulers themselves" (Hooker 1860b, 12).

Hooker was so well known for his principled opposition to discretionary rule that William Pynchon could cite it with irony, for polemic advantage, during a dispute in 1638–9. Pynchon was the chief magistrate of Springfield, farther inland on the Connecticut River, and during the Pequot war he accepted a commission from the colonists at Hartford to ship them extra stores of corn to make up an expected shortfall. In the issue Hooker accused Pynchon of having offered insufficient supplies at extortionate prices and complained specifically of his failure to commandeer canoes from private citizens (Morison 1964, 352–4). Pynchon replied that such an infringement of property rights would have effected "Tyranny," "slavery," and "the lawless law of discretion" (Pynchon 1914, 47–8). Pynchon himself, however, ruled Springfield virtually single-handedly and, after transferring his colony's allegiance from Connecticut to Massachusetts, was a regular Winthrop ally on the board of assistants at Boston during the 1640s (Morison 1964, 348–9, 355–6; Shurtleff 1854, 2:passim). Pynchon's attack on Hooker was designed to put him on the defensive by mocking his reputation as a stickler for accountable rule.

The founding of Connecticut, then, was not only the occasion of and the sequel to political conflict at Boston; it was also fundamentally sympathetic to the idea of democratic accountability associated with the Bay opposition. This basic fact about Connecticut's origins was readily apparent to an older generation of scholars: Johnston's comment that "the settlement of Connecticut was itself the secession of the democratic element from Massachusetts" was mistaken only in implying that none of the "democratic element" remained in the Bay colony (Johnston 1887, 64). But the

Perry Miller school of American puritan studies has denied Hooker's and Connecticut's association with democratic ideology (see Miller 1956, ch. 2; Ahlstrom 1963). Such a view is partly enabled by ignoring the Winthrop-Hooker correspondence of 1638, again departing from the methods of previous scholarship (Johnston 1887, 69–70; Adams 1921, 193–4) – texts that help to undermine the modern scholarly consensus around a supposed New England ideological consensus. A similar sort of corrective must be applied to a primary document that has been misunderstood rather than ignored: the Fundamental Orders of Connecticut (1639). For in their political founding, using a written instrument of government, the Connecticut men gave institutional form to the principles which Hooker had recently defended against Winthrop.

The Fundamental Orders

The breakdown of negotiations for a New England confederation in 1638 prompted the Connecticut men to provide themselves a new instrument of government, formally independent of both England and Massachusetts. The resulting "Fundamental Orders" (Eliot 1910, 63–9) united the three "River Towns" of Hartford, Windsor, and Weathersfield. In this document the settlers of the new towns resolved to "associate and conjoin ourselves to be as one Public State or Commonwealth" and entered "into Combination and Confederation together" for named purposes relating to religious purity and civil order. The structure of the new government contained some imitations of and some departures from that of the Massachusetts colony, but in general it embodied the most salient components of the reformists' agenda there, both those that were enacted as well as some that were not (see Chapter 5 above).

Above all the General Court was named "the supreme power of the Commonwealth" (Art. 10) and was made a representative body by the requirement that towns send deputies (Art. 8) – two of the principal changes made to the Massachusetts constitution in the first few years of its existence. Second, though the governor and magistrates were empowered to convoke special sessions of the General Court besides the two regularly scheduled sessions each year (Art. 6), it was explicitly provided that the freemen could petition against the governor's failure to call a special session, or even against his mismanagement of a regular session; further, that if such a petition were denied the several towns could require their constables to convoke an extraordinary court with full powers. This detailed delineation of the General Court's right of self-assembly effectively pre-empted the sort of standing council that was so controversial at Boston, and its inclusion was judged by Johnston to be "wholly inexplicable" outside the Massachusetts context from which the Connecticut settlers had come (Johnston 1887, 70). He might have added that the Levellers' third and final "Agreement of the People" would, more than ten years later, propose a similar clause providing for the regular election and convocation of representatives by local officers independently of the central authorities (see Chapter 2 above).

In addition to making the representative assembly constitutionally and legally self-sufficient, the Fundamental Orders sought to render all magistrates accountable to that assembly, making them subject to scrutiny "for any misdemeanor" (Art. 10). Another significant codification of the Massachusetts democrats' aspirations, albeit a departure from actual Massachusetts law, was the rule against consecutive terms for governors (Art. 4). On the heels of the Antinomian controversy Winthrop had returned to the governor's chair at Boston for consecutive terms in 1637 and 1638, after Thomas Dudley, John Haynes, and Henry Vane had rotated in that post the previous three years. Such backsliding on the principle of rotation may have provided the immediate impetus for Connecticut's adoption of this provision. This rule against consecutive terms had previously been codified only in Plymouth, in 1636 (Shurtleff and Pulsifer 1968, 1:7).

But the most striking constitutional difference between Connecticut and Massachusetts had to do with the magistrates' "negative voice," the very issue which Hooker's and Haynes's determination to emigrate had brought to the fore in 1634. The Connecticut men showed their sympathy with this vital component of the opposition agenda by providing no magisterial veto over the representative legislature, thus making the magistracy "organically the agent" (Osgood 1907, 1:319) of the General Court rather than its constitutional rival. In effect the governor and the other six magistrates were to have no independent legislative power, again echoing New Plymouth (see Chapter 4 above): their primary duties were judicial and administrative, and otherwise they were merely voting members of the assembly on a par with the other deputies. In the phrase of Hooker's letter to Winthrop, the Connecticut General Court combined "the magistrates and people" in one organ, without a mixing or sharing of sovereignty between distinct chambers.

When set against the Massachusetts background, then, the Fundamental Orders represented a deliberate repudiation of aristocracy, since the colony's better men could not prevent the people's representatives making law by simple majority or even assembling at all. This was precisely the sort of popular unicameral regime which the Bay reformers were never able to push past the magistrates' and ministers' commitment to a "mixed" constitution.

Modern scholars, repulsed by previous Whiggish and jingoistic claims about the Fundamental Orders' anticipatory or pathbreaking significance, have thoroughly deprecated the document's democratic credentials (see Miller 1956, ch. 2; Lucas 1976, 9–10). But this is a misinterpretation predicated on a failure to see Connecticut's first constitution in the terms of its own times.

Democracy in Connecticut

It is noteworthy that those who constructed this new regime in a patent reaction against the discretionary principles prevailing at Boston, like the dissidents directly confronting Winthrop there, never went on record in favor of "democracy." The traditional association of that term with anarchy and mob rule was powerful, but Hooker at least showed signs of dissatisfaction with such traditions even in the 1630s. For one thing, he defended the view that popular rule is safer than princely rule or elite domination. Against Winthrop he wrote, "I must confess, I ever looked at it [magisterial discretion] as a way which leads directly to tyranny, and so to confusion" (Hooker 1860b, 11), thus deliberately shifting the commonplace association of "confusion" with popular participation to elite discretion instead. English publicists like Marchamont Nedham, perhaps in association with the Levellers, would later make a similar point in the middle 1640s, with specific reliance on Machiavelli's *Discourses* (Scott 2003, 136–9).

For Hooker such views were undergirded by the belief that the traditional assumptions about ordinary people's incapacities and the dangers of mob rule were in the process of being made obsolete by divine providence. As he wrote in the preface to *A Survey of the Summe of Church-Discipline* (1648), his *magnum opus*:

These are the times when the people shall be fitted for such privileges, fit I say to obtain them, and fit to use them.... Knowledge shall increase.... The Lord will write his laws in their hearts, and put it into their inward parts.... And whereas it hath been charged upon the people that through their ignorance and unskilfulness they are not able to wield such privileges, and therefore not fit to share in any such power; the Lord hath promised: To take away the veil from all faces in the mountain. (Hooker 1972, a/1a-b; glossing Isaiah 25:7)

This sort of providential populism would later figure centrally in a more heralded and better studied period of democratic thought, the Jacksonian era in the nineteenth-century United States (e.g. Blau 2003, 263–73). But Hooker had a precedent to draw on even in the 1640s, since John Robinson had urged participation by "the less skilful multitude" in the government of churches as a divine imperative (Robinson 1625, 33).

Yet skepticism of Connecticut's democratic credentials has become the conventional wisdom in studies of seventeenth-century New England, in part because the conduct of colony affairs was evidently more aristocratic than theoretic statements or constitutional forms would suggest. By contrast with Massachusetts, there is no record of the impeachment of any magistrates in the Connecticut General Court, nor of the convocation of any General Court against the will of the governor by motion of the freemen. Moreover, though the governor could not serve consecutive terms, re-election was common among the assistants (Osgood 1907, 1:314–15; Jones 1968, 87, 98). It is sometimes thought, therefore, that these aristocratic features of Connecticut life must undermine any effort to make a democratic hero of Hooker. Alternatively it has been alleged, contrary to the evidence of his correspondence with Winthrop, that Hooker never "descended from his pulpit" to get involved in civil affairs (Shuffelton 1977, 232–3).

Certainly as to substantive considerations (suffrage and pluralism) Connecticut was undemocratic – rather like every other early-modern polity – but formal matters of institutions and authority are also important. As consideration of debates in Massachusetts has already shown, and as consideration of constitutional developments in Rhode Island will further show below, a unicameral regime making magistrates accountable to a representative assembly, and representatives themselves accountable to their constituents, came to be recognized as a "democracy" in Hooker's own time. To conceptualize such a system of government, and to give it that name, and further to endorse it as desirable and just, and still further to instantiate it by founding a new state with a written constitution – doing the first of these alone would have been noteworthy in the 1630s; doing them all was a milestone in the modern epoch of the history of democracy. In one sense, of course, the institution, revision, or ratification by popular consent of basic governmental structures represents the kind of politics of which citizens of most late-modern "democracies" can only dream (see Levinson 2006). But the Connecticut founders went still further toward what their contemporaries would have called a democratic "state," in a Bodinian sense, by also introducing regular procedures of accountability in the intervals of moments of consent.

The fact that a small circle of men ordinarily occupied the positions of authority in a small colony cannot undermine Connecticut's achievement. The non-use of the constitutional prophylaxis of accountability as a safeguard against tyranny could as easily be taken to indicate the success as the absence of democratic politics – just as in the modern United States the executive veto is seen to influence legislation even by the possibility rather than the actuality of its use. Moreover, the year-by-year alternation of Haynes and Edward Hopkins in the governor's chair at Hartford (Johnston 1887, 80) is better evidence for the success of the new colony at implementing the Massachusetts opposition's cherished principle of rotation than for its having succumbed to a "political aristocracy" (Jones 1968, 98) of an "unusually oligarchic" kind (Ahlstrom 1963, 418).

If the Connecticut men are to be judged genuine enemies of democratic politics by non-anachronistic standards, the best evidence available has gone wholly unappreciated by modern scholarship. In 1645 an important change was made to the governmental structure laid out in the Fundamental Orders when the magistrates as a body and the deputies as a body were each given a "negative vote" (Trumbull and Hoadly 1890, 1:119). This introduction of functional bicameralism mimicked Massachusetts, with whom Connecticut now had a close and cordial relationship under the aegis of the New England Confederation of 1643.[1] But there is no textual evidence of the rationale for this defection from one of the main articles of the New England democratic creed. It may simply have been down to the puritan tendency to prioritize substantive social concord at the expense of particular institutional forms – a tendency recently activated by civil war in England, which gave New Englanders a larger common cause around which to unite, and by the subsequent, auspicious confederation of all the New England colonies except the contrarian and self-consciously "democratic" Rhode Island.

Not only practices but also ideas are important to the question of Connecticut democracy, and here too contextualization amounts to correction. Miller's mistake about Hooker and Connecticut democracy (see Miller 1956, ch. 2) has been particularly prestigious and baneful. Miller believed he was downgrading Connecticut's democratic significance when he reduced Hooker's political theory to two noteworthy features: "the responsibility of officers to their constituents" and the reference of questions about the founding covenant to popular rather than elite interpretation (47). The second point, as Rossiter long ago pointed out, represented a significant step toward democracy vis-à-vis John Cotton (Rossiter 1953, 169–70). But an equally important consideration for the origins of democratic theory has to do with Miller's first point about "responsibility," where he hit on a crucial

---

[1] The conventional wisdom is that bicameralism did not come to Connecticut, or most other Anglo-American colonies, until after the Glorious Revolution in England in 1689 (Jones 1968, 91; Craven 1969, 135–6), but this judgment refers to physically separate deliberations rather than functionally separate voting.

conceptual development without recognizing it. Miller's failure to appreciate the importance of upholding democratic accountability in the middle seventeenth century supplies a strong argument for integrating the study of American political ideas with the history of political thought more generally.

If Hooker's letters and sermons show his sympathy with the principle of democratic accountability which the Massachusetts opposition deputies both professed and tried to implement, his treatise on church government elaborates his understanding of that principle in not only its ecclesiastic but also its civil applications. More specifically, Hooker's status as a democratic theorist rests on his assembly and deployment of the very conceptual tools found in the modernized ideology of democracy later developed by the Levellers: the commonwealth idea (via the language of *salus populi*), the fiduciary idea (via the language of trust and guardianship), the principle of popular sovereignty, and the accountable conception of political trust.

Trust and Authority

Hooker's *Survey* was meant for an English audience beset by civil war and ecclesiastic uncertainty; in New England, by contrast, the middle 1640s witnessed a convergence of ideological interests and constitutional developments. Initially composed in 1645–6, the manuscript was lost at sea and had to be rewritten in 1647 before its posthumous publication in 1648. Its principal purpose was to defend on behalf of the chief ministers of New England – whose endorsement of the work was indicated in a preface added after Hooker's death – a particular variant of congregational or "Independent" ecclesiology against the Presbyterian attack spearheaded by Samuel Rutherford. But Hooker's *magnum opus* revealed his brand of congregationalism to be more faithful to Robinsonian populism than other New Englanders', even surpassing the Pilgrim Pastor in its powerful analogies between spiritual and temporal government.

Hooker's conception of church authority included the two cardinal principles of consent and accountability, linked by the language of trust. Thus the very existence of a particular church originates in the "covenanting and confederating of the Saints," or in "free consent and mutual engagement" (Hooker 1972, 1:46).[2] It is because of the natural juristic equality of humans – none by nature has "power each over other" – that "free consent" is prerequisite to the existence of "any right or power," and "this appears

---

[2] Because Hooker's *Survey* is divided into four parts, each beginning again with p. 1, it is cited by part:page. The unpaginated preface is cited by sig./fol.

in all covenants betwixt *Prince* and *People, Husband* and *Wife, Master* and *Servant*, and ... in all *confederations* and *corporations*" (1:69). If consent is necessary for the existence of any political society, it is also essential to the designation of specific officers. One of Hooker's chief polemic aims against Rutherford was to establish that "election" is the "causal virtue" assigning a minister to his office and therefore not subordinate and secondary to "ordination," as the Presbyterians held (b/1b). Thus "*Ordination* doth depend upon the *people's lawful Election*, as an *Effect* upon the *Cause*" (2:41).

The popularly elected minister's authority, in turn, Hooker conceived in classically fiduciary terms, using the language of medieval jurisprudence which had been deployed by radical analyses of popular sovereignty in the sixteenth century (see Chapter 2 above). Thus "the faithful Pastors of Christ... all have *Ministerium non Dominium*, are *stewards* not *Lords of God's inheritance*" (Hooker 1972, A/4b). The text is littered with the customary fiduciary labels, together with contrasts between *dominium* and *dispensatio* (cousin to *ministerium*). Thus a pastor is the sort of "shepherd and guide" who holds only an "office and charge," while his flock "submit unto him in the dispensation of his office according to God" (1:72).

Hooker's numerous references to the purposively limited but also accountable character of civil government, particularly at the municipal level, indicate his conviction that the accountable trust applied also to civil power. Generally, as in Robinson, church and state are acknowledged to share the same political nature. Hooker referred to "that resemblance which this policy [of the church] hath with all other bodies politic"; the example then given is "Corporations in towns and cities," an analogy that is resorted to again and again (Hooker 1972, 1:50, 74, 241; 3:2). There is first of all, on Hooker's view, a similarity of origin between the two kinds of authority, in covenant or "confederation": both churches and cities are founded on individuals' "mutual engagements each to other" (1:50). In the city the covenanted community "hath power to choose a Mayor, and to give him authority to do that which they themselves cannot do," but the mayor and other officers, like all other "Agents by counsel," must be steered in their actions "by some common end" (1:187). In short, their authority is purposively limited: "*Salus Populi suprema lex*, it is the highest law in all Policy Civil or Spiritual to preserve the good of the whole" (1:188). Moreover, the people are not powerless, in either church or state, to prevent the betrayal of this purpose: agents may be held accountable, particularly through devices of censure. "They are superior as Officers, when they keep the rule [*salus populi*]; but inferior as Members, and in subjection to any when they break the rule. So it is in any corporation; so in the Parliament. The whole can censure any part" (1:188). Not only did Hooker not shy away from the civil as opposed to ecclesiastic applications of the accountable trust; he explicitly welcomed the comparisons.

If Hooker's fiduciary language was supplied by centuries of European jurisprudence and political philosophy, its democratic import in the *Survey* is best understood in the local context of debates and developments in New England politics. When Hooker first arrived in Massachusetts, John Winthrop had recently answered the Watertown protests by claiming that the colony was more like a parliament than a municipal corporation, meaning that the magistrates could not be called to account outside the annual court of election, and Israel Stoughton later rebutted this argument by likening the Bay magistrates rather to London aldermen (Winthrop 1972, 1:70; Emerson 1976, 149). In the *Survey* Hooker assimilated the two models, parliament and municipality, by placing both under the rubric of the accountable trust, thus reaffirming his affinity with Stoughton's critique of the Massachusetts establishment.

"Censure" and Accountability

In light of the recent acceptance in both colonies of functional bicameralism, there was a convergence between Massachusetts and Connecticut in constitutional form. But in the realm of political theory an important gap was maintained by Hooker's elaboration of the principle of accountability, as illustrated by the analysis of "censure" and "judgment" in Part 3, Chapter 3, of the *Survey*.

The language of censure was an important vehicle for the articulation of ideas of accountability on New England's western frontier, as in the case of Ezekiel Cheever in the New Haven colony, to the south of Connecticut. Cheever, one of New Haven's leading citizens, brought a motion to censure the colony magistrates in 1649. So little did his comrades share his views that his motion not only failed but also triggered his own trial of excommunication from the church he had helped to found – the ultimate censure turned against the would-be censor. In the issue Cheever accepted his excommunication (and concomitant political disfranchisement) and moved to Ipswich (Calder 1934, 93–4), one of the traditional hotbeds of opposition activity in Massachusetts. Hooker's chapter "Of Censures" focused on the process exemplified in the Cheever affair: excommunication by special inquest.

For Hooker the founding covenant of a church implied a duty of "each particular Brother" to keep scrutiny over "all in confederacy with him" (Hooker 1972, 3:33). He recommended that the sanction of wayward members proceed by "a judicial way of process" (3:34), including, for the more serious offenses, a public trial governed by strict rules of evidence designed to establish truth and ensure fairness (3:35–8). Hooker here inserted something of a manual on how to conduct church censures, including two rules for accusers and two for the elders who preside over the trial. After the trial the elders have to present their judgment before the whole congregation, which in turn may answer them and refute their case if the decision seems unjust (3:41–2). This was another example, similar in spirit to but less polemic in purpose than David Calderwood's analysis of parliamentary procedure in *Perth Assembly* (see Chapter 4 above), of the seventeenth-century Calvinist preoccupation with what would now be called "deliberative democracy" – featuring the same goals of justice and conciliation, the same requirements of transparency and "reason-giving."

On this evidence Hooker may have been entertaining a purely discursive notion of democratic accountability, as was typical of Calvinist ecclesiastics. There can be little question about the robustly punitive consequences of censure – banishment in a frontier society – but what appears doubtful relates to the question of who holds power not just to ask questions but actually to settle disputes and render authoritative decisions on censure. In this connection Hooker's *Survey* stands well apart from the previous milestone in the English reception of the New English ecclesiology, John Cotton's *Keyes of the Kingdom of Heaven* (1644). Cotton's work had been seen to press by Thomas Goodwin and Philip Nye, two of the "dissenting brethren" who famously challenged the Presbyterian consensus in the Westminster Assembly, thereby galvanizing the Independent movement in England. Goodwin and Nye's preface to Cotton's *Keyes* torturously attempted to distinguish their favored church polity as a middle way between Presbyterian centralization and "Brownist" anarchy. If Miller and the revisionists were correct in the presumption of widespread consensus around the New England Way, we would expect to find this third way also endorsed in Hooker's *Survey*. Instead we find that Hooker made key departures from the congregational norm, on two registers in particular: the analysis of "judgment" and the classification of regimes.

"Judgment" and Regime

At first blush, some aspects of Hooker's ecclesiastic theory appear to conform to the conventional Aristotelian mixture of aristocracy and democracy. He set out distinct roles for elders and brethren in processes of censure, as we have seen, and he also used the language of "joint" or shared powers between the two groups (e.g. Hooker 1972, 1:191, 3:44). If these gestures were indeed meant to endorse the mixed regime in ecclesiastics, Goodwin's efforts to see Hooker's *Survey* into print (Bremer 1989, 215–16) would have been consistent with the stance taken by him and Nye in the preface to Cotton's *Keyes* four years previously.

But in fact Hooker's analysis of "judgment" decisively undermines the Aristotelian mixed regime in favor of the Bodinian "popular state." Even when speaking of "joint" powers, for instance, Hooker made clear that the elders were superior to the brethren "in *point of rule* and exercising the act of their Office" but inferior "in *point of power of judgment or censure*" (3:45). This distinction between "office" and "judgment" was crucial, corresponding to Bodin's "government" and "state" or Robinson's "government" and "power" (see Chapter 4 above). Hooker even acknowledged his debt to the latter in a passage citing Robinson's *Justification of Separation* for the point that "government" lies in the elders (1:199) but that "the Power of the Keys" lies in the brethren (1:200). He was thereby affirming the view that a true church is, in Bodinian language, a "popular state" though not a "democratic government."

This was the view, as we have seen, first advanced by Robinson, Henry Ainsworth, and John Smyth in opposition to Francis Johnson and other defenders of a more aristocratic regime in the church (see Chapter 4 above). It was against the uncompromising language favored by Smyth in particular that Goodwin and Nye's 1644 preface denied that church power is located "radically and originally" in the people (Cotton 1644, A/2b). It is therefore significant that Hooker's 1648 text directly defies this third-way approach, for he now affirmed exactly the proposition that Goodwin and Nye had recently denied, and in exactly the same terms, by claiming that ecclesiastic power is indeed "radically and originally" in the whole congregation (Hooker 1972, 1:195). The use of this strong Bodinian language set Hooker's *Survey* apart from the usual run of post-Robinsonian congregationalist works.

The proof that Hooker meant to adopt not only the style but also the substance of the Bodinian distinction appears in his treatment of "judgment" as exercised in hard cases of censure. Despite holding, conventionally, that the brethren were normally obliged to accept the elders' sentence in church censures (Hooker 1972, 3:42) – thus appearing to endorse the usual alliance of purely discursive accountability with aristocratic predominance in a mixed regime – Hooker then moved back toward democratic supremacy. If a motion of censure were brought against the elders, he maintained, it cannot be that they "must be complained unto as their own Judges" (3:44), for that would mean that "the inconvenience, which is cross to right reason, remains yet unremoved" (3:45). Rather the "fraternity" is "the supreme Tribunal in point of judgment" (3:43) – a strikingly Bodinian turn of phrase. In this connection Hooker cited Matthew 18:17 ("tell it to the church"), precisely the text to which Robinson and the Pilgrims had given the most populist possible gloss in developing their theory of church power (see Chapter 4 above).

But unlike Robinson, whose advocacy of discursive accountability in the church was designed to forge unity out of diverse opinions, Hooker considered the possibility that unanimity might be impossible to achieve. Thus Hooker's examination of hard cases of censure reveals an even stronger commitment to popular control, as opposed to the mere ratification of elite initiatives, than Robinson had offered. Here he gave a nod to the sort of straight majority voting that Goodwin and Nye had condemned as "democratical" in the church (Cotton 1644, A/4a) and which Winthrop had struggled against in Massachusetts's civil government. In case a church were sharply divided over some question of censure, Hooker first suggested calling in members of other churches as arbitrators, but ultimately, if consensus even then remained elusive, "the major part of the Church hath power and right to proceed and pass the censure according unto Christ, and the rest of the Church dissenting are bound to sit down satisfied therewith" (Hooker 1972, 3:40). This was precisely the rule that had long been followed by the Salem church in contrast to most others in Massachusetts (Gildrie 1975, 53), and it may have been fear of the spread of Salem's example that prompted Goodwin and Nye's protest against "drowning" the elders' voices by unicameralism. Against the congregational norm, then, Hooker's ecclesiastics emphatically excluded the elders' "negative voice," which made quality supreme over quantity.

It is perhaps for this reason that George Lawson, writing a decade after the publication of the *Survey*, called Hooker's ecclesiastics "too democratical" (Lawson 1992, 186). For the ambiguities of "joint" power in Hooker's text are readily resolved within a Robinsonian framework: the "mixture" is not of the Aristotelian but of the Bodinian sort – a democratic "state" reposing legal supremacy in the whole congregation but reserving ordinary administration to a mixed "government." Hooker even followed out the usual implications of Bodin's "popular state" by holding that the people's "causal virtue" of authority in the church did not confine their power "only to consent" (Hooker 1972, 1:197; see also 3:45); popular control must also be included. Accordingly, popular powers of ratification and selection were not enough; accountability was also part of the people's "Power of the Keys" (1:196–7).

Hooker's radically populist conception of authority, his language of "judgment" and "convenience," his contention that exalting discretionary rule over popular control would amount to making trustees judges in their own cases – all this would be rehashed less than half a century later in Locke's *Second Treatise of Government*. For Locke's pithy resolution of disputes over what counts as tyranny replicated Hooker's analysis of church censures in a more legalistic idiom: "who shall be judge of whether his trustee or deputy acts well... but he who deputes him?" (Locke 1988, 2.240). A possible medium of transmission between Hooker and Locke was Lawson, who expressed the difference between fundamental popular power and ordinary governmental power in the language of "real" and "personal majesty" (Lawson 1992, ch. 4) – terms that had first emerged from German commentaries on none other than Bodin in the early seventeenth century (Franklin 1991, 309–12). In turn, Bodin's *Six Books* was a set text at the University of Cambridge (Greenleaf 1964, 125), where a young Lawson matriculated in 1615 at the same college, Emmanuel, from which Hooker departed three years later. Whether from personal remembrances or recent readings, Lawson repeatedly cited Hooker's *Survey* as one of the two most important works on ecclesiology in the congregational vein (Lawson 1992, 13, 155–6, 186, 191–2, 208), and if it is true that Locke read Lawson (Franklin 1978, 88–9, 93–4) then the former might also have found his way to Hooker. The comparison, if not the influence, is especially cogent because Locke's defense of armed resistance offered little scope for regular democratic accountability (see Chapter 2 above). His fiduciary conception of authority and defense of popular judgment were thereby dissociated from institutional means of popular control that had already been realized in Hooker's Connecticut.

Yet Hooker's analysis of church censures also shows how the ecclesiastical model of accountability tends to collapse its two favored mechanisms, special inquests and deselection. A pastor or elder could be tried as occasion arose, and it was clearly understood that the loss of his position was the prime punishment on offer. Hooker supplied an unusually democratic account of the church, but the logic of the church's chief means of accountability could be converted, with minor modifications for civil matters, into the proposition that regular elections alone can effect popular control – as if a motion of censure were offered for every magistrate once a year. This conceptual affinity does not show up in Hooker's text, but it might help to explain why Winthrop's electoral thesis of accountability could find rhetorical purchase with the congregational cast of mind (see Chapter 5 above).

"Democracy"

Like the reformist deputies at Boston, Hooker shunned the language of "democracy"; like Robinson, he applied his political principles directly to churches not civil governments. Yet there is good evidence that Hooker and his readers must have been aware of the favorable implications of his *Survey* for the democratic brand of temporal constitutionalism.

Lawson considered Hooker's ecclesiology "too democratical" because he believed it located supreme power in the *plebs* of the church (the brethren only) rather than the *populus* (the brethren plus the elders) (Lawson 1992, 163). This was certainly a fair interpretation by the standards of Goodwin and Nye's 1644 preface, since Hooker's unicameral and majoritarian scheme would have allowed the quantitatively superior brethren to out-vote the qualitatively superior elders. It is clear that Lawson was also following the Bodinian practice of naming regime types according to "state" rather than "government" (164). In turn, Bodin applied the name "democracy" to precisely the sort of representative, accountable government which the Massachusetts reformers advocated and the Connecticut founders realized. Lawson took a similar analytic view of democracy to Bodin's but regarded it with less normative hostility, observing that "it may be so ordered, as that the exercise of the power may be trusted in the hands of some just, wise, and experienced persons, which either must govern by course, or be removed, lest trusted too long, they engross the power to themselves, or to some few families, or to a faction predominant" (96). Thus Lawson offers the example of a contemporary who regarded the principles of both Connecticut's Fundamental Orders and Hooker's *Survey* as appropriate to democratic politics.

It seems remarkable, then, that Goodwin would have facilitated the publication of a work that defied his and Nye's 1644 preface so directly and, moreover, that leading New England ministers would have publicly supported it. Yet several explanations are available which acknowledge Hooker's patently democratic leanings in favor of formal mechanisms of popular control. In the first place, Hooker stood foursquare with the Massachusetts men against religious toleration (Hooker 1972, a/3b). Since Nye was one of the spokesmen against toleration in the Whitehall debates of 1648 (Taft 2001, 191), he and Goodwin would surely have appreciated the value of Hooker's name as an ally against this key radical demand for substantive rights. Possibly the Independents' solicitation of Hooker to write for an English audience reflected a sense that this matter was of a higher priority than those points on which he patently departed from their norm. Moreover, Cromwell's New Model Army had defeated royalist forces (not once but twice) by 1648, and the army had become an ecclesiastically sympathetic base of power outside the Long Parliament, so that the need for Independents to accommodate Presbyterian sentiment with their structural third way had lessened considerably.

As we have also seen (in Chapter 4 above), mainstream Massachusetts divines were meeting Robinsonian populism halfway by endorsing, in the same year as the publication of the *Survey*, the congregation's right to depose a corrupt minister. Thus the willingness of the likes of Cotton and John Wilson to sign on to Hooker's *Survey* may be considered as part of a general radicalization on questions of extraordinary accountability, including the 1648 Cambridge Platform's countenance of the popular deposition of ministers (Walker 1960, 215) and soon, in civil affairs, Cotton's support of Cromwell in favor of the regicide (Bremer 1980).

Of course not only episodic but also regular accountability was essential for democratic constitutionalism in the civil sphere, and there are signs of Hooker's sympathy for this element of temporal democracy in his treatise on spiritual government. Speaking of his Robinsonian allocation of "judgment" to the brethren and "office" to the elders, Hooker commented, "nor need any man strange at this distinction, when the like is daily obvious in parallel examples" (Hooker 1972, 3:45). Three such civil examples were adduced:

The Lord *Mayor* is above the *Court*: as touching the ways and works of his Office, none hath right, nor can put forth such acts, which are peculiar to his place; and yet the *Court* is *above in point of censure*, and can answerably proceed to punish in a just way, according to the just desert of his sin. Thus the Parliament is above the King, the Soldiers and Captains above their General.

These examples were all taken to illustrate the broadly applicable political principle that "the whole hath power over any member and members, and can preserve her self and safety against any of their power that would annoy or destroy it." All these civil analogies were topical and potent. The first example, of "Mayor" and "Court," invoked the language of not only English municipalities, as we have seen, but also New English colonies, since the assemblies of all the colonies were called "courts." The second, of "King" and "Parliament," signaled New Englanders' sympathy with the original premises of the war against Charles I.

But the third, of "General" and "Soldiers," is the most intriguing because it corresponds with the prominence of populist elements in Cromwell's army associated with the Levellers. As we have seen (in Chapter 5 above), New Englanders were very sensitive about matters of power within military bodies (see also Breen 2001, ch. 1). The Antinomian controversy in 1637 featured threats of mutiny over theological differences, and Winthrop's impeachment in 1645 was precipitated by a dispute over the election of a militia captain. Those who instigated proceedings against Winthrop, in fact, had alleged the right of the soldiers themselves to overrule the appointment of the town and colony magistrates. If Hooker's analogies were part of the first draft of the *Survey* written in 1645–6, fresh in the aftermath of Winthrop's trial and acquittal, they would have amounted to an endorsement of one of the principles behind that impeachment, just as Hooker's analysis of censures endorsed the notion of impeachment in general. During his ordeal Winthrop had recorded his horror at the underlying political theory of his opponents, "as if *salus populi* had been now the transcendent rule to walk by, and that magistracy must be no other, in effect, than a ministerial office" (Winthrop 1972, 1:231). As we have just seen, Hooker explicitly endorsed the maxim of *salus populi* to support his placement of supreme judgment in the whole congregation; as we have also seen (in Chapter 2 above), *salus populi* was among the terms the Levellers had appropriated from the parliamentarians and then radicalized.

The Levellers were, after all, a rising force in Cromwell's army when Hooker's *Survey* was being rewritten in 1647. John Lilburne, Richard Overton, and William Walwyn were then in close cooperation with John Wildman, Thomas Rainsborough, and other "Adjutators" (sometimes called "Agitators") who led a vocal segment of the army's rank and file in challenging Cromwell and his lieutenants to pursue a more radical tolerationist and constitutional agenda. In this context, though opposing the radical agenda as to toleration, Hooker's remark about "the Soldiers and Captains above their General" is striking for what it suggests on the constitutional front. The notion that the principle of democratic accountability also applies to the relationship of soldiers to their commanders could have been a statement of both principled agreement with and moral support for the democratic element of the army, including the Levellers.

This contextual argument about the relation of the *Survey* to contemporary debates in England is bound to remain somewhat speculative, not least because it is far from clear whose ideas the text actually represents. It was a second and probably hastily rewritten draft which was not seen into print by the author himself; at the same time, it is unclear how far the contents of the printed product were determined, or even examined, by the English divines who took it to press or by the New English divines who introduced it with deeply personal tributes to its recently deceased author. What is certain is that at least one conventional assumption about the New England Way must be discarded, either the one about the relation of New England congregationalism to democratic politics or the one about the relation of Hooker to New England congregationalism. For it now appears to be no accident that Hooker had already been involved in something in Connecticut which the Levellers would shortly be promoting in England: the application of the accountable conception of political trust to regular politics through the device of a written constitution.

Democracy in Rhode Island

Only in Rhode Island were the sorts of arguments and constitutional structures developed by the Pilgrims, the Massachusetts opposition, and the Connecticut founders placed explicitly and unreservedly under the rubric of "democracy." This usage was consistently maintained even as the colony moved from a primitive to a modern scale – from a state of nature to village self-government to a federal, representative system. By the later 1640s, after Massachusetts and Connecticut had formed the United Provinces of New England (with Plymouth and New Haven) and subsequently formalized bicameral arrangements in their general courts, the towns around Narragansett Bay stayed on the more democratic path. They formed their own united colony while upholding unicameralism and explicitly applying the language of democracy to it. Their political principles featured not only the democratic prerequisite of popular consent but also a strong form of accountability in service of popular control. If Rhode Island's terminological novelty was initially predicated on the first principle, it was reinforced over time and developed into a settled ideological commitment by reference to the second. Thus Perry Miller's denial of the democratic character of Hooker's commitment to "responsibility" to the people is shown by the example of Rhode Island, in literal terms, to be an anachronism.

Like the towns along the Connecticut River, the plantations around Narragansett Bay originated in the centrifugal forces of dissent in the middle and later 1630s. In the latter case these conflictual origins have been more readily perceived by dint of Roger Williams's famous published exchanges with John Cotton, and the equally well-recorded Antinomian controversy further augmented English settlement in the Narragansett country. While a small party of exiles fled north to present-day New Hampshire, the bulk of them – including John Clarke, William Coddington, and Anne Hutchinson and her husband, William – went south to settle on Aquidneck (a.k.a. Rhode Island proper), across the bay from Williams's town of Providence. These migrants twice over felt themselves to be confronting a legal state of nature, and the principle of consent figured centrally in their search for social order. "We have no patent; nor doth the face of Magistracy suit our present Condition," Williams wrote in Providence's early days; thus "mutual consent hath finished all matters with speed and peace" in fortnightly town meetings (LaFantasie 1988, 1:53). The earliest town record of Providence, a compact made in 1636 whose subscribers were "incorporated together into a town fellowship," with questions to be determined by "major consent" (Rogers 1915, 1:1), set the tone for colonization around Narragansett Bay.

The principle of popular consent, in fact, was of primary importance to the terminological innovation of the Narragansett settlers. The reunion of the Antinomians on Rhode Island in 1640, after a brief split between two towns, Newport and Pocasset (a.k.a. Portsmouth), occasioned a new regime that was denominated a "democratic or popular government" in its founding document (Bartlett 1968, 1:112), a clear instance of a usage not only analytic and non-pejorative but also normative and celebratory. Similarly, when the joint assembly of Rhode Island and Providence Plantations in 1647 declared the new united colony's regime to be "Democratical," they explained that it was "a government held by the free and voluntary consent of all, or the greater part of the free inhabitants" (Staples 1847, 18). The first court of election on the island in 1640 had passed a unanimous resolution to set up a unicameral regime, stipulating that "it is in the power of the body of freemen, orderly assembled, or the major part of them, to make and constitute just laws by which they will be regulated, and to depute from among themselves such ministers as shall see them faithfully executed between man and man" (Kavenagh 1973, 1:343). The Narragansett colonies, then, differed from Connecticut only in their explicit resort to the word "democracy." The absence of predetermined governmental forms required, in both colonies, the construction of new states, and scale was not a differentiating factor: the intimate conditions of the towns around Narragansett Bay were hardly different from the early days of the River Towns. Rhode Island's departure from Connecticut came down to a rhetorical choice made within a distinct political context.

The Colony versus Coddington

Broadly speaking, the political theory of the Connecticut colony followed that of the Massachusetts opposition movement out of which it emerged: democratic in all but name. The Rhode Islanders' use of an unfashionable label was itself a deliberate ideological move, perhaps reflecting a deeper hostility toward Massachusetts whose effects were felt in a series of boundary disputes and other political conflicts throughout the 1640s. But another key ingredient in the democratic persuasion around Narragansett Bay was the galvanizing effect of evidently endemic (albeit patchily documented) intramural conflicts, especially on Rhode Island proper.

Attachment to the term "democracy" originated in the Antinomians' island colonies before moving to Williams's mainland settlement. The fact that this terminology thrived on the island, where land-distribution was based to a much greater degree on ascriptive inequalities of status and rank than it was at Providence (McLoughlin 1978, 21), suggests much about the futility of modern scholars' anachronistic interpretations of seventeenth-century politics. But, equally paradoxically, the fondness for "democracy" on Rhode Island was also related in obscure but important ways to the presence there of one of New England's most aggressive advocates of discretionary rule and elite privilege. William Coddington, whose temperament was once likened to that of a "feudal proprietor" (Andrews 1934, 2:32–3), had been one of the original assistants in the Massachusetts Bay Company when it was first formed in England in 1629. He was regularly elected as a magistrate at Boston and had served as Massachusetts colony treasurer in the middle 1630s before falling in with the losing side of the Antinomian controversy. He joined Clarke, the Hutchinsons, and other exiles on their migration to the Narragansett country but was destined to come into conflict with most of his fellow sojourners at one point or another.

The older histories offer a variety of interpretations of the sometimes confusing records of political conflict around Narragansett Bay. Richman posited an ideological disjunction between the individualism and libertarianism of Williams's Providence and Samuel Gorton's Warwick on the mainland, on the one hand, and a more authoritarian and commercial orientation on the island, on the other (Richman 1902, 1:83–4). Field saw a different divide among the islanders themselves, pitting the democratic tendencies of Portsmouth (led by the Hutchinsons and, for a time, Gorton) against the Newport aristocracy (led by Clarke and Coddington) (Field 1902, 1:47). Neither assessment seems satisfactory.

Only a year after the initial settlement of Portsmouth was made, having been governed by a town meeting professing adherence to Mosaic law, Coddington and Clarke took a party to the other side of the island and founded Newport. The remnant at Portsmouth then made a new compact acknowledging the royal sovereignty of Charles I and naming William Hutchinson governor and eight others assistants. But only a year later, in 1640, the two towns reunited under the governorship of Coddington (Weeden 1991, 53, 57–8). The most plausible explanation of this switch is that the arrival of the eccentric and litigious Gorton in 1639 galvanized differences between Coddington and the Hutchinsons and spurred the former to secede from Portsmouth, but that within a short period Gorton and the Hutchinsons fell out among themselves, allowing the active and ambitious Coddington to return to island-wide pre-eminence (Gura 1984, 368). In any case it is clear that Coddington's ambitions for a kind of personal rule always aroused opposition. Thus the enactment of provisions for making magistrates accountable to the town meeting in 1639 has been interpreted as an anti-Coddington move that may have contributed to his decision to leave Portsmouth in the first place (Weeden 1991, 53; James 2000, 24).

Coddington's relationship with Clarke is an important but obscure part of the story. The two made common cause against Gorton and the Hutchinsons, but by the middle 1640s they seemed to be at odds. Coddington opposed the new parliamentary patent that Williams brought back from London in 1644, as well as the 1647 assembly convened under its aegis, and he intrigued with the Massachusetts authorities in a failed attempt to have Newport annexed by them (as another frontier oligarch, William Pynchon, had already succeeded in doing in Springfield). After the regicide Coddington would obtain his own patent making him governor for life, but this was overturned when Williams, now joined by Clarke, traveled to England and exploited their connections within the Cromwellian regime (Winslow 1957, 244; Warden 1984, 140, 146–7; James 1999, 16–17). On Williams's account it was the 1647 assembly, the one uniting Rhode Island and Providence Plantations as a "Democracy," which instigated a split on the island between one party led by Coddington and another led by Clarke (Easton 1930, 267). Coddington appears to have been motivated by ambition more than doctrine, but the presence of such a determined oligarch may go some way toward explaining Rhode Islanders' unusually active and articulate attachment to democratic accountability.

What is striking is not that Rhode Islanders called the face-to-face democracy of their initial settlements by its conventional name, but that they subsequently clung to the label even after they had united their several towns into a single colony under a federal, representative structure. The difficulty that Coddington encountered in his attempts to realize what he believed to be his due reveals a remarkable degree of consensus among his fellow citizens around an evident ideological attachment. The fact that Williams seems to have had little to do with the early formation of this attachment is noteworthy, but it cannot diminish his importance in developing the fiduciary idea in the political theory underlying Rhode Island's democratic constitutionalism.

Trust and Toleration

Deriving political authority from popular consent, as we have seen (see Chapter 2 above), was more like a fork in the road than the end of the road. Pursuing that road to some practical conclusion about the exercise and limitation of power required passing through the precincts of trust and accountability, making choices along the way about where to turn at key intersections. What are the binding purposes of authority? Who has the right to enforce these purposes? What kind of relationship holds between persons in and out of authority? Williams's writings on politics followed in the usual paths of sixteenth- and seventeenth-century radical constitutionalism, driven largely by the fiduciary idea. This was the engine that powered his famous argument for religious toleration – as in the similar arguments made by contemporary tolerationists in England like the Levellers.

Chief among Williams's writings was *The Bloudy Tenent of Persecution for Cause of Conscience* (1644), the major salvo in his running pamphlet battle with John Cotton. Williams's central point against the meddling of civil government in matters of conscience was supported by analogies of various kinds of "corporation." As Hooker would later do, though more vigorously, Williams insisted that all corporate bodies are essentially alike. The one important point of difference, for Williams, was that the city alone is comprehensive and supreme while all other corporations, including the church, are "particular." Yet the analysis of civil power which followed drew heavily on the classic radical configuration of popular sovereignty, the fiduciary idea, and *salus populi* to produce a limited conception of legitimate authority which excluded all jurisdiction over individual consciences in spiritual affairs. "The Sovereign, original, and foundation of civil power lies in the people.... Such governments as are by them erected and established, have no more power, nor for no longer time, than the civil power or people consenting and agreeing shall betrust them with" (Williams 1644, 137). Williams later put this point even more directly in *The Bloody Tenent Yet More Bloody* (1652): "every lawful Magistrate, whether succeeding or elected, is not only the Minister of God, but the Minister or servant of the people also ... and that Minister ... goes beyond his commission, who intermeddles with that which cannot be given him in commission from the people" (Williams 1652, 96). Therefore it cannot be "lawful for people to give power to their Kings and Magistrates thus to deal with them their subjects for their conscience; nor for Magistrates to assume a tittle more than the people betrust them with" (Williams 1644, 246).

This conception of political power in terms of fiduciary authorization put Williams in line with Englishmen on both sides of the Atlantic. But is civil authority a matter of accountable or discretionary trust? Williams's language of commission and custody implied the former, but no elaboration was forthcoming. In England Richard Overton's *Arrow Against All Tyrants* (1646) would shortly use the accountable trust to define religious persecution as tyranny par excellence and to defend resistance (Sharp 1998, 54–72). But to provide a similar defense Williams would have had to move beyond the limited terms of his analysis and perhaps of his moral compass as well. *The Bloudy Tenent* ultimately does not say what if anything should be done about magistrates who persecute, and it is an essential fact about Williams as a political thinker that he had no theory of resistance. Williams's dialogues against Cotton feature two interlocutors, "Truth" and "Peace." His political theory was tailored especially to the demands of the latter; hence subjects' and especially Christians' obligation, commensurate to would-be persecutors', not to disrupt civil peace. Accordingly Williams's advocacy of toleration came with the indispensable proviso that "good assurance [be] taken according to the wisdom of the civil state for uniformity of civil obedience from all sorts" (Williams 1644, pref.). The closest Williams came to advocating resistance was in his qualified valorization of struggle and strife. On the one hand, he primarily wanted to argue that religious persecution was a form of war-making which fundamentally disturbed the peace of both bodies and souls, thus flouting a variety of Christian imperatives. On the other, Williams did concede that conflict could be necessary, honorable, and godly – precisely against "oppressing, persecuting Nimrods" – but it is not clear that he meant any sort of resistance other than by "religious and spiritual artillery" (17).

It is noteworthy, more broadly, that the early Anglo-American colonies produced no theory of resistance to civil government. The genre itself presupposes a fixed, claustrophobic arena of social action characterized by a kind of political scarcity; also, perhaps, a sense of moral complexity, according to which normally criminal and antisocial behavior may not be quite what it seems. These two prerequisites did not reliably hold on the puritan frontier. The early New Englanders could resist authority in ways outside the scope of classic resistance theory. When one can simply pick up and leave, as Hooker did, there is little need to take up arms against one's rulers or to develop a theoretic justification for doing so. At the same time, the newness and fragility of the early colonies made their inhabitants and especially their governors particularly sensitive about the notion of rebellion. Maintaining even the thinnest frontier veneer of order required that all hints of criminal activity be regarded as straightforwardly unjustifiable.

In short, the institutional state of nature in which English America found itself called for construction not destruction. For this reason the accountable conception of trust had to be channeled away from war and resistance and into the paths of regular constitutional process. Williams's analysis of trust led directly to his colony's attachment to written law: the first articulated legal limitation and the second attempted to provide its institutional vehicles. But Rhode Island's democratic ideology showed itself through constitutional as well as literary practice.

The Rhode Island Assembly of 1647

The earliest documents relating to the government of the Narragansett towns show that their citizens always joined Hooker's two democratic principles: consent through elections was always paired with accountability through non-electoral procedures. At the town's founding in 1639 the citizens of Portsmouth stipulated that within their town "the Judge [governor] with the Elders shall be accountable unto the Body [of freemen] once every quarter of the year," when acts of government were "by them [the freemen] to be scanned and weighed by the word of Christ" (Bartlett 1968, 1:63–4). This formulation of the brethren's right to censure the elders in civil affairs anticipated Hooker's *Survey* by several years but was consonant with the populist, Robinsonian strain in New England ecclesiastics more generally, with accountability as its central principle. The Providence men followed the same principle in 1640 when they superseded their original plantation covenant by creating a board of arbitrators who were to be regularly accountable to the town meeting (Osgood 1907, 1:340).

But the capstone of democratic constitutionalism in Rhode Island was the assembly of 1647. Several months prior to the publication of the Levellers' first Agreement of the People (see Chapter 2 above), Williams's colony put together a framework of government, together with a charter of liberties, which applied the principle of democratic accountability to a representative legislature through the device of a written constitution. Moreover, at a time when both Massachusetts and Connecticut had formalized bicameralism, Rhode Island reaffirmed unicameralism.

The assembly of 1647 compiled a law code, including a statement of immunities similar to (though much shorter than) the Massachusetts Body of Liberties (see Chapter 5 above), and laid down a number of orders relating to basic constitutional procedure. The colony's General Court was to meet at least once a year as a court of election open to all freemen. In other sessions a "representative committee" of the General Court would meet, composed of six commissioners from each of the four towns. The process of legislation was peculiarly federal: either the four distinct town meetings must all initiate a bill, to be ratified by the representative committee; or else the committee must propose a bill subject to the ratification of all four town meetings. In either case, a bill thus passed was to stand as law only until the next annual meeting of the General Court of election, where the whole body of freemen then had the right to accept or reject it (Staples 1847, 12–13).

The magistracy included a colony-wide president and a board of assistants, one drawn from each town, as well as a secretary and treasurer. These and other officers of the colony had to swear an oath "to execute the commission committed unto you, and do hereby promise to do neither more nor less, in that respect, than that which the Colony have [illegible in original] you to do, according to the best of your understanding" (Staples 1847, 13). This sort of limited commission was a cornerstone of the regime of 1647 in Rhode Island, for Article 2 of the law code further reinforced the imperative that an officer not "presume to do more or less than those that had power to call him did authorize him to do" (18). In an evident nod to John Winthrop's rivals in the recent Hingham controversy (see Chapter 5 above), this code also provided for a colony-wide militia in which the members themselves were permitted to "agree of their form and choose their officers" (15). Most importantly, procedures of accusation and impeachment were detailed for different grades of colony officer, so that "no officer in this Colony shall think it strange or hard dealing, to be brought to his fair trial and judgment for what he has done amiss" (60–1). Thus the Hookerian scheme of popular censure of church officers was realized in Rhode Island's constitutional practice. But whereas Connecticut's impeachment provisions are not known to have been used, two Rhode Island magistrates, including the arch-oligarch Coddington, were put out of office in 1648 (Richman 1902, 1:261–2).

This was the regime which the 1647 General Assembly declared "Democratical" (Staples 1847, 18). Their premise was that "Popularity" need not be equated with either "Tyranny" or "Anarchy" (Rogers 1915, 1:156, 158). Even in 1650, when it was provided that the General Court would contain only representatives with town authorization, not freemen on their own account, it was not considered necessary to abjure that form of self-identification. The Rhode Islanders appear to have decided that, in a modern context, a representative government accountable to the whole body of freemen counted as a "democracy."

It is important to note that it was not only magistrates but also legislative representatives who were subjected to a kind of democratic control. Indeed this was the norm all around New England. Practices of close control were central to the self-government of the Massachusetts towns, for instance, where inhabitants kept their elected officials "constantly under their thumb," particularly through the use of written instructions to direct the conduct of affairs. Similar devices were applied to colony-wide representation (see Chapter 5 above).

The township basis of the New England colonies was thus an important factor in representative accountability, and the heritage of English local government supplied some precedent in this respect (Thompson 2001, 49). The municipal corporation seemed especially conducive, by comparison with larger units of local government, to deliberation on how and whether to bind deputies with a particular mandate. Shires in England rarely issued instructions to their knights in parliament, whereas it was not uncommon for corporations and boroughs to do so with their burgesses (Colegrove 1920, 421–3). In 1647, then, the town of Providence found itself following standard New England practice. A set of instructions that their "committees" (as they called their deputies) were required to observe was drafted by Williams and read as follows:

we the greatest part of the Inhabitants of this plantation of Providence, having orderly chosen you at our Town meeting... do hereby give you full power and Authority as Followeth –... Act and Vote for us... as if we our selves were in person... in all General Affairs; and for the settling of the Island in peace and Union; And for all matters that shall concern this particular Town. (LaFantasie 1988, 1:229)

The townsmen, "desiring a careful respect unto these ensuing Instructions," then articulated their most pressing concerns. And they concluded, much in the manner of the metropolitan principals of the Massachusetts Bay and Virginia Companies, with the proviso that "we give you full power on our behalves, to move, and procure any things, (besides these Instructions) that in your wisdom you conceive, may tend unto the General peace and Union of the Colony and our own particular Liberties and privileges, provided you do all or the most of you Unanimously agree therein" (1:229). These instructions show that the freemen of Providence regarded the accountable trust with respect to their most important purposes as consistent with a modicum of discretion in their agents.

The unified Rhode Island regime of 1647 brings the story of the colonial American origins of modern democratic thought to its culmination, applying principles from the earliest conceptions of fidelity and accountability for Anglo-American colonial agency (see Chapter 3 above) to political relations between representatives and their constituents within the government of federated towns. The fiduciary model's non-electoral modes of sanction and localized sites of popular control provided alternatives to some of the classical and ecclesiastical models' features and would soon form part of the Levellers' democratic constitutionalism in England.

The Other New England Way

In ecclesiastics, the Independents allied with Cromwell's New Model Army were more or less in sympathy with the congregationalism celebrated by ministers like John Cotton as "the New England Way." In politics, Cromwell's radical gadflies followed a different sort of precedent recently established in New England.

When advocates of toleration and constitutional reform in England turned the language of trust from king to parliament, they often recounted mythic histories about the origins of representative institutions. The radical line – and one that would be repeated on both sides of the Atlantic throughout the colonial period, down to Milton, Penn, and Paine (see epigraph above) – was that political representation was a practical convenience rather than a moral necessity, that the freemen of England had been accustomed to assemble in person to transact public affairs, and that members of parliament had originated as mere "attorneys," or mandatories, in other words agents to be held strictly accountable to their principals. The Levellers used this historical argument, among others, to press for annual elections, constituent instructions, and a written constitution specifically noting the conditions on which political authority was held, as in a trust-deed (see Chapter 2 above).

But in the 1640s this story about the nature and origins of representative government was more than mythic. The experiences of Connecticut and Rhode Island had recently made it real again.

7

Conclusion

Anglophone Radicalism and Popular Control

Those whom I have been calling the first modern democrats in the pages above made three key theoretic moves in the middle seventeenth century: they advanced (a) the accountable over the discretionary conception of political trust, (b) popular over elite or representative bodies as agencies of accountability, and (c) regular procedures within a legal order over emergent moments of war and resistance as occasions of accountability. In terms of institutional design, they made non-electoral mechanisms of accountability a necessary supplement to the authorization of governors through regular elections. In short, they reconstructed the ancient conception of democratic accountability to fit distinctively modern conceptions of legitimacy, consent, and representation.

Those who first made these theoretic moves were colonists in New England in the 1630s who sought to bring colony officers under the control of the whole body of freemen, whether by reforming existing laws in Plymouth and Massachusetts or by creating new constitutions in Connecticut and Rhode Island. Though these colonial reformers' rationales and arguments are not well represented in the extant documentary record, there are indications from the Rhode Island assembly of 1647 and the town of Providence's instructions to its deputies that they considered their representatives strictly accountable to their local constituents; and, from the correspondence of Israel Stoughton, that they regarded Athenian-style practices of audit, impeachment, and rotation as necessary to control magistrates independently of regular elections. The Levellers' proposals for constitutional reconstruction in England in the later 1640s, rather more amply documented, show more clearly the assimilation of ideas of accountable trusteeship and other forms of revocable agency (attorneys, proxies, stewards, etc.) to the language of representation. However we may conceive representatives today, the seventeenth-century democrats deliberately construed all kinds of political agency according to the accountable trust. At the same time they also accommodated non-electoral accountability, via general legal liability as well as special inquests, alongside regular electoral selection and deselection.

There were two prime alternatives to this kind of radical democracy which attempted to honor the general demand for political accountability while in fact undercutting popular control. The classic Calvinist substitution of an elite "ephoral" body for popular bodies, as popularized in the sixteenth-century debates on resistance, was newly rationalized in England in the next century by resort to the language of representation. Thus the scrutiny and sanction of the monarch by the parliament might be considered "popular" or "democratic" by dint of parliament's representative or microcosmic status vis-à-vis the whole people. Between ephoral theorists' obvious preference for elite action and their apparent desire to have it count as genuinely popular action, there were persistent tensions inherited from Huguenot theorists of resistance. This was the strain of thought which the Levellers attempted to appropriate and radicalize by shifting the locus of democratic accountability from the relation of king to parliament to the relation of representatives to represented.

The other alternative to the radical theory of democratic accountability was contrived in the context of Massachusetts's debates over constitutional reform in the 1630s. John Winthrop remained firmly committed to the discretionary conception of political trust throughout his life, but he was also a shrewd and often conciliatory polemicist. His attempts to beat back campaigns for popular control by directly defending the principle of magisterial discretion always failed to convince a substantial segment of deputies and freemen at Boston. Much more successful, however, was his argument that unicameralism, legal limitation, and non-electoral accountability were not only dangerous but in any case unnecessary for popular control because regular elections were a sufficient mechanism of accountability.

Something like a combination of these two anti-democratic approaches to accountability may be found in the arguments of *The Federalist* on behalf of the United States Constitution of 1787. Winthrop's ironic polemic maneuver in particular underwrote what has since become one of the basic building blocks of modern democratic thought: the electoral thesis of accountability. Perhaps even more ironically, the Levellers appear to have been the first after Winthrop to suggest that regular elections render elected officers accountable to voters by supplying a deterrent incentive against flouting voters' welfare. Yet the Levellers, unlike Winthrop, did not rest their whole case for democratic accountability on this institutional mechanism in order to exclude all other possibilities. They also let it stand on general legal liability and special inquests like audit and impeachment. Thus they followed their colonial precursors by demanding robust institutions of accountability alongside basic democratic institutions of selection and ratification – in other words, a strong conception of popular control alongside popular consent.

This concluding chapter will attempt to spell out how my findings might reorient and provoke future research in several areas: the historical relationships of influence between colonial American and English political ideas, the theoretic contours of models of democratic accountability, the conceptual coherence and practical traction of current theories of democratic deliberation and constitutionalism, and the ways in which democratic accountability might feature in institutional design.

Precedence and Influence

The fact of American precedence begs the question of influence. The scheme of regular accountability proposed for Virginia, in John Bargraves's "Forme of Polisie," languished in manuscript form in the Lord Treasurer's files until the early twentieth century (Newton 1914, 559). New Englanders' ideas of democratic accountability were drawn not from Bargraves or Virginia but rather from their own immersion in classical-republican history, fiduciary-legal tradition, Bodinian jurisprudence, and Calvinist ecclesiology. Though these sources of ideas of accountability were equally available to their contemporaries in England, the American colonists were the first to deploy them in constructing a modern constitutional "popular state," followed shortly by the Levellers on the metropolitan side of the Atlantic. What eastward-moving, trans-oceanic influence could have been at work, if any?

Generally speaking, Englishmen noticed the tiny New England colonies from time to time out of commercial, strategic, ecclesiological, or anthropological interest – not for lessons in civil government. Descriptive and promotional tracts on America included only brief and often inaccurate passages on local government. In private correspondence political questions could be more directly posed, as when William Bradford was required to address the charge that New Plymouth was governed democratically. But the tenor of these exchanges generally can be gauged from the contents of this particular challenge: it had been reported in England that women and children were allowed to vote in Plymouth's General Court (Langdon 1966, 91). The same charge was later laid at the Levellers' door (Harris 2001, 231n).

On the whole, what private correspondence has survived shows relatively scant exchange of political ideas or even political news from New England (see Emerson 1976). Israel Stoughton's letter to his brother John in 1635 is the outstanding exception in this regard but by itself cannot make an argument for significant or lasting influence. What is more suggestive in this connection is Israel's evident expectation that word of the turmoils of the 1634 General Court in Massachusetts would reach John in England independently of Israel's letter on the subject (Emerson 1976, 144).

If news of New England politics was indeed traveling fast to England, there might have been real influence behind certain parallels between constitutional reforms enacted in New England in the middle 1630s and subsequently by the Long Parliament in 1641, the year before civil war broke out. The Triennial Act superseded laws long on the books providing for annual parliaments which had gone unenforced: in the event the king failed to convoke a session of parliament at least once every three years, local constables were now required to arrange for members to be selected and sent to Westminster (Gardiner 1906, 144–55). A similar provision for local initiation of regular assemblies (albeit annual rather than triennial) had already been included in the Fundamental Orders of Connecticut in 1638 (see Chapter 6 above). Also passed in 1641, the Act against Dissolution prohibited the king from dissolving the Long Parliament specifically without that body's own consent (158–9), just as the Fundamental Orders had done vis-à-vis Connecticut's governor and General Court. The correspondence of Winthrop and John Cotton with puritan nobles in England during the 1630s shows that some transatlantic discussion of issues of constitutional design took place, and it may be that Englishmen entered the tumultuous 1640s with some knowledge of the New England democrats' ambitions and achievements. And the English debate over the king's "negative voice" just prior to the outbreak of civil war in 1642 (see Skinner 2002) came several years after Stoughton first wrote home about the debate over a similar power in Massachusetts's board of assistants.

Other evidence for an eastward transatlantic influence relating to ideas of democratic accountability may lie in personal contacts. After the calling of the Long Parliament late in 1640, its notable legislative and other achievements over the course of 1641, and especially the eruption of civil war in 1642, many New Englanders returned to aid the cause of reformation in England (Sachse 1948). Some of these returning migrants, like Israel Stoughton, were veterans of the reformist campaigns in the constitutional conflicts in Massachusetts who would never see New England again. Others, like Roger Williams, took important business on behalf of their colonies into England's new political climate before returning to America. The argument from personal contacts is peculiarly difficult to document, and without undertaking a comprehensive examination I will merely draw its outlines with respect to the figures of Williams and Stoughton.

Williams returned to England in 1644 to negotiate with the parliamentary commission on foreign plantations for a new charter uniting his mainland colony of Providence with Rhode Island proper. While in London he took the opportunity to enter, on the side of toleration and "Independency," the ecclesiastic debates gripping puritan reformers of all stripes. He was reported to have attended the Westminster Assembly of divines and lobbied against a Presbyterian settlement subordinating particular congregations to regional and national councils of elders (Winslow 1957, 186-7). Famously, he also saw into print his *Bloudy Tenent of Persecution for Cause of Conscience* (1644), in which he launched a wide-ranging attack on Massachusetts's policy of criminalizing heterodox opinions and banishing their holders. Williams's fame on this account was such that the *Bloudy Tenent* was publicly burned and named by a preacher before the Long Parliament as one of the four most dangerous books in favor of toleration (198-200). Another of these four was *The Compassionate Samaritane* (1644), standardly attributed to the Leveller William Walwyn (McMichael and Taft 1989, 97-9). At this time the Levellers – Walwyn, Richard Overton, and John Lilburne – had published a great deal on toleration and as yet rather little on constitutional questions.

The association of Williams with the Levellers has often been made in unfortunately vague and complacent terms (e.g. Brockunier 1940, 151), but there is at least good textual evidence for his influence on Overton in particular (Ernst 1931). The Levellers' arguments for freedom of conscience showed some affinity to Williams's, as Overton acknowledged in his *Araignement of Mr. Persecution* (1645). One of the characters in Overton's dialogue, named "Truth-and-Peace" in allusion to both characters in Williams's dialogue, cites *The Bloudy Tenent* as having established the "Impiety, Treason, Blood-shed, etc." of religious persecution (Overton 1645, E/4b, 31). Williams's other friendships within pro-toleration circles included John Milton and Henry Vane. Milton's printer brought out Williams's *Key into the Language of America* (1643) and then followed Williams on his return to Providence in 1645 (Spurgin 1989, 37). Vane and Williams had met during their brief stints in Massachusetts in the middle 1630s, and their friendship was particularly strong during the 1650s, when Williams once again traveled to London to settle his colony's legal status, this time with Vane's and Oliver Cromwell's help. Speaking in 1659 on the eve of the Restoration,

Vane was probably exaggerating his own former feelings for the Leveller program when he said that "it seemed plain to me [in 1649] that all offices had their rise from the people, and that all should be accountable to them" (Judson 1969, 32). But this remark, and his last-ditch proposal that a convention of elected delegates meet to remodel the English constitution (44–5), may have owed something to the example of Williams's colony in 1647, and perhaps to the Levellers' subsequent Agreement of the People.

Another Leveller connection with colonists returning from New England went through Israel Stoughton, who was just one of many Massachusetts men with friends of high consequence in the English Civil War. Stoughton had served with distinction in the war with the native Pequots in 1637 and returned to England in 1643 to join a newly formed infantry regiment under the command of Col. Thomas Rainsborough (Brailsford 1961, 198; Winthrop 1972, 2:245). Two other New Englanders, Nehemiah Bourne and John Leverett, were major and captain in Rainsborough's regiment, respectively, while Stoughton served as his lieutenant-colonel (Williamson 1949, 113). Rainsborough was the symbolic champion of the radicals in the New Model Army whose fame was resurrected by scholars in the twentieth century on account of his speeches at the 1647 army debates at Putney, where he opposed Cromwell by favoring manhood suffrage. He was also a member of the Long Parliament from 1646, one of the army negotiators with King Charles, and among the first public figures to countenance the idea of regicide (117, 122–8). Rainsborough was said to have told Cromwell that "one of us must not live" (109), and after the fulfilment of that prophecy in 1648 the former's funeral was attended by a procession of thousands through the streets of London, with a eulogy appearing in the Leveller newsbook *The Moderate* (140–1). The Levellers wore sea-green ribbons at the funeral and thereafter adopted that color as their own (Ashcraft 1986, 143) because of the Rainsborough family's long tradition of naval service; Thomas himself had fought at sea both before and after his stint in the infantry.

Rainsborough's New England connections revolved around the Winthrops and the Stoughtons: his sister Martha was John Winthrop's second wife, and another sister married Winthrop's son Stephen. His brothers William and Edward joined their sisters in New England in the later 1630s before returning to fight in the parliamentary armies in the 1640s, bringing Stephen Winthrop back with them: William led a regiment of horse which Stephen joined (Williamson 1949, 110). William Rainsborough had been in the Massachusetts militia and was therefore probably well known to Israel Stoughton, and this connection may explain how the latter ended up in Thomas Rainsborough's regiment. Though William's life in Massachusetts is not well documented, he spoke in support of his brother at the Putney debates and later greeted the regicide with enthusiasm. His identification with the Levellers was such that, after their violent suppression by Cromwell's lieutenants in 1649, William was among those discharged from the army (Stephen and Lee 1901, q.v. "Rainborough"). He may well have been the "Rainsborrow" who joined Roger Williams among the grantees of Charles II's royal patent for Rhode Island in 1663, after the Restoration (Bartlett 1968, 2:6).

The influence of Stoughton and his political ideas on the Rainsboroughs and other like-minded soldiers can only remain a matter of circumstantial conjecture. But it is striking how Stoughton's intramural fight against John Winthrop in the middle 1630s appears as a more temperate antecedent of the Rainsboroughs' and other Levellers' intramural fight against Cromwell in the later 1640s. The contests in the Massachusetts General Court and in the New Model Army both pitted unicameralism coupled with democratic accountability against the classical mixed regime coupled with elite discretion (Maloy 2007).

The evidence of American influence on England, then, is more suggestive than conclusive. But the story of the colonial American origins of modern democratic thought more generally, like all such stories, begs as many historical questions as it answers; in short, it begs further research. Its interest for political theorists in any case must also depend on the conceptual insights it offers.

Three Models of Accountability

The most basic lesson for modern democratic theory arising from the story of the genre's origins has to do with the centrality of the principle of accountability as distinct from notions of consent and institutions of selection and ratification. None of the first modern democrats denied the primary importance of popular consent – in fact they loudly proclaimed it – but what distinguished their political theories from their contemporaries', and from most democratic theories today, was the firm partnership with popular control to which consent was tethered. Respecting this seventeenth-century partnership would require embracing robust non-electoral institutions of accountability, whether these be regular or occasional, periodic or episodic. In this connection the stories of theoretic development recounted above have highlighted three models of democratic accountability which encapsulate important conceptual resources for renewing democratic theory's commitment to accountability.

The *classical*-republican model of accountability draws inspiration from historical republics, especially ancient ones, in which public liberty or welfare is regarded as the result of mutual checks, including relations of scrutiny and sanction, among various political bodies. Classical accountability is thus predicated on the sort of mixed regime analyzed in Aristotle, Polybius, and Machiavelli, in which agencies rooted in specific social classes check one another's maneuvers toward domination. The popular bodies in charge of scrutiny and sanction are either randomly sampled from or else representative of the lower classes, as in the Athenian *dikasteria* (jury courts) or Roman tribunes. The classical model's favored mechanism of control is the quasi-judicial inquest, as in John Bargraves's proposed standing grand jury for political crimes in Virginia, as well as the episodic trials of impeachment advocated and practiced by Winthrop's opponents in Massachusetts.

The *ecclesiastical* model is derived from the Calvinist notion that every member of a particular church is subject to the scrutiny of every other and to sanctions handed down by those in authority; holding figures of authority themselves accountable is a special case of this. The favored mechanism of ecclesiastic censure was the special inquest, specifically a public trial of impeachment. In English puritan churches, where a pastor or elder typically held his position for life, this was simultaneously the principal means of deselection, by which the congregation could depose its pastor and install a replacement. In civil government, however, the notion of regular elections intervened to offer a distinct avenue of deselection. The importance of the latter mechanism in the ecclesiastical model arises from the characteristic puritan zeal for bringing high men low when they err, and it is probably from this motive that English Calvinists arrived at their innovative conception of regular elections as devices of punishment rather than merely procedures of selection. The prime agency of accountability in this model is one of universal composition, in other words the whole congregation, and the guiding rationale is some kind of metaphysical truth – the maintenance of true religion, the fulfilment of divine justice, and so on – with the harmony and cohesion of the community itself often considered corequisites of this.

The *fiduciary*-legal model of accountability begins by conceiving political power in terms of relations of agency such as guardianship and trusteeship. It emphasizes the right of a unitary, Bodinian legal superior to control its delegated agents by scrutiny and sanction, relying on the sorts of judicial procedures and rules of liability found in Roman and English law. Fiduciary accountability is versatile as to mechanisms of control, running the gamut from special punishments following regular audits or episodic

Conclusion

trials, to general legal liability, to deselection and replacement. The fiduciary model militates against representative agencies in favor of randomly sampled or universal ones. This tendency of thought was crystallized by the Levellers, who recognized that a body of representative agents holding others accountable on behalf of the people merely begged the question, within a fiduciary framework, of how to hold the representative agents themselves accountable. As to rationale, the formal logic of this model suggests popular control as an end in itself, or perhaps as the prime criterion of legal justice – what some might call "democratic legitimacy" today. But all kinds of higher purposes could be attributed to the people as trustor and thereby made enforceable against the trustee, and the Levellers alone loaded divinely given natural rights, positive English liberties, the communal imperative of *salus populi* ("the safety of the people is the supreme law"), and the restoration of true religion onto democratic accountability's burden of expectation.

The classical and ecclesiastical models appear to suggest contrasting and influential approaches to democratic accountability. The classical approach is quite comfortable with class-specific and representative agencies, which it seeks to endow with punitive powers in the name of robust popular control – accountability with teeth. The ecclesiastical approach insists on the participation of the entire membership but endows it with more limited discursive functions that stop at selection and ratification – accountability by the tongue. With some modifications, the contrast between these two models of accountability reflects basic differences between more "republican"- and more "liberal"-leaning approaches to democratic theory today: the first countenancing a more active but perhaps less inclusive politics; the second, one more inclusive but perhaps less active.

Both these models embody definite aristocratic or elitist tendencies. The classical model has historically been inseparable from a mixed-regime republicanism which, on the one hand, invites institutional competition in which elite bodies usually prevail over their popular rivals (McCormick 2003, 630–1); and, on the other, allows the popular agencies themselves to be taken over by elite elements, as modern legislatures and political parties have powerfully demonstrated. In short, the classical model's reliance on mutual checks among centralized, national institutions sits uneasily with the norm of popular control. For its part the ecclesiastical model is equally prone to underwriting elite domination. In the hands of most English puritan ministers, to begin with, it was often assimilated to the classical ideal of the mixed regime in order to give the elders decisive sway over the brethren. But the reason for this elitism goes deeper than historical imagination: the maintenance of true religion and communal purity was considered to require what

McCormick has found is also typical of the dominant "oligarchic" strain of republicanism – that ordinary people "acclaim but not determine" the major public decisions taken by their betters (630–1). The roots of this aristocratic strand of the ecclesiastical model are best seen in John Winthrop's claim of elite superiority as to *logos* generally and scriptural as well as legal interpretation more specifically.

The classical and ecclesiastical models of accountability, then, are each a house divided. John Robinson and Thomas Hooker set up on the democratic side of the second house, in opposition to the usual Calvinist presumption of elite superiority, by identifying popular control itself as part of a grand providential design. McCormick has recognized a similar split in the first house and has urged Machiavelli as the champion of the democratic side thereof, since he made a formally similar sort of presumption (McCormick 2003): that the many are more trustworthy than the few, not by reference to providential ends but in respect of guarding public liberty.

Ultimately what distinguished the first modern democrats' political thought, however, was more than their populist sensibilities; it was their overcoming of the aristocratic tendencies in the classical and ecclesiastical conceptual frameworks by resort to the third, fiduciary model of accountability. This sort of move was explicitly theorized for the church by Robinson and Hooker and debated and practiced for the state by the Massachusetts opposition and the Connecticut and Rhode Island founders in the 1630s and 1640s. The civil reformers in particular went beyond the discursive or acclamatory function associated with selection and ratification by introducing Athenian, Bodinian, and English-law precepts of accountability: they radicalized the ecclesiastical model, placing it on more securely democratic foundations, only by importing institutions of power from other traditions.

Later, in England, the move was executed again by the Levellers; only in this context they were transcending rather the classical model. The Roman tribunes cited in some early Leveller writings were hardly more promising as vehicles of democratic power than the Spartan ephors dear to the Huguenots. If it is true that Marchamont Nedham was behind the handful of Leveller pamphlets that explicitly invoked Machiavelli, Nedham's subsequent opportunistic turns as a royalist and a Cromwellian caution against taking the notion of Leveller Machiavellism too seriously. In the end the Levellers did not embrace the idea that England could have tribunes, since the only plausible institution for that service turned out to be, in their eyes, a very corrupt parliament. Instead they relocated sites of political accountability from the center to the periphery, in other words to local constituencies, precisely in order to make the would-be tribunes themselves subject to popular control. In this respect they were repeating what had happened in New England, where non-electoral accountability was extended (most explicitly in Rhode Island) even to relations between constituencies and their representatives. The legal fiction of a unitary Bodinian trustor was thereby disaggregated into a reality of localized sites of popular control. Whereas Tocqueville famously credited the New England town meeting with fostering America's democratic culture, the seventeenth-century democrats show that, through its powers to convoke central assemblies and to control their members, its primary achievement was to institutionalize democratic power in a modern setting.

Deliberationism and Constitutionalism

My analysis of the three seventeenth-century models of accountability puts us in a position to see that democratic theory's recent excursions into the concept of deliberation are reminiscent of the ecclesiastical model in particular. Their treatment of the cardinal principle of modern democratic thought, accordingly, carries a credible threat of passing off aristocratic power as "democracy." This distant genealogy of deliberationism is doubly important because, notwithstanding some critics' allegations of impracticality, Cass Sunstein has given recent theories of deliberation a plausible point of entry into the worldly concerns of constitutional design.

The term "accountability" is frequent in deliberationist writing and names a chapter in Amy Gutmann and Dennis Thompson's *Democracy and Disagreement* (Gutmann and Thompson 1996, ch. 4) in recognition of its place among "the chief standards regulating the conditions of deliberation" (Gutmann and Thompson 2004, 133). Compared with the seventeenth-century Anglo-American democrats, however, deliberationists employ a notion of accountability which has not only a smaller stature but also a different character. Only one of fifteen chapters in a collection responding to *Democracy and Disagreement* gives accountability more than a passing mention (Macedo 1999, ch. 14), and the more astute readers of deliberationist theory tend to pass over accountability in favor of the other two "chief standards" (e.g. Garsten 2006, 176, 194). More to the point, however, the general criticism that deliberationism ignores power (see Shapiro 1999) applies with full force to its rationalist and purely discursive conception of democratic accountability.

The thesis of Gutmann and Thompson's chapter is that deliberative processes within a given jurisdiction must be "accountable to" those formally outside the jurisdiction who are nonetheless affected by a given policy (Gutmann and Thompson 1996, 145–51). What is required is that outsiders' points of view be taken into consideration, not that they hold any authority in the decision-making process itself or wield any means of sanction over the decision-makers. "To respect the principle of accountability, representatives must give reasons to their constituents and respond to criticisms from them" (351), and the injunction to "listen to and communicate with" them appears to close the issue (Gutmann and Thompson 2004, 30). This is the language of scrutiny but not sanction, leaving little in the way of power – that is, little *kratos* for the *demos*. It depicts the face of democratic accountability with a tongue but no teeth.

This aloofness from active, coercive power helps to explain deliberationists' regular declarations against "direct" popular participation (Sunstein 2001, 7; Pettit 2003, 154; Gutmann and Thompson 2004, 30–1). But the choice between the inert ballot-casting consumer and the full-time active citizen would have held little appeal for the first modern democrats – and it may also be a false alternative today. Though democratic deliberation is itself an attempt to conceive a middle range of participation between these alternatives, pejorative references to "direct" democracy raise the historically grounded suspicion that Platonic guardianship is behind this fight for the supremacy of *logos* (cf. Shiffman 2004). Nadia Urbinati, by contrast, has recently sought out a new conception of democratic participation by reconceiving representation in terms that are simultaneously "deliberative" and "democratic" (Urbinati 2006, 3–4), but the first modern democrats' structures of regular accountability offer a straighter path to popular control. They meant to confer this control not only on leisured elites but also on ordinary citizens who left their farms and trades only a few times a year. Granted that modern mores may require modifications in how agencies of accountability are substantively composed, their formal principles might yet be institutionalized today, as we will shortly see.

The origins of the deliberationist embrace of the discursive, rationalist facets of accountability lie in Calvinist ecclesiastics. When faced with the threat of disagreement and heresy, the opponents of democratization in the church relegated popular power to a merely auditory, consensual, and acclamatory role. Even the exceptionally populistic John Robinson contemplated a purely discursive notion of accountability in his later confrontations with problems of ecclesiastic disunity (see Chapter 4 above); a parallel move was made for civil government by anti-democrats in Massachusetts. The story of their rivals, by contrast, reminds us that modern democracy was originally about not just reason but also power. In light of deliberationists' frankly stated aim to remodel democracy to meet the demands of deliberation (Gutmann and Thompson 1996, 347; Pettit 2003, 138), we might turn to the seventeenth-century Anglo-American radicals to recall what the substantive ("democracy") meant before it succumbed to the adjective ("deliberative").

Reorienting democratic theory's conceptual compass toward accountability and popular control would also affect how we assess basic problems of legal theory and constitutional design. The story of the first modern democrats offers a distinctive and critical angle of vision on four points of conceptual contact between democracy and constitutionalism: (a) respecting *constituent power* but without resort to legal entrenchment, (b) accepting *legal limitation* but on different terms, (c) doing without *judicial review* thanks to regular accountability, and (d) undermining the democratic credentials of *multicameralism*, with its "checks and balances" among differentiated agencies of government.

The least problematic issue between democracy and constitutionalism is the idea of *constituent power*, which embodies the legal supremacy of the whole people in paramount law. This principle was adduced whenever Bodinian sovereignty was radicalized by being reposed in the whole community. The New England democrats substantially recognized this principle in various ways, but not by strategies of legal entrenchment, such as applying different voting rules for changing ordinary as opposed to fundamental laws. Regular forms of accountability were presumed to activate the supremacy of the people over governing elites, as expressed by the fiduciary logic of superior and inferior powers in government. As recent work on the intellectual history of legal entrenchment has shown, it is the fruit of an anti-democratic family tree (Schwartzberg 2007).

Entrenchment is conceptually distinct from *legal limitation* and its current institutional companion, judicial review. The most notable recent attempt to reconcile these with democratic values is Sunstein's deliberationist approach to constitutional design, in which the purpose of legal limitation and judicial review is not so much to invalidate acts of government as to suspend them until their enactment or ratification by a truly deliberative process, so that "government power will be unavailable to those who have not spoken with those having competing views" (Sunstein 2001, 4–5, 240–1). This reasonable proposal participates in a long tradition, as we can now see, of *logos* over *kratos*, ratification over accountability, and consent over control.

The first modern democrats' embrace of legal limitation in charters of fundamental rights was not based on such faith in a reasonable aristocracy. The Massachusetts law-reform movement's achievements were meant to bind the magistrates but not the General Court; in this sense legal limitation shared the same rationale of popular control as non-electoral procedures of accountability. But most distinctively oriented toward popular control was the first modern democrats' pioneering use of written codes. The essential relevant fact was that the law was (as it still is) an established institution of social power, an arena in which individuals and families can be made and unmade. Turning the law to popular purposes was therefore a common objective among puritans and other legal reformers on both sides of the Atlantic in the seventeenth century (Warden 1978). As the Levellers and others made clear, codification and simplification of the law were meant to make the resources of this power more widely available – or at least the ability to avoid its potential depredations. John Lilburne referred to a notion of justice both cosmic and social in describing the rationale behind the Agreement of the People:

The conclusion that I draw from God's subjecting of all men equally alike to his law is by way of advice to all my countrymen... that the powers of King, Parliament, and people may be distinctly and particularly declared and settled, so that we may be no longer in confusion, by having the little ones to be subject to the punishment of the law, and the great ones to be subject to none but their lusts and the law of their own wills. (Lilburne 1648, proem)

Thus written constitutions were part of a wide-ranging democratic literacy campaign, one component of which was a leveling of the playing field inside courts of justice; another, the provision of a sort of trust-deed by which the people might be able to judge, and then to sanction, the performance of their political trustees. Using a written constitution to democratize politics in this way was later behind Thomas Paine's celebration of the 1776 Pennsylvania constitution as a "political Bible" that belonged in every household (Paine 1987, 287).

Recent defenses of the democratic credentials of legal limitation, however, assume a very different character by dint of their attachment to *judicial review*, which is conventionally taken for granted as its primary enforcement mechanism. The first modern democrats had no use for it: limitations were supposed to be enforced by ordinary (elected and accountable) officers, not an insular council of expert interpreters. By the same token the Levellers, for instance, belong to the tradition of democratic thought which identifies legislators rather than judges as the most appropriate agents of legal change (Schwartzberg 2007, ch. 3). The nearest equivalents today to the negative voice belonging to the magistrates in early Massachusetts, arguably, are the powers of the United States Supreme Court and equivalent bodies within

American states. Modern judicial review could only be passed off as an instrument of democratic accountability after genuinely popular agencies had already been relegated to consent rather than control vis-à-vis officers of government.

This passing-off was the historic achievement of *The Federalist*, no. 78. As we can now appreciate, judicial review was polemically placed in its by now entrenched position in the American political tradition, in the 1780s, by the same kind of argument by which the electoral thesis of accountability was first broached in the 1630s and 1640s. In defense of the newly proposed Constitution, the pseudonymous "Publius" exalted the federal judiciary as a kind of guardian protecting the people from their representatives – much as the Huguenots had done by interposing ephoral elites between the French people and their king. The wonder of this image's continuing power in American political culture generally, and in political and legal theory particularly, lies in its strategic irony. Publius had previously attacked the very idea of democratic accountability as dangerous and unnecessary (*The Federalist*, nos. 10, 51), and an unsympathetic reader of no. 78 might have considered that its argument for judicial guardianship begged the question of why the people had been demoted to the status of legal minority in the first place. But at times Publius also claimed, polemically, that the Anti-Federalists' opposition to the Constitution was self-defeating, that they were unwittingly undermining their own values. No. 8 had cleverly made this point about their opposition to a standing army; no. 57 had done similarly for the Constitution's electoral arrangements by arguing, in the spirit of Winthrop, that biennial elections would place representatives under their constituents' control through a variety of psychic pressures. Now no. 78 was making the same polemic gesture again by suggesting that the federal judiciary (of which the Anti-Federalists were intensely suspicious) would in fact be the vehicle for the people's constituent power (of which the Anti-Federalists heartily approved). This was Winthrop's polemic strategy all over again: he always opposed democratic accountability as a general principle and appeared to accept it only when striving to convince his opponents to give up their specific institutional demands. Winthrop's irony has been even more successful in the long run than it was in its own day, just like the irony of *The Federalist*, no. 78. Thus America's contribution to two of modern democracy's cardinal propositions about institutional design began with this sort of anti-democratic irony.

A fourth idol of modern constitutionalism, perhaps even more universally revered than judicial review (the American instantiation of which is peculiar), is *multicameralism*. The New England reformers and the Levellers, it is true, were at times opportunistic about questions of structure. After all, the Bodinian protocols of regime analysis allowed "government" to be mixed while the "state" remained unitarily democratic. Yet the Anglo-American democrats tended to favor a unicameral voting assembly: when faced with disagreement between popular and elite sectors within their communities their solution was the power of the former not the reason of the latter. On the other side, the committed partisans of the Aristotelian mixed regime, whether in church or state, were constantly marshaling arguments against "drowning" the votes of the notable few in a single chamber. Though advocates of a deliberationist approach to constitutional design have recently reaffirmed their commitment to the mixed regime (e.g. Sunstein 2001, 7), latter-day constitutional reformers have begun to cast doubts on multicameral arrangements (e.g. Levinson 2006, 29–49). We are now in a position to see that this second perspective represents a rehoisting of the tattered standard of modern democracy.

Institutional Design

Ultimately the challenge posed by the first modern democrats for political theory today is to investigate the possibilities for institutional designs responsive to their distinctive version of democratic constitutionalism and its core principle of accountability. Their perspective, contrary to that of some recent critics (see Shiffman 2004, 113; Garsten 2006, 14, 20, 200–9), would find no remedy for deliberationism's defects in the institutional status quo of the present-day United States. Political crisis in Virginia produced a wave of institutional-reform proposals in the 1620s, but no similar wave has appeared in American political thought in a hundred years or more. Yet the fiduciary model of accountability bids us to think outside conventional institutional bounds, and in particular beyond two tempting targets of reform: elections and parties.

The electoral thesis of accountability is still widely accepted today, in defiance of not only the logic of the first modern democrats but also the evidence of considerable modern experience (see Przeworksi et al. 1999). It has been especially crucial for the conventional rational-choice model of American democracy – as opposed to the neo-Schumpeterian, "minimalist" model for which accountability represents dispensable and in any case unrealizable values (e.g. Przeworski 1999). Thus the "electoral connection" between individual representatives and their constitutencies was seen in the later twentieth century as a rescue for democratic accountability from the perceived decline of political parties in the United States (Mayhew 2004, xi, 6). Mass parties, in turn, have usually been conceived as tribune-like institutions, but their oligarchic operations in fact are not only a formidable obstacle in their own right but also, arguably, a key reason for the failure of elections as mechanisms of democratic accountability.

In light of this failure Manin and others have recently called for the creation of non-electoral, nonpartisan "accountability agencies" (Manin et al. 1999a, 50; Manin 1999b, 24). The classical model, with its emphasis on an old-fashioned conception of active democratic control, has something to offer in this regard. But it needs to find ways to render its favored centralized agencies, which tend to suggest representative assemblies and national parties, invulnerable to elite domination and subject to popular control. One possibility is that selection by lottery rather than election might neutralize the model's vulnerabilities to aristocratic power – a device that could conceivably help to staff formal institutions of decision-making but not political parties as we currently understand them.

McCormick's proposal of a Tribunate Assembly for the United States, for instance, partially answers the call for specialized bodies of accountability by accentuating the populist, Machiavellian strand of the classical-republican tradition (McCormick 2006). The powers of McCormick's Assembly would include one veto per year in each of the legislative, executive, and judicial fields of action; one calling of a national referendum; and one impeachment of an officer of the national government (160). If this body, selected by a mixture of random and representative sampling – that is, by a lottery weighted to ensure descriptive representation – could be considered a microcosm of the whole citizenry, its vetoes would strengthen the element of popular ratification in American national politics, as would its power of referendum. But those powers still leave out accountability properly speaking – scrutiny and sanction – which the impeachment power of McCormick's Assembly is meant to satisfy. This last power renders it, in part at least, a specialized accountability agency similar to John Bargraves's proposed Syndex for Virginia (see Chapter 3 above), except that the former is lotteried while the latter was elected. In any case the Tribunate Assembly, like the Syndex, would have real authority, not just the right to ask questions and have them heard; thus it captures the spirit of the first modern democrats better than the current deliberationist alternatives.

Another essential feature of McCormick's proposal which partakes of the classical model of accountability is its predication on the old-fashioned class-based understanding of politics found in the Renaissance Italian city-republics. Given today's patterns of political and socio-economic stratification, it would be natural if democratic theory's rediscovery of class (see

Hanson 1989) went hand in hand with its re-emphasis on power. Here is another stark difference between the classical and ecclesiastical models of accountability, since the latter tended to deny class distinctions.

But the first modern democrats' fiduciary model bids us to go beyond McCormick's partial answer to the call for non-electoral "accountability agencies." The scrutinizing and sanctioning functions of New England's colonial courts might be relocated to the local levels of a large modern state, as in the Levellers' proposals for local commissions for auditing individual members of parliament (see Chapter 2 above). Among the three mechanisms of regular accountability that we have encountered, only one featured prominently in all three models of accountability in the early-modern period: the special inquest. And this is the one that is most salient today, whether in periodic or episodic form. The current challenge for institutional design, then, may most usefully focus on the two principal vehicles of the special inquest: regular audits and episodic impeachments.

The "citizen jury" has been recently proposed in the name of "deliberation," to make ordinary people more reasonable but not more powerful (Fishkin 1991, 1995). A similar sort of body might be made acquainted with *kratos* at the same time as *logos* if one were assigned to every elected officer of the United States and given powers not of advice but of scrutiny and sanction. A national lottery for the president, state-wide lotteries for members of the Senate, and district-wide lotteries for members of the House of Representatives could be used to staff these juries, and the massive pools of citizens even in the congressional districts could justify a lifetime limit of one term of jury service per citizen.

Following the first modern democrats' example, the powers of a "constituent jury" might be both periodic and episodic. On the one hand, a regular audit of each elected officer might be conducted at six- or twelve-month intervals, with a schedule of rewards and punishments to apply according to the jury's verdict. At the same time, the jury might have the episodic power to suspend an officer, pending a trial of impeachment (as was done to guardians in Roman law; see Chapter 2 above), by vote of some supermajority on any emergent occasion. Such a scheme would institute powers contemplated by the New England reformers, apply them at the Levellers' preferred level of representative-constituency relations, and locate them in a single-purpose body after the example of Bargraves.

Whereas a prime worry of deliberationist theory today concerns the dangers of "direct" popular participation, participation on these "constituent juries" would not be more frequent, intense, or "direct" than service on juries for civil and criminal trials. The prime concern that has always underlain opposition to the Anglo-American trial jury is that ordinary people cannot be relied on to get at the truth – the same motive behind those seventeenth-century exponents of the ecclesiastical model of accountability who sought to prevent heresy by hedging popular power.

As with McCormick's Tribunate Assembly, my proposal of a "constituent jury" may be regarded as in the first instance heuristic, since key questions of institutional design remain to be resolved. One in particular concerns the substantive question of the jury's composition, and indeed McCormick's analysis of selection techniques (McCormick 2006, 156–9) and suggestion of a weighted lottery for his Tribunate Assembly are promising by comparison with the electoral means of selection preferred by Bargraves and, generally, the New England reformers. It would be in the intersection of the substantive themes arising from the institutional heuristic I have introduced, and the formal principles arising from my analysis of the colonial American origins of modern democratic thought, that the details of a revised conception of democratic participation might be worked out. As the first modern democrats might have reflected after the mixed results of their various battles, there is work yet to be done.

Bibliography

Adams, J. T. 1921. *The Founding of New England*. Boston: Atlantic Monthly.
Ahlstrom, S. E. 1963. "Thomas Hooker: Puritanism and Democratic Citizenship." *Church History* 32: 415–31.
Ainsworth, H. 1608. *A Counterpoyson*. Amsterdam: G. Thorpe.
Althusius, J. 1995. *Politica*, trans. F. S. Carney. Indianapolis: Liberty Fund.
Ames, W. 1968 (1629). *The Marrow of Theology*, trans. J. D. Eusden. Boston: Pilgrim.
Anderson, D. 2003. *William Bradford's Books*. Baltimore: Johns Hopkins Univ. Press.
Andrews, C. M. 1933. *Our Earliest Colonial Settlements*. New York: New York Univ. Press.
　1934. *The Colonial Period of American History*. 4 vols. New Haven: Yale Univ. Press.
Aristotle. 1998. *Politics*, trans. C. D. C. Reeve. Indianapolis: Hackett.
Armitage, D. 2000. *The Ideological Origins of the British Empire*. Cambridge, U.K.: Cambridge Univ. Press.
Ashcraft, R. 1986. *Revolutionary Politics and Locke's Two Treatises of Government*. Princeton: Princeton Univ. Press.
Ashton, R. 1851. "The Exiles and Their Churches in Holland." *Works of John Robinson*, vol. 3. London: J. Snow.
　1852. "Memoir of Rev. John Robinson." *Collections of the Massachusetts Historical Society* 1 (4th ser.): 111–64.
Bacon, F. 1864. *Works*, eds. J. Spedding, R. L. Ellis, & D. D. Heath. 15 vols. Boston: Taggard & Thompson.
Ball, T., & R. Dagger. 1999. *Political Ideologies and the Democratic Ideal*. 3rd ed. New York: Longman.
Bargraves, J. 1914 (1623). "A Forme of Polisie," ed. A. P. Newton. *American Historical Review* 19: 560–78.
　1922 (1623). "Proposicions Concerning Virginia," ed. A. P. Newton. *American Historical Review* 27: 511–14.

Bartlett, J. R. (ed.). 1968 (1865). *Records of the Colony of Rhode Island and Providence Plantations*. 10 vols. New York: A.M.S.
Battis, E. 1962. *Saints and Sectaries: Anne Hutchinson and the Antinomian Controversy in Massachusetts Bay Colony*. Chapel Hill: Univ. of North Carolina Press.
Baumgold, D. 1993. "Pacifying Politics: Resistance, Violence, and Accountability in Seventeenth-Century Contract Theory." *Political Theory* 21: 6–27.
Billings, E. 1659. *A Mite of Affection*. London.
Blau, J. L. (ed.). 2003 (1954). *Social Theories of Jacksonian Democracy*. Indianapolis: Hackett.
Block, J. E. 2002. *A Nation of Agents: The American Path to a Modern Self and Society*. Cambridge, Mass.: Harvard Univ. Press.
Bodin, J. 1962 (1606). *The Six Bookes of a Commonweale*, trans. R. Knolles, ed. K. D. McRae. Cambridge, Mass.: Harvard Univ. Press.
 1986 (1593). *Six Livres de la Republique*, eds. C. Fremont, M.-D. Couzinet, & H. Rochais. 6 vols. Paris: Fayard.
 1992. *On Sovereignty*, trans. J. H. Franklin. Cambridge, U.K.: Cambridge Univ. Press.
Borgeaud, C. 1894. *The Rise of Modern Democracy in Old and New England*, trans. A. B. Hill. London: S. Sonnenschein.
Bradford, W. 1952. *Of Plymouth Plantation, 1620–47*, ed. S. E. Morison. New York: Knopf.
Brailsford, H. N. 1961. *The Levellers and the English Revolution*. London: Cresset.
Breen, L. A. 2001. *Transgressing the Bounds: Subversive Enterprises among the Puritan Elite in Massachusetts, 1630–92*. Oxford: Oxford Univ. Press.
Breen, T. H. 1970. *The Character of the Good Ruler: A Study of Puritan Political Ideas in New England, 1630–1730*. New Haven: Yale Univ. Press.
Bremer, F. J. 1980. "In Defence of Regicide: John Cotton on the Execution of Charles I." *William and Mary Quarterly* 37 (3rd ser.): 103–24.
 1989. *Puritan Crisis: New England and the English Civil Wars, 1630–70*. New York: Garland.
 2003. *John Winthrop: America's Forgotten Founding Father*. Oxford: Oxford Univ. Press.
Brennan, E. E. 1931. "The Massachusetts Council of the Magistrates." *New England Quarterly* 4: 54–93.
Bridge, W. 1643. *The Wounded Conscience Cured*. London: B. Allen.
Brockunier, S. H. 1940. *The Irrepressible Democrat, Roger Williams*. New York: Ronald.
Brown, A. (ed.). 1890. *The Genesis of the United States*. 2 vols. Boston: Houghton Mifflin.
 1968 (1901). *English Politics in Early Virginia History*. New York: Russell & Russell.
 1969 (1898). *The First Republic in America*. New York: Russell & Russell.
Brown, B. K. 1954. "A Note on the Puritan Concept of Aristocracy." *Mississippi Valley Historical Review* 41: 105–12.
Bruce, P. A. 1910. *Institutional History of Virginia in the Seventeenth Century*. 2 vols. New York: Putnam.

Buchanan, G. 2004. *De Jure Regni apud Scotos*, trans. R. A. Mason & M. S. Smith. Aldershot, U.K.: Ashgate.
Buckland, W. W. 1931. *The Main Institutions of Roman Private Law*. Cambridge, U.K.: Cambridge Univ. Press.
  1950. *A Text-Book of Roman Law from Augustus to Justinian*. 2nd ed. Cambridge, U.K.: Cambridge Univ. Press.
Burgess, W. H. 1920. *The Pastor of the Pilgrims: A Biography of John Robinson*. New York: Harcourt, Brace, & Howe.
Burrage, C. 1912. *The Early English Dissenters, 1550–1641*. 2 vols. Cambridge, U.K.: Cambridge Univ. Press.
Butler, J. 2004. *Becoming America: The Revolution before 1776*. Cambridge, Mass.: Harvard Univ. Press.
Butler, N. 1882. *Historye of the Bermudaes or Summer Islands*, ed. J. H. Lefroy. London: Hakluyt Society.
Calder, I. M. 1934. *The New Haven Colony*. New Haven: Yale Univ. Press.
Calderwood, D. 1619. *Perth Assembly*. Leiden: W. Brewster.
Carney, F. S. 1995 (1964). "Introduction." *Politica*, ed. F. S. Carney. Indianapolis: Liberty Fund.
Carter, A., & G. Stokes. 2002. "Introduction." *Democratic Theory Today*, eds. A. Carter & G. Stokes. Cambridge, U.K.: Cambridge Univ. Press.
Cohen, J. 1996. "Procedure and Substance in Deliberative Democracy." *Democracy and Difference*, ed. S. Benhabib. Princeton: Princeton Univ. Press.
Coke, E. 1650. *The Compleat Copy-Holder*. London.
Colegrove, K. 1920. "New England Town Mandates." *Publications of the Colonial Society of Massachusetts* 21: 411–49.
Cook, K. S., R. Hardin, & M. Levi. 2005. *Co-Operation without Trust?* New York: Russell Sage.
Cooper, J. F., Jr. 1999. *Tenacious of Their Liberties: The Congregationalists in Colonial Massachusetts*. New York: Oxford Univ. Press.
Cotton, J. 1644. *The Keyes of the Kingdom of Heaven*. London: H. Overton.
  1648. *The Way of Congregational Churches Cleared*. London: M. Simmons.
  n.d. (1630). "God's Promise to His Plantations." *Old South Leaflets*, no. 53. Boston.
Cowel, J. 1651. *The Institutes of the Lawes of England*. London: J. Ridley.
Crashaw, W. 1610. *A Sermon Preached in London before the Right Honorable the Lord Lawarre*. London.
Craven, W. F. 1932. *The Dissolution of the Virginia Company*. New York: Oxford Univ. Press.
  1949. *The Southern Colonies in the Seventeenth Century*. Baton Rouge: Louisiana State Univ. Press.
  1969. "And So the Form of Government Become Perfect." *Virginia Magazine of History and Biography* 77: 131–45.
Cushman, R. 1846 (1621). *The Sin and Danger of Self-Love*. Boston: C. Ewer.
Davenport, J. 1663. *A Discourse about Civil Government in a New Plantation Whose Design Is Religion*. Cambridge, Mass.: S. Green.
Dexter, H. M. 1880. *The Congregationalism of the Last Three Hundred Years*. New York: Harper.

1890. "Elder Brewster's Library." *Proceedings of the Massachusetts Historical Society* 25: 37–85.
Dry, M., & H. J. Storing (eds.). 1985. *The Anti-Federalist*. Chicago: Univ. of Chicago Press.
Dunn, J. 2005. *Setting the People Free: The Story of Democracy*. London: Atlantic.
Dzelzainis, M. 2005. "History and Ideology: Milton, the Levellers, and the Council of State in 1649." *Huntington Library Quarterly* 68: 269–88.
Easton, E. 1930. *Roger Williams, Prophet and Pioneer*. Boston: Houghton Mifflin.
Eisenach, E. 1978. "Cultural Politics and Political Thought: The American Revolution Made and Remembered." *American Studies* 20: 71–97.
Eliot, C. W. (ed.). 1910. *American Historical Documents, 1000–1904*. New York: P. F. Collier.
Emerson, E. (ed.). 1976. *Letters from New England: The Massachusetts Bay Colony, 1629–38*. Amherst, Mass.: Univ. of Massachusetts Press.
Ernst, J. E. 1931. "Roger Williams and the English Revolution." *Collections of the Rhode Island Historical Society* 24: 1–58.
Fairfax, T. 1647. *The Case of the Armie Truly Stated*. London.
Fearon, J. D. 1999. "Electoral Accountability and the Control of Politicians." *Democracy, Accountability, and Representation*, eds. A. Przeworski, S. C. Stokes, & B. Manin. Cambridge, U.K.: Cambridge Univ. Press.
Field, E. 1902. *The State of Rhode Island and Providence Plantations at the End of the Century: A History*. 3 vols. Boston: Mason.
Figgis, J. N. 1998 (1916). *Studies of Political Thought: From Gerson to Grotius, 1414–1625*. 2nd ed. Bristol: Thoemmes.
Fishkin, J. S. 1991. *Democracy and Deliberation: New Directions for Democratic Reform*. New Haven: Yale Univ. Press.
　1995. *The Voice of the People: Public Opinion and Democracy*. New Haven: Yale Univ. Press.
Fitzmaurice, A. 1999. "The Civic Solution to the Crisis of English Colonization, 1609–25." *Historical Journal* 42: 25–51.
　2003. *Humanism and America: An Intellectual History of English Colonisation, 1500–1625*. Cambridge, U.K.: Cambridge Univ. Press.
Fontana, B., C. J. Nederman, & G. Remer. 2004. "Deliberative Democracy and the Rhetorical Turn." *Talking Democracy: Historical Perspectives on Rhetoric and Democracy*, eds. B. Fontana, C. J. Nederman, & G. Remer. University Park: Pennsylvania State Univ. Press.
Franklin, J. H. 1963. *Jean Bodin and the Sixteenth-Century Revolution in the Methodology of Law and History*. New York: Columbia Univ. Press.
　(ed.). 1969. *Constitutionalism and Resistance in the Sixteenth Century*. New York: Pegasus.
　1973. *Jean Bodin and the Rise of Absolutist Theory*. Cambridge, U.K.: Cambridge Univ. Press.
　1978. *John Locke and the Theory of Sovereignty*. Cambridge, U.K.: Cambridge Univ. Press.
　1991. "Sovereignty and the Mixed Constitution: Bodin and His Critics." *The Cambridge History of Political Thought, 1450–1700*, ed. J. H. Burns. Cambridge, U.K.: Cambridge Univ. Press.

Gardiner, S. R. (ed.). 1906. *The Constitutional Documents of the Puritan Revolution, 1625–60.* 3rd ed. Oxford: Oxford Univ. Press.
Garnett, G. (ed.). 1994. *Vindiciae contra Tyrannos.* Cambridge, U.K.: Cambridge Univ. Press.
Garsten, B. 2006. *Saving Persuasion: A Defense of Rhetoric and Judgment.* Cambridge, Mass.: Harvard Univ. Press.
van Gelderen, M. 1992. *The Political Thought of the Dutch Revolt, 1555–90.* Cambridge, U.K.: Cambridge Univ. Press.
von Gierke, O. F. 1900. *Political Theories of the Middle Age,* trans. F. W. Maitland. Cambridge, U.K.: Cambridge Univ. Press.
Gilbert, F. 1965. *Machiavelli and Guicciardini: Politics and History in Sixteenth-Century Florence.* Princeton: Princeton Univ. Press.
Gildrie, R. P. 1975. *Salem, Massachusetts, 1626–83: A Covenant Community.* Charlottesville: Univ. of Virginia Press.
Glover, S. D. 1999. "The Putney Debates: Popular vs. Elitist Republicanism." *Past and Present* 164: 47–80.
Gooch, G. P. 1927. *English Democratic Ideas in the Seventeenth Century.* 2nd ed. Cambridge, U.K.: Cambridge Univ. Press.
Goodwin, J. 1649. *Right and Might Well Met.* London: M. Simmons.
Goodwin, T., P. Nye, S. Simpson, J. Burroughs, & W. Bridge. 1963 (1644). *An Apologeticall Narration,* ed. R. S. Paul. Philadelphia: United Church.
Gough, J. W. 1950. *John Locke's Political Philosophy.* Oxford: Clarendon.
Gray, R. 1609. *A Good Speed to Virginia.* London: F. Kingston.
Greenberg, J. R. 2001. *The Radical Face of the Ancient Constitution.* Cambridge, U.K.: Cambridge Univ. Press.
Greenleaf, W. H. 1964. *Order, Empiricism, and Politics: Two Traditions of English Political Thought, 1500–1700.* Oxford: Oxford Univ. Press.
Guicciardini, F. 1969. *The History of Italy,* trans. S. Alexander. New York: Macmillan.
Gura, P. F. 1984. *A Glimpse of Sion's Glory: Puritan Radicalism in New England, 1620–60.* Middletown, Conn.: Wesleyan Univ. Press.
Gutmann, A., & D. F. Thompson. 1996. *Democracy and Disagreement.* Cambridge, Mass.: Harvard Univ. Press.
2004. *Why Deliberative Democracy?* Princeton: Princeton Univ. Press.
Habermas, J. 1996. "Three Normative Models of Democracy." *Democracy and Difference,* ed. S. Benhabib. Princeton: Princeton Univ. Press.
Hakluyt, R. 1850. *Divers Voyages Touching the Discovery of America,* ed. J. W. Jones. London: Hakluyt Society.
Hall, C. C. (ed.). 1910. *Narratives of Early Maryland, 1633–84.* New York: Scribner.
Hall, D. D. 1972. *The Faithful Shepherd: A History of the New England Ministry in the Seventeenth Century.* Chapel Hill: Univ. of North Carolina Press.
1987. "On Common Ground: The Coherence of American Puritan Studies." *William and Mary Quarterly* 44 (3rd ser.): 193–229.
Hamilton, A., J. Madison, & J. Jay. 2005 (1788). *The Federalist,* ed. J. R. Pole. Indianapolis: Hackett.
Hansen, M. H. 1999. *The Athenian Democracy in the Age of Demosthenes,* trans. J. A. Crook. Norman: Univ. of Oklahoma Press.

Hanson, R. L. 1989. "Democracy." *Political Innovation and Conceptual Change*, eds. T. Ball, J. Farr, & R. L. Hanson. Cambridge, U.K.: Cambridge Univ. Press.

Harris, J. R., & S. K. Jones. 1987 (1922). *The Pilgrim Press*. Nieuwkoop: De Graaf.

Harris, T. 2001. "The Leveller Legacy: From the Restoration to the Exclusion Crisis." *The Putney Debates of 1647: The Army, the Levellers, and the English State*, ed. M. Mendle. Cambridge, U.K.: Cambridge Univ. Press.

Herne, J. 1663. *The Law of Charitable Uses*. 2nd ed. London.

Herodotus. 1938. *Histories*, trans. A. D. Godley. Cambridge, Mass.: Harvard Univ. Press.

Hobbes, T. 1996 (1651). *Leviathan*, ed. R. Tuck. Cambridge, U.K.: Cambridge Univ. Press.

Hoffer, P. C., & N. E. H. Hull. 1978. "The First American Impeachments." *William and Mary Quarterly* 35 (3rd ser.): 653–67.

Hoffert, R. W. 1992. *A Politics of Tensions: The Articles of Confederation and American Political Ideas*. Niwot: Univ. of Colorado Press.

Holdsworth, W. S. 1923. "The English Trust: Its Origins and Influence in English Law." *Tijdschrift voor Rechtsgeschiedenis* 4: 367–83.

  1927. *A History of English Law*. 4th ed. 16 vols. London: Methuen.

Holmes, S. 1995. *Passions and Constraint: On the Theory of Liberal Democracy*. Chicago: Univ. of Chicago Press.

Hooker, T. 1860a (1639). "Abstracts of Two Sermons." *Collections of the Connecticut Historical Society* 1: 19–22.

  1860b (1638). "Letter to Governor Winthrop." *Collections of the Connecticut Historical Society* 1: 1–18.

  1972 (1648). *A Survey of the Summe of Church-Discipline*. New York: Arno.

Howe, M. D., & L. F. Eaton Jr. 1947. "The Supreme Judicial Power in the Colony of Massachusetts Bay." *New England Quarterly* 20: 291–316.

Hudson, W. 1942. *John Ponet, Advocate of Limited Monarchy*. Chicago: Univ. of Chicago Press.

Hutchinson, T. (ed.). 1865 (1769). *A Collection of Original Papers Relative to the History of the Colony of Massachusetts Bay*. Albany, N.Y.: Prince Society.

Jacob, H. 1610. *The Divine Beginning and Institution of Christs True Visible or Ministeriall Church*. Leiden: H. Hastings.

James, S. V. 1999. *John Clarke and His Legacies*. University Park: Pennsylvania State Univ. Press.

  2000. *The Colonial Metamorphoses in Rhode Island*, eds. S. L. Skemp & B. C. Daniels. Hanover, N.H.: Univ. Press of New England.

Jefferson, T. 1979. *Selected Writings*, ed. H. C. Mansfield Jr. Wheeling, Ill.: Harlan Davidson.

Johnson, R. 1947 (1612). *The New Life of Virginea*. Repr. in *Tracts and Other Papers*, ed. P. Force., vol. 1. New York: P. Smith.

Johnston, A. 1887. *Connecticut: A Study of a Commonwealth-Democracy*. Boston: Houghton, Mifflin.

Jones, H. M. 1946. "The Colonial Impulse: An Analysis of the 'Promotion' Literature of Colonization." *Proceedings of the American Philosophical Society* 90: 131–61.

Jones, M. J. A. 1968. *Congregational Commonwealth: Connecticut, 1636–62.* Middletown, Conn.: Wesleyan Univ. Press.
Jordan, D. W. 1987. *Foundations of Representative Government in Maryland, 1632–1715.* Cambridge, U.K.: Cambridge Univ. Press.
Jourdain, S. 1947 (1613). *A Plaine Description of the Barmudas.* Repr. in *Tracts and Other Papers*, ed. P. Force., vol. 3. New York: P. Smith.
Judson, M. A. 1969. *The Political Thought of Sir Henry Vane, the Younger.* Philadelphia: Univ. of Pennsylvania Press.
Kateb, G. 1992. *The Inner Ocean.* Ithaca, N.Y.: Cornell Univ. Press.
Kavenagh, W. K. (ed.). 1973. *Foundations of Colonial America: A Documentary History.* 3 vols. New York: Chelsea House.
King, H. R. 1994. *Cape Cod and Plymouth Colony in the Seventeenth Century.* Lanham, Md.: Univ. Press of America.
Kingsbury, S. M. (ed.). 1935. *The Records of the Virginia Company of London.* 4 vols. Washington, D.C.: Government Printing Office.
Kukla, J. 1989. *Political Institutions in Virginia, 1619–60.* New York: Garland.
LaFantasie, G. W. (ed.). 1988. *The Correspondence of Roger Williams.* 2 vols. Providence, R.I.: Univ. Press of New England.
Langdon, G. D. 1966. *Pilgrim Colony: A History of New Plymouth, 1620–91.* New Haven: Yale Univ. Press.
Laski, H. J. (ed.). 1924. *A Defence of Liberty against Tyrants.* London: G. Bell.
Laslett, P. 1988. "Introduction." *Two Treatises of Government*, ed. P Laslett. Cambridge, U.K.: Cambridge Univ. Press.
Lawson, G. 1992 (1660). *Politica Sacra et Civilis*, ed. C. Condren. Cambridge, U.K.: Cambridge Univ. Press.
Levinson, S. 2006. *Our Undemocratic Constitution: Where the Constitution Goes Wrong (and How We the People Can Correct It).* Oxford: Oxford Univ. Press.
Lewy, G. 1960. *Constitutionalism and Statecraft during the Golden Age of Spain.* Geneva: E. Droz.
Lilburne, J. 1645a. *An Answer to Nine Arguments.* London.
  1645b. *Englands Birth-Right Justified.* London.
  1648. *The Peoples Prerogative and Priviledges.* London.
  1649. *The Trial of the Lieutenant Colonel John Lilburne.* London.
Lloyd, H. A. 1991. "Constitutionalism." *The Cambridge History of Political Thought, 1450–1700*, ed. J. H. Burns. Cambridge, U.K.: Cambridge Univ. Press.
Locke, J. 1988 (1689). *Two Treatises of Government*, ed. P. Laslett. Cambridge, U.K.: Cambridge Univ. Press.
Lockwood, S. 1997. "Introduction." *On the Laws and Governance of England*, ed. S. Lockwood. Cambridge, U.K.: Cambridge Univ. Press.
Lokken, R. N. 1959. "The Concept of Democracy in Colonial Political Thought." *William and Mary Quarterly* 16 (3rd ser.): 568–80.
Lovejoy, D. S. 1990. "Plain Englishmen at Plymouth." *New England Quarterly* 65: 232–48.
Lucas, P. R. 1976. *Valley of Discord: Church and Society along the Connecticut River, 1636–1725.* Hanover, N.H.: Univ. Press of New England.
Macedo, S. (ed.). 1999. *Deliberative Politics: Essays on Democracy and Disagreement.* New York: Oxford Univ. Press.

Main, J. T. 1966. "Government by the People: The American Revolution and the Democratization of the Legislatures." *William and Mary Quarterly* 23 (3rd ser.): 391–407.

Maitland, F. W. 1936. "Trust and the Law of Corporations." *Maitland: Selected Essays*, ed. H. D. Hazeltine. Cambridge, U.K.: Cambridge Univ. Press.

Malcolm, J. L. (ed.). 1999. *The Struggle for Sovereignty: Seventeenth-Century English Political Tracts*. 2 vols. Indianapolis: Liberty Fund.

Malcolm, N. 1981. "Hobbes, Sandys, and the Virginia Company." *Historical Journal* 24: 297–321.

Maloy, J. S. 2007. "The Paine-Adams Debate and Its Seventeenth-Century Antecedents." *Thomas Paine: Common Sense for a New Era*, eds. R. F. King & E. Begler. San Diego: San Diego State Univ. Press.

Manin, B. 1997. *The Principles of Representative Government*. New York: Cambridge Univ. Press.

Manin, B., A. Przeworski, & S. C. Stokes. 1999a. "Elections and Representation." *Democracy, Accountability, and Representation*, eds. A. Przeworski, S. C. Stokes, & B. Manin. Cambridge, U.K.: Cambridge Univ. Press.

1999b. "Introduction." *Democracy, Accountability, and Representation*, eds. A. Przeworski, S. C. Stokes, & B. Manin. Cambridge, U.K.: Cambridge Univ. Press.

de Mariana, J. 1948. *The King and the Education of the King*, trans. G. A. Moore. Washington, D.C.: Country Dollar.

Mather, R. 1643a. *An Apologie of the Churches in New-England for Church-Covenant*. London: B. Allen.

1643b. *Church-Government and Church-Covenant Discussed*. London: B. Allen.

1712. *An Answer to Two Questions*, ed. I. Mather. Boston: B. Green.

Mayhew, D. R. 2004. *Congress: The Electoral Connection*. 2nd ed. New Haven: Yale Univ. Press.

McCormick, J. P. 2001. "Machiavellian Democracy: Controlling Elites with Ferocious Populism." *American Political Science Review* 95: 297–313.

2003. "Machiavelli against Republicanism: On the Cambridge School's Guicciardinian Moments." *Political Theory* 31: 615–43.

2006. "Contain the Wealthy and Patrol the Magistrates: Restoring Elite Accountability to Popular Government." *American Political Science Review* 100: 147–63.

McLoughlin, W. G. 1978. *Rhode Island: A Bicentennial History*. New York: Norton.

McMichael, J. R., & B. Taft (eds.). 1989. *The Writings of William Walwyn*. Athens: Univ. of Georgia Press.

Mendle, M. 1995. *Henry Parker and the English Civil War: The Political Thought of the Public's Privado*. Cambridge, U.K.: Cambridge Univ. Press.

Miller, J. I. 1991. *The Rise and Fall of Democracy in Early America, 1630–1789*. University Park: Pennsylvania State Univ. Press.

Miller, P. 1939. *The New England Mind: The Seventeenth Century*. New York: Macmillan.

1948. "The Religious Impulse in the Founding of Virginia." *William and Mary Quarterly* 5 (3rd ser.): 492–522.

1956. *Errand into the Wilderness*. Cambridge, Mass.: Harvard Univ. Press.

1958. "Introduction." *A Vindication of the Government of New-England Churches*. Gainesville, Fla.: Scholars' Facsimiles.

Morgan, E. S. 1958. *The Puritan Dilemma: The Story of John Winthrop*. Boston: Little, Brown.

(ed.). 2003 (1965). *Puritan Political Ideas, 1558–1794*. Indianapolis: Hackett.

Morison, S. E. 1951. "The Mayflower's Destination and the Pilgrim Fathers' Patents." *Publications of the Colonial Society of Massachusetts* 38: 387–98.

1956. *The Intellectual Life of Colonial New England*. 2nd ed. New York: New York Univ. Press.

1964. *Builders of the Bay Colony*. 2nd ed. Boston: Houghton Mifflin.

Morton, R. L. 1960. *Colonial Virginia*. Chapel Hill: Univ. of North Carolina Press.

Murrin, J. M. 1984. "Political Development." *Colonial British America*, eds. J. P. Greene & J. R. Pole. Baltimore: Johns Hopkins Univ. Press.

Nederman, C. J., 1996. "Constitutionalism, Medieval and Modern." *History of Political Thought* 17: 179–94.

Newton, A. P. 1914. "A New Plan to Govern Virginia, 1623." *American Historical Review* 19: 559–60.

Norton, J. 1913 (1643). "The Negative Vote." *Proceedings of the Massachusetts Historical Society* 46: 276–85.

1958 (1648). *The Answer to the Whole Set of Questions of the Celebrated Mr. William Apollonius*, trans. D. Horton. Cambridge, Mass.: Harvard Univ. Press.

Ober, J. 1998. *Political Dissent in Democratic Athens*. Princeton: Princeton Univ. Press.

2003. "Conditions for Athenian Democracy." *The Making and Unmaking of Democracy*, eds. T. K. Rabb & E. N. Suleiman. New York: Routledge.

Osgood, H. L. 1891. "The Political Ideas of the Puritans." *Political Science Quarterly* 6: 1–28, 201–31.

1907. *The American Colonies in the Seventeenth Century*. 3 vols. New York: Macmillan.

Overton, R. 1645. *The Araignement of Mr. Persecution*. London.

1646. *Vox Plebis*. London.

1647. *An Appeale from the Degenerate Representative Body*. London.

Pagden, A. 1995. *Lords of All the World: Ideologies of Empire in Spain, Britain, and France, ca. 1500–1800*. New Haven: Yale Univ. Press.

Paine, T. 1987. *The Thomas Paine Reader*, eds. M. Foot & I. Kramnick. New York: Penguin.

Parker, H. 1644. *Jus Populi*. London.

Parrington, V. L. 1987 (1927). *The Colonial Mind, 1620–1800*. Norman: Univ. of Oklahoma Press.

Pateman, C. 1970. *Participation and Democratic Theory*. Cambridge, U.K.: Cambridge Univ. Press.

Peltonen, M. 1995. *Classical Humanism and Republicanism in English Political Thought, 1570–1640*. Cambridge, U.K.: Cambridge Univ. Press.

Pettit, P. 1999. "Republican Freedom and Contestatory Democratization." *Democracy's Value*, eds. I. Shapiro & C. Hacker-Cordon. Cambridge, U.K.: Cambridge Univ. Press.

2000. "Democracy, Electoral and Contestatory." *Designing Democratic Institutions*, eds. I. Shapiro & S. Macedo. New York: New York Univ. Press.

2003. "Deliberative Democracy, the Discursive Dilemma, and Republican Theory." *Debating Deliberative Democracy*, eds. J. S. Fishkin & P. Laslett. Malden, Mass.: Blackwell.

2008. "Three Conceptions of Democratic Control." *Constellations* 15: 46–55.

Pitkin, H. F. 1967. *The Concept of Representation*. Berkeley: Univ. of California Press.

Plato. 1995. *Statesman*, trans. C. J. Rowe. Warminster, U.K.: Aris & Phillips.

Plooij, D. 1932. *The Pilgrim Fathers from a Dutch Point of View*. New York: New York Univ. Press.

Pocock, J. G. A. 1975. *The Machiavellian Moment*. Princeton: Princeton Univ. Press.

Pollock, F., & F. W. Maitland. 1899. *The History of English Law before the Time of Edward I*. 2nd ed. 2 vols. Cambridge, U.K.: Cambridge Univ. Press.

Ponet, J. 1972 (1556). *A Shorte Treatise of Politike Power*. New York: Da Capo.

Przeworski, A. 1999. "Minimalist Theory of Democracy: A Defence." *Democracy's Value*, eds. I. Shapiro & C. Hacker-Cordon. Cambridge, U.K.: Cambridge Univ. Press.

Przeworski, A., S. C. Stokes, & B. Manin (eds.). 1999. *Democracy, Accountability, and Representation*. New York: Cambridge Univ. Press.

Purchas, S. (ed.). 1907 (1625). *Hakluytus Posthumus; or, Purchas His Pilgrimes*. 20 vols. Glasgow: J. MacLehose.

Pynchon, W. 1914. "Letters." *Proceedings of the Massachusetts Historical Society* 48: 35–56.

Quinn, D. B. 1976. "Renaissance Influences in English Colonization." *Transactions of the Royal Historical Society* 26 (5th ser.): 73–93.

Rabb, T. K. 2003. "Institutions and Ideas: Planting the Roots of Democracy in Early Modern Europe." *The Making and Unmaking of Democracy*, eds. T. K. Rabb & E. N. Suleiman. New York: Routledge.

Raleigh, W. 1829. *Works*, eds. W. Oldys & T. Birch. 8 vols. Oxford: Oxford Univ. Press.

Richman, I. B. 1902. *Rhode Island: Its Making and Its Meaning*. 2 vols. New York: Putnam.

Riley, F. L. 1896. "Colonial Origins of New England Senates." *Johns Hopkins University Studies in Historical and Political Science* 14(3).

Roberts, J. T. 1982. *Accountability in Athenian Government*. Madison: Univ. of Wisconsin Press.

Robinson, J. 1625. *A Just and Necessary Apologie of Certain Christians*. n.p.

1851. *Works*, ed. R. Ashton. 3 vols. London: J. Snow.

Rogers, H. (ed.). 1915. *The Early Records of the Town of Providence*. 21 vols. Providence, R.I.: Snow & Farnham.

Rolfe, J. 1971 (1616). *A True Relation of the State of Virginia*. Charlottesville: Univ. of Virginia Press.

Rossiter, C. L. 1953. *Seedtime of the Republic: The Origin of the American Tradition of Political Liberty*. New York: Harcourt, Brace.

Rutman, D. B. 1965. *Winthrop's Boston: Portrait of a Puritan Town, 1630–49*. Chapel Hill: Univ. of North Carolina Press.

Bibliography

Sachse, W. L. 1948. "The Migration of New Englanders to England, 1640–60." *American Historical Review* 53: 251–78.

Salmon, J. H. M. 1959. *The French Religious Wars in English Political Thought*. Oxford: Clarendon.

　1996. "The Legacy of Jean Bodin: Absolutism, Populism, or Constitutionalism?" *History of Political Thought* 17: 500–22.

Sargent, M. L. 1992. "William Bradford's Dialogue with History." *New England Quarterly* 65: 389–421.

Savonarola, G. 2006. *Selected Writings: Religion and Politics, 1490–8*, trans. A. Borelli & M. P. Passaro. New Haven: Yale Univ. Press.

Scharf, J. T. 1967. *History of Maryland, from the Earliest Period to the Present Day*. 3 vols. Hatboro, Pa.: Tradition.

Schumpeter, J. A. 1942. *Capitalism, Socialism, and Democracy*. New York: Harper.

Schwartzberg, M. 2007. *Democracy and Legal Change*. New York: Cambridge Univ. Press.

Schwoerer, L. G. 1990. "Locke, Lockean Ideas, and the Glorious Revolution." *Journal of the History of Ideas* 51: 531–48.

Scott, J. 2000. *England's Troubles: Seventeenth-Century English Political Instability in European Context*. Cambridge, U.K.: Cambridge Univ. Press.

　2003. *Commonwealth Principles: Republican Writing of the English Revolution*. Cambridge, U.K.: Cambridge Univ. Press.

Shain, B. A. 1994. *The Myth of American Individualism: The Protestant Origins of American Political Thought*. Princeton: Princeton Univ. Press.

Shapiro, I. 1999. "Enough of Deliberation: Politics Is about Interests and Power." *Deliberative Politics: Essays on Democracy and Disagreement*, ed. S. Macedo. New York: Oxford Univ. Press.

　2003. "John Locke's Democratic Theory." *Two Treatises of Government*, ed. I. Shapiro. New Haven: Yale Univ. Press.

Sharp, A. (ed.). 1983. *Political Ideas of the English Civil Wars, 1641–9*. London: Longmans.

　1988. "John Lilburne and the Long Parliament *Book of Declarations*." *History of Political Thought* 9: 19–44.

　(ed.). 1998. *The English Levellers*. Cambridge, U.K.: Cambridge Univ. Press.

Shiffman, G. 2004. "Deliberation vs. Decision: Platonism in Contemporary Democratic Theory." *Talking Democracy: Historical Perspectives on Rhetoric and Democracy*, eds. B. Fontana, C. J. Nederman, & G. Remer. University Park: Pennsylvania State Univ. Press.

Shuffelton, F. 1977. *Thomas Hooker, 1586–1647*. Princeton: Princeton Univ. Press.

Shurtleff, N. B. (ed.). 1854. *Records of the Governor and Company of the Massachusetts Bay*. 5 vols. Boston: W. White.

Shurtleff, N. B., & D. Pulsifer (eds.). 1968. *Records of the Colony of New Plymouth*. 12 vols. New York: A.M.S.

Simpson, A. 1956. "How Democratic Was Roger Williams?" *William and Mary Quarterly* 13 (3rd ser.): 53–67.

Skinner, Q. 1978. *The Foundations of Modern Political Thought*. 2 vols. Cambridge, U.K.: Cambridge Univ. Press.

1992. "The Italian City-Republics." *Democracy: The Unfinished Journey, 508 B. C. To A. D. 1993*, ed. J. Dunn. Oxford: Oxford Univ. Press.

2002. "Classical Liberty and the Coming of the English Civil War." *Republicanism: A Shared European Heritage*, vol. 2, eds. M. van Gelderen & Q. Skinner. Cambridge, U.K.: Cambridge Univ. Press.

Smith, J. 1986. *Complete Works*, ed. P. L. Barbour. 3 vols. Chapel Hill: Univ. of North Carolina Press.

Smyth, J. 1609. *Paralleles, Censures, Observations*. Middelburg: R. Schilders.

Sommerville, J. P. (ed.). 1994. *James I and VI: Political Writings*. Cambridge, U.K.: Cambridge Univ. Press.

Sprunger, K. L. 1972. *The Learned Doctor William Ames*. Urbana: Univ. of Illinois Press.

1994. *Trumpets from the Tower: English Puritan Printing in the Netherlands, 1600–40*. Leiden: E. J. Brill.

Spurgin, H. 1989. *Roger Williams and Puritan Radicalism in the English Separatist Tradition*. Lewiston, N.Y.: E. Mellon.

Staples, W. R. (ed.). 1847. *The Proceedings of the First General Assembly of Providence Plantations*. Providence, R.I.: Knowles & Vose.

Stephen, L., & S. Lee (eds.). 1901. *The Dictionary of National Biography*. 66 vols. London: Smith, Elder.

Stourzh, G. 1988. "Constitution: Changing Meanings of the Term from the Early Seventeenth to the Late Eighteenth Century." *Conceptual Change and the Constitution*, eds. T. Ball & J. G. A. Pocock. Lawrence: Univ. of Kansas Press.

Strachey, W. 1947 (1612). *Lawes Divine, Morall, and Martiall*. Repr. in *Tracts and Other Papers*, ed. P. Force, vol. 3. New York: P. Smith.

1953. *The Historie of Travell into Virginia Britannia*, eds. L. B. Wright & V. L. Freund. London: Hakluyt Society.

Suarez, F. 1944. *Selections from Three Works*, trans. G. L. Williams, A. Brown, J. Waldron, & H. Davis, ed. J. B. Scott. 2 vols. Oxford: Oxford Univ. Press.

Sunstein, C. 2001. *Designing Democracy: What Constitutions Do*. Oxford: Oxford Univ. Press.

Taft, B. 2001. "From Reading to Whitehall: Henry Ireton's Journey." *The Putney Debates of 1647: The Army, the Levellers, and the English State*, ed. M. Mendle. Cambridge, U.K.: Cambridge Univ. Press.

Taylor, E. G. R. (ed.). 1935. *The Original Writings and Correspondence of the Two Richard Hakluyts*. 2 vols. London: Hakluyt Society.

Thompson, D. F. 2002. *Just Elections: Creating a Fair Electoral Process in the United States*. Chicago: Univ. of Chicago Press.

Thompson, R. 2001. *Divided We Stand: Watertown, Massachusetts, 1630–80*. Amherst: Univ. of Massachusetts Press.

Thornton, J. M. III 1968. "The Thrusting Out of Governor Harvey: A Seventeenth-Century Rebellion." *Virginia Magazine of History and Biography* 76: 11–26.

Travers, W. 1617 (1574). *A Full and Plaine Declaration of Ecclesiastical Discipline*, trans. T. Cartwright. Leiden: W. Brewster.

Trumbull, J. H., & C. J. Hoadly. 1890. *The Public Records of the Colony of Connecticut, 1636–1776*. 15 vols. Hartford: Lockwood & Brainard.

Tuck, R. 1993. *Philosophy and Government, 1572–1651*. Cambridge, U.K.: Cambridge Univ. Press.

2001. "Hobbes and Rousseau". Benedict Lectures, Boston University.

2006. "Hobbes and Democracy."*Rethinking the Foundations of Modern Political Thought*, eds. A. Brett & J. Tully. Cambridge, U.K.: Cambridge Univ. Press.

Tyler, L. G. (ed.). 1907. *Narratives of Early Virginia, 1606–25*. New York: Scribner.

Urbinati, N. 2006. *Representative Democracy: Principles and Genealogy*. Chicago: Univ. of Chicago Press.

Walker, W. (ed.). 1960 (1893). *The Creeds and Platforms of Congregationalism*. Boston: Pilgrim.

Wall, R. E. 1972. *Massachusetts Bay: The Crucial Decade, 1640–50*. New Haven: Yale Univ. Press.

1990. *The Membership of the Massachusetts Bay General Court, 1630–86*. New York: Garland.

Warden, G. B. 1978. "Law Reform in England and New England, 1620–60." *William and Mary Quarterly* 35 (3rd ser.): 668–90.

1984. "The Rhode Island Civil Code of 1647." *Saints and Revolutionaries*, eds. D. D. Hall, J. M. Murrin, & T. W. Tate. New York: Norton.

Warren, M. E. 1996. "Deliberative Democracy and Authority." *American Political Science Review* 90: 46–60.

2002. "Deliberative Democracy." *Democratic Theory Today*, eds. A. Carter & G. Stokes. Cambridge, U.K.: Cambridge Univ. Press.

Waters, J. J. 1968. "Hingham, Massachusetts, 1631–61: An East Anglian Oligarchy in the New World." *Journal of Social History* 1: 351–70.

Weeden, W. B. 1991 (1910). *Early Rhode Island: A Social History of the People*. Bowie, Md.: Heritage.

White, B. R. 1971. *The English Separatist Tradition*. Oxford: Oxford Univ. Press.

White, J. 1947 (1630). *The Planters Plea*. Repr. in *Tracts and Other Papers*, ed. P. Force, vol. 2. New York: P. Smith.

White, S. D. 1979. *Sir Edward Coke and the Grievances of the Commonwealth, 1621–28*. Chapel Hill: Univ. of North Carolina Press.

Wildman, J. 1645. *Englands Miserie and Remedie*. London.

Williams, R. 1644. *The Bloudy Tenent of Persecution for Cause of Conscience*. London.

1652. *The Bloody Tenant Yet More Bloody*. London.

Williamson, H. R. 1949. *Four Stuart Portraits*. London: Evans Bros.

Wingfield, E.-M. 1860 (1608). "A Discourse of Virginia." *Transactions of the American Antiquarian Society* 4: 76–103.

Winslow, E. 1974 (1622). *Mourt's Relation*. Norwood, N.J.: W. J. Johnson.

Winslow, O. E. 1957. *Master Roger Williams: A Biography*. New York: Macmillan.

Winthrop, J. 1972. *The History of New England, 1630–49*, ed. J. Savage. 2 vols. New York: Arno.

n.d. (1629). "Conclusions for the Plantation in New England." *Old South Leaflets*, no. 50. Boston.

Winthrop, R. C. (ed.). 1971 (1867). *Life and Letters of John Winthrop*. 2 vols. New York: Da Capo.

Wise, J. 1958 (1717). *A Vindication of the Government of New-England Churches*. Gainesville, Fla.: Scholars' Facsimiles.

Wolin, S. S. 1989. *The Presence of the Past: Essays on the State and the Constitution*. Baltimore: Johns Hopkins Univ. Press.

　1996. "Fugitive Democracy." *Democracy and Difference*, ed. S. Benhabib. Princeton: Princeton Univ. Press.

Wood, G. S. 1969. *The Creation of the American Republic, 1776–87*. Chapel Hill: Univ. of North Carolina Press.

Wootton, D. 1986. "Introduction." *Divine Right and Democracy*, ed. D. Wootton. London: Penguin.

　1990. "From Rebellion to Revolution: The Crisis of the Winter of 1642/3 and the Origins of Civil War Radicalism." *English Historical Review* 105: 654–69.

Worden, B. 1995. "Wit in a Roundhead: The Dilemma of Marchamont Nedham." *Political Culture and Cultural Politics in Early Modern England*, eds. S. D. Asmussen & M. A. Kishlansky. Manchester, U.K.: Manchester Univ. Press.

Wright, L. B. (ed.). 1964. *A Voyage to Virginia in 1609: Two Narratives*. Charlottesville: Univ. of Virginia Press.

Wright, T. G. 1920. *Literary Culture in Early New England, 1620–1730*. New Haven: Yale Univ. Press.

Young, A. (ed.). 1844. *Chronicles of the Pilgrim Fathers*. 2nd ed. Boston: Little, Brown.

Zagorin, P. 1954. *A History of Political Thought in the English Revolution*. London: Routledge.

Index

absolutism, 34, 40, 42
Acadia, 126, 129
accountability: conceptualization, 7–10; consent and, 101, 107, 151, 156, 167; democratic theory and, 1, 2–3, 8, 9, 16–18, 19, 177–83; institutional forms, 5, 8–9, 17, 18, 27–8, 55, 82–3, 111, 115, 137, 147, 157, 173 (*see also* audit; impeachment; liability); intellectual history, 1–2, 5, 6, 15, 25–6, 27, 33, 39, 41, 51–2, 55, 76, 84, 94, 109, 115, 116, 121, 137, 149, 150–1, 153, 161, 168, 169, 172, 176, 177; popular control and, 1, 2, 22, 48, 101, 107, 114, 161, 182; popular sovereignty, joined to, 3, 16, 87, 108, 141; selection, distinguished from, 7–8, 17–18, 51, 101, 133, 156; *see also* elections; models of accountability; trust
Adams, J. T., 14
Adams, John, 22
Aeschylus, 28
Agreement of the People, 44–5, 147, 167, 184
Ainsworth, Henry, 86, 102, 103, 155
Alcibiades, 50
Allerton, Isaac, 94
Almain, Jacques (*see* Sorbonnists)
Althusius, Johannes, 34, 35–6, 42, 51, 54, 89, 96, 183
American colonies: influence on England, 173–7
American Revolution, 15–16, 114, 140–1
Ames, William, 105–6
Andrews, C. M., 115, 141
Anglicanism (*see* England, Church of)
Anti-Federalists, 21, 22, 138, 185
Antinomianism, 105, 121–3, 124, 125, 128, 136, 145, 159, 161
Aquinas, Thomas, 28, 107
aristocracy, 12, 14, 22, 50, 83, 112, 147, 179, 187; "democracy," passing for, 15, 181; regime type, 51, 96, 102, 130, 131–2, 155; social elites, 17, 26, 115, 135, 149
Aristotle, 28, 47; "mixed" regime and, 13, 35, 89, 96, 100, 105, 106, 131, 135, 154, 156, 186
Athens (ancient): accountability in, 33, 48, 50, 120, 135, 178; government, 27–8; historic example, 24, 34, 51, 127–8, 129, 130
audit, 8, 27–8, 33, 35, 48–9, 66, 82, 115, 120, 128, 134, 135, 173, 188
Augustine of Hippo, 29
authority (political) (*see* accountability; discretion; trust)

205

Index

Bacon, Francis, 38
Bahamas, 13
Ball, William, 43
Baltimore (Cecilius Calvert, Lord), 84
Barbados, 13
Bargaves, John, 5, 57, 58–9, 84, 178, 187, 188, 189; on accountability, 59, 76, 82–3; "A Forme of Polisie," 59, 81–4, 173; Virginia Company and, 78–80
Barrow, Henry, 86, 97
Bartolus, 30, 31, 32
Baxter, Richard, 49
Bellingham, Richard, 119, 125
Berkeley, William, 84
Bermuda, 4, 13, 57, 60, 62, 68, 74, 87, 90, 94
Bermuda Compact, 90
Beza, Theodore, 31, 98
Bible: Acts, 98; Isaiah (25:7), 148; Matthew (18:17), 99, 100, 102, 156; Proverbs (11:14), 100; Psalms (118), 39, 94; Psalms (146), 94
bicameralism (*see* multicameralism)
Billings, Edward, 48
bills of rights, 124–5, 141, 167, 183; *see also* civil liberties; legal limitation
Bodin, Jean, 5, 11, 12; on accountability, 34, 36, 89, 96, 149; influence and precedence, 12–13, 40, 42, 51, 53, 85, 89, 95, 100–1, 102, 106–7, 115, 127, 129, 130, 132, 157, 158, 173, 183; on regime types, 12, 34–6, 95–6, 103, 105, 131, 135, 149, 155–6; on sovereignty, 34, 106
Borgeaud, Charles, 14
Boston (Massachusetts), 122, 123
Bourne, Nehemiah, 176
Bradford, William, 91, 94, 95, 104, 110, 111, 173
Breen, Timothy, 14
Brewster, William, 92, 95, 106, 109
Brooke (Robert Greville, Lord), 133
Browne, Robert, 97

"Brutus, Stephanus Junius" (*see* Vindiciae contra Tyrannos)
Buchanan, George, 32–3, 38, 40, 42, 54, 55
Burke, Edmund, 26
Butler, Nathaniel, 68–9, 76

Calderwood, David, 109–10, 154
Calvin, Jean (*see* Calvinism)
Calvinism, 11, 35, 49, 85, 89, 97, 122, 133, 154, 172, 173; *see also* congregationalism; Huguenots; Marian exiles; Presbyterianism; puritanism; separatism
Cambridge (Massachusetts), 119, 143
Cambridge, University of, 12, 95, 132, 157
Cambridge Platform, 96, 107, 159
Cartwright, Thomas, 98
Catholicism, 31, 129
Cavendish, William, 77–8, 80
censure (ecclesiastic), 11, 101, 102, 123, 152, 153
Chancery, court of, 37, 38, 40, 78, 96
Charles I (king of England), 40, 41, 51, 71, 75, 84, 91, 129, 163, 176
Charles II (king of England), 177
"checks and balances" (*see* multicameralism)
Cheever, Ezekiel, 153
Child, Robert, 137–8
Christianity, 58, 61, 62, 87, 166; *see also* Catholicism; evangelism; Protestantism
Chrysostom, 101
Cicero, 29
civil liberties, 11, 15, 179, 183
Clarke, John, 161, 163, 164
Clarkson, Lawrence, 48
class (social), 11, 15, 28, 48, 60–1, 83, 104, 106, 116, 131, 132, 163, 178, 187–8
Coddington, William, 161, 163–4, 168
Coke, Edward, 38, 40
Columbus, Christopher, 61, 68
commerce, 62, 64, 91–2, 93, 112

Index

common good (*see* commonwealth values; *salus populi*)
commonwealth values, 69, 82; applied to American colonies, 57, 58, 61, 62–4, 76, 81, 87, 93; fiduciary authority, joined to, 57, 79; intellectual history, 59, 75, 84, 112, 142, 151
congregationalism, 97, 102, 106–8, 138, 141, 142, 151, 157, 158, 169, 175; *see also* New England Way; Westminster Assembly
Connecticut, 14, 119, 123, 140–61, 162, 170, 171; government, 149, 167 (*see also* Fundamental Orders); Massachusetts, relations with, 143, 150; royal charter, 141
consent: intellectual history, 3, 5, 25, 144; popular control, distinguished from, 2, 7–8, 9–10, 16, 45, 53, 59, 82, 87, 98, 156, 161, 173, 185; popular sovereignty, following from, 141–2; *see also* accountability; democracy; elections
conspiracies, 61–2, 78–9
constituent power, 20–1, 44, 183, 185
constitution: political founding by, 1, 142, 170; terminological history, 86; *see also* Pennsylvania; United States
constitutionalism (*see* constituent power; constitution; democracy; entrenchment; judicial review; legal limitation; multicameralism)
Cooper, James F., Jr., 113
corporation (*see* local politics, municipal analogies)
corruption (*see* virtue and vice)
Cortez, Hernan, 68
Cotton, John, 87–9, 92, 95, 118, 124, 128, 132–3, 135, 159, 161, 165, 174; ecclesiology, 105, 107, 123, 170; *Keyes of the Kingdom of Heaven*, 106, 126, 154, 155; political ideas, 108, 131, 135, 150

covenant, 112, 141, 150, 152
Crashaw, William, 62
Cromwell, Oliver, 43, 47, 50, 159, 160, 164, 170, 175, 176–7; *see also* New Model Army
Cushman, Robert, 92

Davenport, John, 108
Delaware (Thomas West, Lord), 60, 65, 67, 72
delegation vs. alienation (*see ministerium non dominium*)
deliberation: in contemporary theory, 3, 5, 9–10, 18–19, 104, 181–3, 186, 187, 188; in historical perspective, 45, 55, 110, 154
democracy: ancient, 6, 11, 25, 34–5; consent and, 5, 130, 149, 161–2, 177; constitutionalism and, 20–2, 51–2, 169, 171, 183–6; formal vs. substantive aspects, 6–7, 9, 16, 26, 110, 189; modern, 1, 141, 149; popular control essential to, 3, 7, 96, 101, 179; terminological history, 12, 14, 15, 16, 49–52, 77–8, 96, 114, 118, 126, 127, 130–2, 142, 148, 149, 156, 157, 161, 162–3, 164, 168; *see also* popular sovereignty
democratic theory: modern origins, 1–2, 3, 5, 14–15, 25, 36, 52, 59, 83, 84, 138, 142, 168, 171–2; today, 2–3, 12, 18–19, 22–3, 48, 186 (*see also* deliberation); *see also* accountability
Demosthenes, 99
de Soto, Hernando, 68
discretion, 29, 30, 40, 53, 66–70, 93–4, 96, 115, 116–17, 125, 135, 136, 145, 169, 177; legal limitation and, 118, 123–4, 131; *see also* trust
Dorchester (Massachusetts), 122, 143
Dudley, Thomas, 119, 122, 147
Dunn, John, 15
Dutch colonies, 62
Dutch (United) Provinces, 48, 86, 98, 101–2, 105, 106–7, 109

ecclesiology, 14, 49, 50, 84–5, 86–9, 96–109, 115, 126–7, 133, 151–7, 158, 167; *see also* congregationalism; New England Way
Eisenach, Eldon, 15
elections, 43–4, 55, 58, 82, 114, 130, 170; accountability and, 2, 9, 17, 21, 45–9, 83, 110, 116, 117, 132–5, 152, 172, 185, 186–7; aristocracy and, 17, 115, 132; consent in, 107, 167; deterrent effect, 9, 17, 45–6, 140, 178, 185; intellectual history, 129, 138, 142, 153, 157; practical problems, 17, 186
electoral thesis of accountability (*see* elections, accountability and)
Eliot, Hugh, 61
elites (*see* aristocracy)
Elizabeth I (queen of England), 97
Emden, 38
Endecott, John, 90, 94, 122
England, 71–2, 169; Church of, 87, 100, 104, 105, 106, 110; civil war, 26, 34, 41–52, 55, 84, 87, 101, 106, 133, 137, 150, 151, 159–60, 174, 176; Elizabethan period, 38, 57, 58–9, 75, 83, 87, 92; Glorious Revolution, 55, 150; Restoration, 141, 175, 177
English law, 37–8, 40, 42–3, 44, 91, 137; *see also* Magna Carta; Petition of Right
entrenchment (legal), 20–1, 183
ephors, 32, 35, 83, 109, 172, 180, 185
equality, 6, 151
Essex County (Massachusetts), 125, 126, 128, 132, 143
evangelism, 62–4, 91

Federalist, The, 17, 21, 25, 114, 140, 172, 185
fiduciary agency, 11, 26, 29, 31–2, 37, 38, 42, 54, 58, 93–4, 116–17, 136, 183
Field, Edward, 163

Five Knights' Case (1627), 40
Flaminius, 50
Florence, 129
Florida, 129
form and substance (*see* democracy, formal vs. substantive aspects)
France, 2, 15–16, 31–2, 33, 129
Frankfurt, 38, 97
Franklin, Julian, 36, 96
"fugitive democracy," 22
Fuller, Samuel, 104
Fundamental Orders (of Connecticut), 146–8, 150, 158, 174

Gates, Thomas, 67, 69, 72
Geneva, 24, 35, 36, 38, 79, 98, 131
George III (king of England), 140
Gilbert, Humphrey, 83
Glorious Revolution (*see* England)
Goodwin, John, 43
Goodwin, Thomas, 106, 107, 108, 126–7, 154, 155, 156, 158
Gorges, Ferdinando, 90
Gorton, Samuel, 163
Gray, Robert, 63
Greece (ancient), 7, 10, 99, 115, 132; *see also* Athens; democracy, ancient
Grotius, Hugo, 53
guardianship (*see* fiduciary agency)
Guicciardini, Francesco, 129–30
Gutmann, Amy, 181–2

Hakluyt, Richard (the younger), 57, 58, 62–3, 64, 75, 77
Hartford (Connecticut), 141, 145, 146
Harvard College, 105
Harvey, John, 84
Hathorne, William, 125
Haynes, John, 119, 123, 125, 143, 147, 150
Heath, Robert, 40
Herodotus, 27
Hingham (Massachusetts), 135–6, 137, 168
historiography, 13, 49, 62, 72, 110, 150, 163; "patriotic" (American),

13, 71, 80; "progressive" (American), 13, 175; revisionist (American), 13–14, 101, 105, 115, 120, 135, 137, 146, 148, 149, 150–1, 154
Hobbes, Thomas, 5, 26, 52–3, 55, 77–8, 80, 96, 101
Hooker, Thomas, 5, 14, 95, 97, 119, 123, 143, 147, 148–60, 165, 166, 167, 168, 180; influence and precedence, 141–2, 156–7; *Survey of the Summe of Church-Discipline*, 148–60; Winthrop, correspondence with, 144–5, 147, 148, 149
Hopkins, Edward, 150
Hotman, François, 31
Huguenots, 31–2, 38, 39, 41, 42, 54, 89, 172, 180, 185
humanism (classical), 57, 61, 62–4, 84, 87, 91, 112
Hutchinson, Anne, 105, 122, 123, 124, 130, 161, 163
Hutchinson, William, 161, 163

impeachment, 8, 28, 34, 46, 50, 51, 82, 84, 115, 125, 128, 135, 149, 160, 168, 173, 187, 188
incumbent re-eligibility (*see* rotation in office)
Independency (ecclesiastic) (*see* congregationalism)
Indians (American), 59, 62, 66, 69–70, 75, 94, 105, 122, 136, 144, 145, 176
institutional design, 12, 22–3, 59, 186–9
instructions (political), 111, 134, 168–9, 170
Ipswich (Massachusetts), 124, 131, 153
Ireland, 51, 69, 83
Ireton, Henry, 43
irony, 2, 15, 21, 36, 135, 138, 172, 185
Italy, 129–30, 132, 187

Jacksonian democracy, 148
Jacob, Henry, 105–6

James I (king of England), 31, 39, 71, 79, 80, 90, 109–10; political ideas, 40, 53, 55, 115
Jamestown (Virginia), 59–61, 62, 67, 69, 73
Jefferson, Thomas, 17
Jesus Christ, 99, 105, 106–7, 124
John of Paris, 30
Johnson, Francis, 101, 102, 105, 155
Johnson, Robert, 66, 74, 78, 79
Johnston, Alexander, 145, 147
joint-stock companies, 58, 77–8, 79, 110, 114
judicial review, 20, 21, 183, 184–5
juries, 27–8, 46, 82, 178, 188–9
justice, 9, 11, 18, 106, 178, 179, 184; *see also* virtue and vice

Knolles, Richard, 95

Laud, William, 143
law (*see* constitutionalism; English law; fiduciary agency; liability; Roman law)
Lawson, George, 141–2, 156, 157, 158
legal limitation, 20, 21, 115, 118, 123–5, 137, 138, 145, 166, 183
Levellers, 22, 148, 159, 170, 175–7; on accountability, 45–9, 135, 180, 188; on democracy, 49–52; historic significance, 5, 16, 26, 55–6, 151, 169, 171, 172; Hobbes and, 52–3; Locke and, 53–5; name, 40; polemics, 41–2, 43–4, 138, 160, 172; on toleration, 165; *see also* Agreement of the People
Leverett, John, 176
lex regia, 30, 31, 32
liability (legal), 30, 34, 46, 47, 48, 55, 173
liberalism, 6, 22, 179; *see also* civil liberties
Lilburne, John, 42, 45, 46–7, 49, 52, 160, 175, 184

local politics, 47, 55, 134–5, 146–7, 168–9, 171, 174, 180–1, 188; municipal analogies, 108, 152, 159, 165
Locke, John, 5, 52, 53–5, 142, 157
Long Island (New York), 141
Long Parliament, 42, 43, 50, 51, 106, 138, 158, 174, 176
lottery (selection by), 9, 25, 27–8, 51, 187, 188, 189
Ludlow, Roger, 119, 120, 121, 123, 125, 143

Macedonian empire, 24
Machiavelli, Niccolò, 13, 35, 49–50, 69, 96, 129, 130, 148, 180, 187
Madison, James, 16, 17, 25, 138
Magellan, Ferdinand, 68
Magna Carta, 40
Maine, 13, 141
Mair, John (*see* Sorbonnists)
majoritarian voting, 79, 81, 98, 120, 125, 126–7, 130, 147, 156, 162
Manin, Bernard, 15, 22, 187
Mariana, Juan de, 33
Marian exiles, 38, 97
marriage, 136
Marsilius, 30
Martin, Christopher, 94
Martin, John, 62, 76, 78, 83
Mary I (queen of England), 38, 39, 97
Maryland, 13, 66, 84
Massachusetts, 14, 22, 87, 91–4, 114–39, 141, 171, 182; Bay Company, 90, 91, 114, 116, 119, 163; Body of Liberties, 124–5, 128, 134, 135, 138, 167; churches, 104–5, 112–13, 156, 175 (*see also* Cambridge Platform); conflicts within, 22, 117–22, 123–8, 130–8, 142, 156, 172, 174, 177; Connecticut, relations with, 143–5, 150; government, 146–7, 167, 168 (*see also* "negative voice"; "standing council"); legal charters, 117, 118, 120, 123; reform movement (of 1634), 118–19, 123, 129, 143, 145, 151, 158, 161, 162; Rhode Island, relations with, 162, 164
Mather, Richard, 87–9, 103, 105, 106, 107, 109, 123
Mayflower Compact, 90
McCormick, John P., 180, 187–8, 189
Medici family, 129
medieval period, 28, 30, 33, 152
Mercurius Britannicus, 43, 50
Middlesex (Lionel Cranfield, Lord), 80, 81
militias, 135–6, 159, 168, 176
Miller, Perry, 13–14, 146, 150–1, 154, 161
Milton, John, 170, 175
ministerium non dominium, 31, 32, 35, 121, 152
mixed regime, 83, 99, 100, 118, 126–7, 133, 134, 147, 177, 179; Aristotelian vs. Bodinian, 13, 35, 89, 96, 105–6, 131–2, 135, 154–5, 156
models of accountability, 2, 10–12, 27, 177–81; classical, 10, 12, 36, 47, 51, 55, 59, 83, 112, 116, 130, 134, 169, 178, 179, 180, 187; ecclesiastical, 11, 12, 38, 39, 87, 103, 108, 112, 116, 157, 169, 178, 179–80, 181, 182, 188, 189; fiduciary, 11–12, 30, 33, 36, 47, 48, 51, 55, 106, 112, 116, 130, 169, 178–9, 180–1, 186, 188
Moderate, The, 176
monarchy, 24, 40, 42, 51, 76, 78, 79–80, 96
Moore, Richard, 68, 90
multicameralism, 20, 22, 114, 126, 127, 132, 150, 153, 161, 185–6; *see also* unicameralism

Nederman, Cary, 31
Nedham, Marchamont, 50, 51, 148, 180
"negative voice" 22, 119–21, 125–7, 132, 134, 136–7, 143, 147, 150, 156, 174, 184

Index

New England, 2, 13; colonization, 90; confederation (a.k.a. United Colonies), 144, 146, 150, 161; conflict within, 14, 19, 139, 143; democratic tradition, 168–9, 171, 181; influence on old England, 173–7; intellectual life, 85, 108, 128–9, 130; resistance theory absent, 166; solidarity within, 93, 112, 151; town meetings, 168, 181; *see also* Connecticut; Massachusetts; New Haven; Plymouth; Rhode Island
New England Way, 87–9, 105–8, 132, 154, 170
Newfoundland, 13, 83
New Hampshire, 13, 141, 161
New Haven, 108, 153, 161
New Model Army, 43, 49, 158, 159, 160, 169, 176–7; *see also* Putney debates
Newport (Rhode Island), 162, 163–4
Norton, John, 95, 106, 107, 108, 112, 131–2, 133–4, 135
Nova Scotia, 13
Nye, Philip, 106, 108, 126–7, 154, 155, 156, 158

Osgood, H. L., 14
Otanes, 27, 28
Overton, Richard, 41, 43, 46–7, 50, 54, 160, 165, 175

Paine, Thomas, 17, 22, 140, 142, 170, 184
Parker, Henry, 41, 42, 51–2, 53, 133
Parliament and parliamentarians, 22, 40, 41–2, 43, 47, 50, 55, 114, 152, 159, 172; *see also* Long Parliament
Parrington, V. L., 14–15
participation, 2, 16, 18, 100, 103, 105, 108, 149, 179, 182, 188, 189
parties, 179, 186–7
Penn, William, 170
Pennsylvania: Constitution (of 1776), 184
Peter, Hugh, 95, 109

Petition of Right, 40, 72
Pilgrims, 86–95, 104, 110; Dutch exile, 98, 109; ecclesiology, 98, 123, 126, 156 (*see also* Robinson, John); Virginia Company and, 80, 90; *see also* Mayflower Compact; Plymouth
Pitkin, Hannah, 26
Pizarro, Francisco, 68
Plato, 28, 29, 95, 182
pluralism, 7, 19, 149
Plymouth (New), 104, 116, 144, 161, 171, 173; government, 89, 97, 108, 110, 112, 134, 147; *see also* Pilgrims
Polybius, 13, 35, 96
Ponet, John, 38–9, 41, 42, 94, 97, 109
popular control (*see* accountability; democracy; power vs. reason)
popular sovereignty, 59, 98, 112, 132, 152, 165; democracy and, 3, 5, 83, 84, 142, 151; *see also* accountability; consent
Portsmouth (Rhode Island), 162, 163–4, 167
Pory, John, 60
power vs. reason, 3, 18, 19, 45, 104, 154, 181–2, 183, 188
Presbyterianism, 50, 103, 106, 137, 138, 151, 152, 154, 158, 175
property, 29–30, 145
Protestantism, 31; *see also* Calvinism
Providence (Rhode Island), 161, 163, 167, 169, 171
providentialism, 148, 180
Przeworski, Adam, 22
Purchas, Samuel, 61, 62, 64
puritanism, 13, 14, 40, 80, 86–7, 103, 129, 150, 178, 184
Putney debates, 43, 176, 177
Pynchon, William, 145, 164

quod omnes tangit, 100

Rainsborough, Edward, 176
Rainsborough, Thomas, 160, 176–7
Rainsborough, William, 176–7

Raleigh, Walter, 51, 61, 68, 129, 130
Ratcliffe, John, 62
rational-choice theory, 186
reason of state, 40, 122
regime types, 12, 35–6, 51–2, 89, 130–2, 154; *see also* Bodin, Jean; mixed regime; sovereignty, administration
Renaissance (*see* Italy)
representation, 2, 3, 5, 26–7, 41, 44, 52–3, 83, 142, 149, 168, 170, 179, 182
republicanism, 18, 49–51, 76, 130, 173, 179, 187; *see also* models of accountability, classical
resistance theory, 30, 31–3, 35–6, 38–9, 41, 54, 100, 107–9, 157, 165–6
Rhode Island, 14, 16, 130, 140–2, 161–9, 170, 171; conflicts within, 162–4; legal charters, 141, 164, 175, 177; relations with neighbor colonies, 150, 162, 164; 1647 assembly, 162, 164, 167–8; *see also* Newport; Portsmouth; Providence; Warwick
Rich, Nathaniel, 79–80
Richman, Irving, 163
rights, 6, 11, 16, 20, 21, 179
Riley, F. L., 114
Roanoke, 61
Robinson, John, 86, 89, 92, 96–104, 107, 180, 182; ecclesiology, 97–106, 108, 156; influence and precedence, 112, 142, 148, 151, 159, 167; on regime types, 106–7, 131, 155
Rogers, Ezekiel, 128
Rolfe, John, 73
Roman law, 29, 31–2, 37, 38, 100, 188; *actio furti*, 32; *fiducia*, 29, 37; *procuratio*, 29, 30, 32, 53; *see also lex regia*; *quod omnes tangit*; *salus populi*
Rome (ancient), 10, 24, 28, 30, 34, 35, 36, 50, 63, 128, 129, 131
Rossiter, Clinton, 150

rotation in office, 2, 9, 47, 48, 51, 115, 128, 129, 137, 138, 147, 150
Rutherford, Samuel, 151

St. Kitts, 13
Salamonio, Mario, 31
Salem (Massachusetts), 90, 93, 104, 156
Salmon, J. H. M., 36, 96
Saltonstall, Richard, 125, 143
salus populi, 42, 53, 54, 137, 151, 152, 160, 165, 179
Sandys, Edwin, 66, 70–1, 73, 74–5, 76, 77, 79–80, 83, 90, 92
Savonarola, Girolamo, 129
Saye and Sele (William Fiennes, Lord), 133, 134
Schumpeter, Joseph, 16, 186
Scotland, 32, 33, 109–10
Scott, Jonathan, 55
senate, 34, 35
Seneca, 29
separatism (religious), 80, 86, 87, 97–8, 104, 105, 106, 126, 154
Shepard, Thomas, 95
Sherley, James, 94
Sieyes, E. J. (l'Abbé), 16
Smith, Capt. John, 5, 57–9, 60, 61, 62, 75, 76, 77, 83; *Description of New England*, 63, 90, 92; influence and precedence, 84, 87, 92, 93, 117; moral criticism, 60–1, 63–4; theory of colonial agency, 67–8, 69–70, 71
Smyth, John, 101–2, 103, 106, 107, 126, 155
Smythe, Thomas, 64, 66, 70–1, 72–3, 74, 75, 78–80, 81
Somers, George, 60
Sorbonnists, 30, 35
sovereignty, 11, 25, 31, 42, 53, 65, 89, 96, 147; administration, distinguished from, 12, 35, 95–6, 100–1, 102, 103, 106, 132, 155 (*see also* regime types); *see also* absolutism; *ministerium non dominium*; popular sovereignty
Spain, 61, 68, 129; Inquisition in, 33

Index

Sparta, 24, 32, 180
Spottiswood, John, 109–10
Springfield (Massachusetts), 145, 164
"standing council," 121, 125, 126, 131, 137, 147
state of nature, 55, 141, 161, 166
Statute of Uses (1535), 37
Stokes, Susan, 22
Stoughton, Israel, 5, 115, 122–3, 124, 125, 131, 136, 143, 174, 176–7; political ideas, 118, 119–21, 128, 153, 171
Stoughton, John, 118, 174
Strachey, William, 60, 61, 62
Suarez, Francisco, 31, 40, 53
suffrage, 6, 7, 16, 49, 53, 110, 149, 176
Sunstein, Cass, 181, 182

term limits (*see* rotation in office)
territorial scale, 3, 25, 162
Themistocles, 50
Thompson, Dennis, 181–2
Thorne, Robert, 61
Tocqueville, Alexis de, 181
toleration, 6, 43, 44, 80, 111, 142, 158, 160, 165–6, 170, 175
Travers, Walter, 98, 101
tribunes, 34–5, 50, 51, 178, 180–1, 187
trust, 26, 34, 38–9, 40, 51, 53–4, 57, 62, 64, 69, 71, 130, 151, 164, 165; accountable vs. discretionary conceptions, 3, 17, 30, 59, 70–2, 93, 116, 118, 120, 134, 145, 165, 171; in English Civil War, 26, 41–3, 44, 137; in English law, 37–8; as fiduciary authorization, 64, 65–6, 79, 93, 142, 151; *see also* virtue and vice, fidelity
trusteeship (*see* fiduciary agency)
Tuck, Richard, 28
tyrannicide (*see* resistance theory)
tyranny, 32, 39, 78, 81, 101, 109, 145, 148, 157, 168

Underhill, John, 122
unicameralism, 186; in the American Revolution, 22; in congregational churches, 156, 158; in Connecticut, 141, 147; in the Levellers, 44, 177; in Massachusetts, 114, 126–7, 132, 134, 137, 138, 177; in Plymouth, 89, 110–11; in Rhode Island, 141, 161, 162, 167; *see also* majoritarian voting; multicameralism
United States, 186, 187; Constitution (of 1787), 17, 138, 140, 172, 185; Supreme Court, 184
Urbinati, Nadia, 15, 182
utopianism, 72, 81, 83

Vane, Henry, 122, 123–4, 145, 147, 175–6
Vassall, William, 137
Venice, 24, 129
Vindiciae contra Tyrannos, 31–2, 33–4
Virginia, 4, 13, 57–84, 87, 90, 92–3, 94, 112, 129, 173, 186; government, 59, 72–4; House of Burgesses, 74–5, 80, 82, 84; *see also* Jamestown
Virginia Company, 57–8, 74, 90; commissions, 65–6, 67–70, 169; conflicts within, 66, 77–80; dissolution, 72, 75, 81, 110; legal charters, 59, 72, 77; promotional literature, 62–3, 92
virtue and vice, 57, 63, 65, 69, 92; avarice, 60–1, 64; fidelity, 57, 65, 67, 79, 87, 93, 169; justice, 61, 63, 69; pride, 60–1

Wall, Robert, 115
Walwyn, William, 42, 160, 175
Ward, Nathaniel, 115, 124, 128
Warwick (Robert Rich, Lord), 91
Warwick (Rhode Island), 163
Watertown, 117, 132, 143, 153
Weathersfield (Connecticut), 146
Westminster Assembly, 106, 154, 175
Whalley, Edmund, 49
White, John (of Massachusetts), 90, 91
White, John (of Roanoke), 61
Wildman, John, 160

Williams, Roger, 5, 14, 95, 142, 161, 164–6, 167, 174–6, 177
Wilson, John, 95, 122, 159
Windsor (Connecticut), 146
Wingfield, Edward-Maria, 61, 62, 65
Winthrop, John, 5, 14, 91, 95, 114–15, 168, 174, 176; Hooker, correspondence with, 144–5, 147, 148, 149; influence and precedence, 16, 21, 138–9, 157, 185; political ideas, 17, 21, 92, 93, 115–17, 124, 127, 129, 131, 132–8, 144–6, 153, 172, 180; political office, 91, 116, 117–24, 126, 128, 143, 156, 159–60
Winthrop, John, Jr., 95
Winthrop, Martha, 176
Winthrop, Stephen, 176
Wise, John, 86, 89
Wither, George, 24
Wittenberg, 97
Wootton, David, 53

Yeardley, George, 66